The

Complete Book

of

Dog Obedience:

A Guide for Trainers

by BLANCHE SAUNDERS

HOWELL BOOK HOUSE INC.

845 THIRD AVENUE, NEW YORK, N.Y. 10022

L.C. Cat. Card No.: 65–25633
ISBN 0-87605-457-2

First printing ...... September, 1954
Second printing .... May, 1955
Third printing .... March, 1963
Fourth revised printing 1965
Fifth printing 1966
Sixth printing 1967
Seventh printing 1968
Eighth revised printing 1969
Ninth printing 1970
Tenth printing 1971

Published by Howell Book House Inc., *New York. By arrangement with* Prentice-Hall, Inc., *Englewood Cliffs, N.J.*

Foreword

It is no mere coincidence that the phenomenal increase in America's dog population in recent years has paralleled the burgeoning of the dog obedience training movement.

From the very beginning, of course, America has had dogs. When the country was largely rural, it was the most natural thing in the world to allow its dogs to run and roam. As cities multiplied and grew larger, this practice was found incompatible with urban living, and dogs in the metropolitan centers lagged far behind the dog population generally. The introduction of dog obedience training, with its promise of fully controlled, well-behaved pets, set a trend toward dog ownership in an environment considered by many as inhospitable to canines. Today many of America's finest dogs are to be found within the confines of cities and their adjoining suburbs.

And one of the leaders in bringing about this remarkable change was Blanche Saunders, author of the present work.

Dog obedience and Blanche Saunders in this country are synonymous. She was the nearest thing we have to a "Miss Obedience." She was in obedience training at its very birth, and stayed in it until her death on December 8, 1964. There are few phases of obedience in which she did not play a part. Through her classes, her judging, her films, and her writings, she was daily promulgating sound constructive thinking on obedience training to thousands who, in turn, will similarly influence additional thousands in the years to come.

The *Complete Book of Dog Obedience* is in line with the sort of good thing we had come to expect of Blanche Saunders. I read the manuscript, and every page turned increased my admiration of the author's coverage of her subject. She had done not only a complete and thorough job but an exceedingly competent one, and in a field which urgently needed attention. There is a real need for a book of this type, and I predict that its exceptionally valuable and practical contents will appeal to a great many more besides those who now or in the future turn to obedience training as a vocation or as an avocation. I will go a step further and predict that this work will give a fillip to obedience which will carry it past anything heretofore dreamed for it in this country.

This book of Blanche Saunders' did not come a minute too soon. In every section of the country there is an acute lack of experienced trainers. With the aid of this work and conscientious application, almost any member of a training group can develop a proficiency that would be most helpful to his fellow-members.

From various parts of the nation also comes a cry of another order—complaints of trainers so untutored or inept as virtually to take money under false pretenses from persons entrusting them with their dogs for training. Here the book can serve a double purpose—as a guide for such a trainer in improving his work and for his clients in checking on whether he really knows what he is doing.

The writer of these lines happens to be associated with a group—the Gaines Dog Research Center—which believes that if obedience training in this country is to continue to progress, there will have to be either licensing of obedience training instructors by the American Kennel Club, or the certification of instructors by institutions of higher learning upon completion of a definite course of study. There is no longer any reason for colleges and universities to refrain from offering such special courses when Blanche Saunders has provided them with the ideal textbook.

HARRY MILLER

Preface

The success of dog obedience training is largely due to Mrs. Whitehouse Walker, who in 1936 persuaded the American Kennel Club to assume jurisdiction of obedience rules. At that time you could count the number of dog trainers and class instructors on the fingers of one hand. The growth of dog obedience training has been so phenomenal that every dog owner today is a potential trainer or training director in one of the hundreds of training classes throughout the world.

The amateur becomes expert through skill and knowledge. Skill is acquired through personal experience; knowledge can be gained from books that give the experiences of others. My purpose in writing this book (the first of its kind) is to give the reader the benefit of twenty years of classroom teaching. If others can profit from what I have learned, then I will feel that I have contributed something of value to dogs and to their training.

I have been very fortunate in having the cooperation of many friends in writing this book. I am sincerely grateful to Laura Abbott Dale for helping me edit the manuscript, and I owe a special vote of thanks to Mary Priscilla Keyes for the many illustrations portraying instruction procedures and techniques.

I received permission to use various photographs, charts, and previously published material, for which I express appreciation, from the following persons, companies, and societies: Jerome B. Behrend, Louise Branch, Frank Dill, and William Shell; Doubleday and Company; The American Kennel Club, The Mountain City Obedience Club (Montreal), The So-

ciety for the Prevention of Cruelty to Animals, and The Suf-
folk Obedience Training Club.

BLANCHE SAUNDERS

*The publishers wish to thank Miss Elinor E. Mason, devoted
friend and associate of Miss Saunders, for her assistance in
bringing this classic work up-to-date. The information on
show ring Obedience has been revised to conform with com-
prehensive changes recently made in the American Kennel
Club rules and regulations for Obedience. We extend thanks,
too, to the Ralston Purina Company, makers of Purina Dog
Chow, for allowing us to reproduce the new judging sheets
which they provide to show-giving clubs.*

Table of

Contents

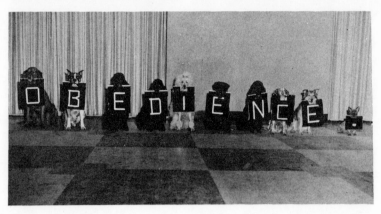

VOICE COMMANDS USED IN
OBEDIENCE TRAINING

"COME": Command used to bring the dog in to the handler.

"COME FORE": Command used to bring the dog from the side of the handler to a position where he sits and faces him.

"DOWN": Command used to make the dog drop to the ground in a prone position.

"FIND IT" (or LOOK FOR IT): Command used to make a dog seek an object that he will recognize only by smell, such as when seeking a lost article, doing scent discrimination or tracking.

"GO": Command used to send the dog away from the handler.

"HEEL": (a) Command used to make the dog walk at the handler's left side. (b) Command used to make the dog go to heel position from the come-fore position.

"HUP": Command used to make the dog jump.

"NO": A word used to caution the dog or to let him know he has done wrong.

"OUT": Command used to make the dog release his hold on whatever object he has in his mouth.

"PHOOEY": An expression used to correct a dog when he has made a mistake.

"SIT": Command used to make the dog sit down.

"STAND": Command used to bring and keep the dog on all four feet.

"STAY": Command used to make the dog remain in either the sitting, the lying down, or the standing position.

"TAKE IT" (or "FETCH"): Command used to make the dog take an object either from the hand or off the ground.

HAND SIGNALS USED IN OBEDIENCE TRAINING

"COME": A motion across the body from the side toward the opposite shoulder.

"COME FORE": A motion from the left side to the front of the handler to make the dog come around and sit in front.

"DIRECTED JUMPING": Arm extended full length to the side and parallel to the ground. Right arm indicates right hurdle. Left arm indicates left hurdle.

"DOWN": (a) Arm raised shoulder height in a striking motion if handler is facing the dog. (b) Left arm down with elbow straight, wrist bent, and palm and fingers parallel to floor if the dog is at heel position.

"GO": Arm extended full length in front of the handler.

"HEEL": (a) A forward motion of the left hand parallel to the floor to make the dog start walking at heel. (b) A swinging motion of the left hand from in front of the handler to his side to make the dog go to heel.

"JUMPING": (Broad Jump) The left arm moved with a quick motion parallel to the hurdle.

"SIT": When facing the dog, either hand extended palm upward. Fingers flip up with a quick wrist motion. (No signal is used to make the dog sit at the handler's side.)

"STAND-STAY": Same as signal to Stay.

"STAY": Arm extended downward, palm back, and held momentarily in front of the dog's muzzle.

COMMANDS OF INSTRUCTOR OR
JUDGE TO HANDLER

"ABOUT-TURN": Handler makes a counter turn to the right to go in the opposite direction.

"ARE YOU READY?": The question asked the handler before starting each exercise.

"BACK TO YOUR DOG": Handler returns to his dog.

"CALL YOUR DOG": Handler brings in his dog on command or signal.

"DOWN YOUR DOGS": Handlers to prepare for the long down.

"DROP YOUR DOG": Handler makes his dog lie down.

"EXERCISE FINISHED": An expression indicating the dog is no longer being judged in that particular exercise.

"FAST": Handler executes a running pace.

"FIGURE-8": Handler prepares his dog for the Figure-8 exercise.

"FINISH": Handler to complete the exercise by making the dog go to heel position from the come-fore position.

"FORWARD": Handler to walk briskly with the dog at heel.

"HALT": Handler to stop walking and dog to sit at heel.

"LEAVE YOUR DOG": Handler to leave the dog by himself.

"LEFT TURN": Handler to make a 90-degree angle turn to the left.

"NORMAL": Handler resumes a natural brisk walking pace.

"RIGHT TURN": Handler to make a 90-degree angle turn to the right.

"SEND YOUR DOG": Handler orders the dog to obey a command or signal.

"SIT YOUR DOG": (a) Handler prepares for the Long Sit. (b) Handler sits the dog at a distance from the down position in the signal exercise.

"SLOW": Handler executes a slow walk.

"STAND YOUR DOG": (a) Handler poses or stands his dog for the group examination. (b) Handler signals the dog to stand at heel in the signal exercise.

"STAND FOR EXAMINATION": Handler to pose or stand his dog, then faces him at the end of a loose leash.

"TAKE IT": Handler takes whatever object the dog is holding.

"THROW IT": Handler throws the dumbbell.

1

The Training Club
and Classes

OBEDIENCE TRAINING, having become one of America's favorite pastimes, has resulted in several hundred obedience clubs and training classes, where owners are learning the art of training and the technique of handling their own dogs.

Which comes first, the class or the club? The answer is, either! Most clubs originate for the purpose of giving training instruction, but a good many others are formed as the result of successful classes. A few such groups operate primarily to teach the house pet good manners but the majority are interested in having their members exhibit at dog shows to gain their dog's obedience titles.

The purpose of the OBEDIENCE CLUB is threefold: to promote obedience training, to sponsor training classes, and to hold obedience trials. To accomplish its objective, the club must overcome the handicap of inexperience and insufficient knowledge, very often due to lack of cooperation, to poorly conducted training classes and incompetent leadership. Not every club will triumph over adversity.

To have a prosperous club, those in authority must be willing to act for the good of all concerned. It must be agreed that a club divided in any way is condemned to failure. To be further assured of success, the obedience club must select the best trainers available. Obedience training is a skill that requires the use of various methods, for dogs are not all trained alike and instructors do not teach in the same manner. However, best results will be achieved under expert guidance, and when the problems are solved with patience and ingenuity.

It is well for the club members to discuss controversial ideas on training with the training director. The instructor can only receive the full support of the members when they approve of his methods of teaching. The instructor inadvertently shoulders the blame for the dogs that react badly to training and for the handlers who fail to live up to expectations. He should, by the same token, be given credit for the good examples of the system under which the dogs are trained. But if, at any time, the instructor or his manner of teaching fails to meet with the approval of the majority, another should be elected to take his place.

The next step is for the obedience club to establish a constitution and by-laws that will meet the requirements of the American Kennel Club. Few persons realize that every club must fulfill specific and basic rules or it will not be recognized. A solid constitution and set of by-laws is insurance against friction and ultimate disaster. Their use will prevent mistakes and long delays in getting established. A constitution and by-laws for an all-breed club may be applied to an obedience club. Following is a sample copy of such rules and regulations, published by the American Kennel Club, 51 Madison Avenue, New York, N.Y. 10010.

SAMPLE CONSTITUTION AND BY-LAWS
FOR AN ALL-BREED CLUB

Many clubs seek the assistance of the American Kennel Club in the preparation of their constitutions and by-laws. This specimen is prepared purely as a service for such clubs. It is recognized that varying viewpoints and conditions exist and that some clubs will wish to modify or elaborate upon these suggestions.

This specimen does represent extensive experience of many clubs, and it is especially designed to meet the problems which most frequently arise. It is prepared particularly for an all-breed club which operates on a local basis; it presumes that a substantial number of the members will be able to attend important club meetings.

Clubs applying to The American Kennel Club to conduct shows or trials under its rules are required to submit their by-laws with their applications. This form, under present American Kennel Club policies, could be readily approved. It does not follow that any deviation from this form would be disapproved.

For instance, some clubs may wish to provide a special dues rate for husband and wife (Article II, Section 2); the number of officers and directors is purely optional (Article IV); and the dates for fiscal and official year are simply examples (Article V).

However, it should be pointed out that the wording of Article I, Section 3, and Article IX is thought to be helpful in avoiding tax problems; that more than one class of membership has been the source of much club trouble (Article II, Section 1); that a fixed location for club meetings has been found desirable (Article III); that the provisions for notices as they appear throughout the sample are important; that the suggested procedure for elections and nominations best meets the need of the average club of the type described (Article V, Sections 3 and 4). The procedures for disciplining in Article VII should be closely followed for the protection of all concerned, though Section 1 in this Article is optional and is included only because many clubs have some such provision in their by-laws. Close adherence to Article VIII on amendments is recommended.

—THE AMERICAN KENNEL CLUB

ARTICLE I

NAME AND OBJECTS

SECTION 1. The name of the Club shall be ....
....

SECTION 2. The objects of the Club shall be:

(a) to further the advancement of all breeds of pure-bred dogs;

(b) to conduct dog shows (field trials) (obedience trials) and sanctioned matches under the rules of The American Kennel Club;

SECTION 3. The Club shall not be conducted or operated for profit and no part of any profits or remainder or residue from dues or donations to the Club shall inure to the benefit of any member or individual.

ARTICLE II

MEMBERSHIP

SECTION 1. *Eligibility.* There shall be one type of membership, open to all persons eighteen years of age and older who are in good standing with The American Kennel Club and who subscribe to the purposes of this Club.

While membership is to be unrestricted as to residence, the Club's primary purpose is to be representative of the breeders and exhibitors in its immediate area.

SECTION 2. *Dues.* Membership dues shall be $......... per year, payable on or before the 1st day of January of each year. No member may vote whose dues are not paid for the current year. During the month of November, the Secretary shall send to each member a statement of his dues for the ensuing year.

SECTION 3. *Election to Membership.* Each applicant for membership shall apply on a form as approved by the Board of Directors and which shall provide that the applicant agrees to abide by these constitution and by-laws and the rules of The American Kennel Club. The application shall state the name, address and occupation of the applicant and it shall carry the endorsement of two members. Accompanying the application, the prospective member shall submit dues payment for the current year.

All applications are to be filed with the Secretary and each application is to be read at the first meeting of the Club following its receipt. At the next Club meeting the application will be voted upon and affirmative votes of ¾ of the members present and voting at that meeting shall be required to elect the applicant.

Applicants for membership who have been rejected by the Club may not re-apply within six months after such rejection.

SECTION 4. *Termination of Membership.* Memberships may be terminated:

(a) *by resignation.* Any member in good standing may resign from the Club upon written notice to the Secretary; but no member may resign when in debt to the Club. Dues obligations are considered a debt to the Club and they become incurred on the first day of each fiscal year.

(b) *by lapsing.* A membership will be considered as lapsed and automatically terminated if such member's dues remain unpaid 90 days after the first day of the fiscal year; however, the Board may grant an additional 90 days of grace to such delinquent members in meritorious cases. In no case may a person be entitled to vote at any Club meeting whose dues are unpaid as of the date of that meeting.

(c) *by expulsion.* A membership may be terminated by expulsion as provided in Article VII of these constitution and by-laws.

ARTICLE III

Meetings and Voting

SECTION 1. *Club Meetings.* Meetings of the Club shall be held in the city of .... on the first .... in the months of January, ... and December in each year, at such hour and place as may be designated by the Board of Directors. Written notice of each such meeting shall be mailed by the Secretary at least 10 days prior to the date of the meeting. The quorum for such meetings shall be 20% of the members in good standing.

SECTION 2. *Special Club Meetings.* Special Club meetings may be called by the President, or by a majority vote of the members of the Board who are present and voting at any regular or special meeting of the Board, or by the Secretary upon receipt of a petition signed by five members of the Club who are in good standing. Such special meetings shall be held in the City of .... and at such hour and place as may be designated by the person or persons authorized herein to call such meetings. Written notice of such meeting shall be mailed by the Secretary at least 5 days and not more than 15 days prior to the date of the meeting; and said notice shall state the purpose of the meeting and no other Club business may be transacted thereat. The quorum for such a meeting shall be 20% of the members in good standing.

SECTION 3. *Board Meetings.* Meetings of the Board of Directors shall be held in the City of .... on the first .... in the months of .... and .... in each year, at such hour and place as may be designated by the Board. Written notice of each such meeting shall be mailed by the Secretary at least 5 days prior to the date of the meeting. The quorum for such a meeting shall be a majority of the Board.

SECTION 4. *Special Board Meetings.* Special meetings of the Board may be called by the President or by the Secretary upon receipt of a written request signed by at least three members of the Board. Such special meetings shall be held in the City of .... and at such hour and place as may be designated by the person author- ized herein to call such meeting. Written notice of such meeting shall be mailed by the Secretary at least 5 days and not more than 10 days prior to the date of the meeting, or telegraphic notice shall be filed at least 3 days and not more than 5 days prior to the date of the meeting. Any such notice shall state the purpose of the meeting and no other business shall be transacted thereat. A quorum for such a meeting shall be a majority of the Board.

ARTICLE IV

DIRECTORS AND OFFICERS

SECTION 1. *Board of Directors.* The Board shall be comprised of the President, Vice-President, Secretary, Treasurer and five other persons all of whom shall be members in good standing and all of whom shall be elected for one-year terms at the Club's annual meeting as provided in Article V. General management of the Club's affairs shall be entrusted to the Board of Directors.

SECTION 2. *Officers.* The Club's officers, consisting of the President, Vice-President, Secretary and Treasurer shall serve in their respective capacities both with regard to the Club and its meetings and the Board and its meetings.

    (a) The President shall preside at all meetings of the Club and of the Board, and shall have the duties and powers normally appurtenant to the office of President in addition to those particularly specified in these constitution and by-laws.

(b) The Vice-President shall have the duties and exercise the powers of the President in case of the President's death, absence or incapacity.

(c) The Secretary shall keep a record of all meetings of the Club and of the Board and of all matters of which a record shall be ordered by the Club. He shall have charge of the correspondence, notify members of meetings, notify new members of their election to membership, notify officers and directors of their election to office, keep a roll of the members of the Club with their addresses and carry out such other duties as are prescribed in these constitution and by-laws.

(d) The Treasurer shall collect and receive all moneys due or belonging to the Club. He shall deposit the same in a bank satisfactory to the Board, in the name of the Club. His books shall at all times be open to inspection of the Board and he shall report to them at every meeting the condition of the Club's finances and every item or receipt or payment not before reported; and at the annual meeting he shall render an account of all moneys received and expended during the previous fiscal year.

SECTION 3. *Vacancies.* Any vacancies occurring on the Board during the year shall be filled for the unexpired term of office by a majority vote of all the then members of the Board at its first regular meeting following the creation of such vacancy.

ARTICLE V

The Club Year, Annual Meeting, Elections

SECTION 1. *Club Year.* The Club's fiscal year shall begin on the 1st day of January and end on the 31st day of December.

The Club's official year shall begin immediately at the conclusion of the election at the annual meeting and shall continue through the election at the next annual meeting.

SECTION 2. *Annual Meeting.* The annual meeting shall be held in the month of January at which directors and officers for the ensuing year shall be elected by secret, written ballot from among those nominated in accordance with Section 4 of this Article. They shall take office immediately upon the conclusion of the election and each retiring officer shall turn over to his successor in office all properties and records relating to that office within 30 days after the election.

SECTION 3. *Elections.* The nominated candidate receiving the greatest number of votes for each office shall be declared elected. The three nominated candidates for other positions on the Board who receive the greatest number of votes for such positions shall be declared elected.

SECTION 4. *Nominations.* No person may be a candidate in a Club election who has not been nominated. During the month of September, the Board shall select a nominating committee consisting of three members and two alternates, not more than one of whom shall be a member of the Board. The Secretary shall immediately notify the committeemen and alternates of their selection. The Board shall name a Chairman for the Committee and it shall be his duty to call a committee meeting which shall be held on or before November 1st.

(a) The Committee shall nominate one candidate for each office and five candidates for the five other positions on the Board, and, after securing the consent of each person so nominated, shall immediately report their nominations to the Secretary in writing.

(b) Upon receipt of the Nominating Committee's report, the Secretary shall before November 15th notify each member in writing of the candidates so nominated.

(c) Additional nominations may be made at the December meeting by any member in attendance provided that the person so nominated does not decline when his name is proposed, and provided further that if the proposed candidate is not in attendance at this meeting, his proposer shall present to the Secretary a written statement from the proposed candidate signifying his willingness to be a candidate. No person may be a candidate for more than one position, and the additional nominations which are provided for herein may be made only from among those members who have not accepted a nomination of the Nominating Committee.

(d) Nominations cannot be made at the annual meeting or in any manner other than as provided in this Section.

ARTICLE VI

COMMITTEES

SECTION 1. The Board may each year appoint standing committees to advance the work of the Club in such matters as dog shows (field trials), (obedience trials), trophies, annual prizes, membership and other fields which may well be served by committees. Such committees shall always be subject to the final authority of the Board. Special committees may also be appointed by the Board to aid it on particular projects.

SECTION 2. Any committee appointment may be terminated by a majority vote of the full membership of the Board upon written notice to the appointee; and the Board may appoint successors to those persons whose service has been terminated.

ARTICLE VII

DISCIPLINE

SECTION 1. *American Kennel Club Suspension.* Any member who is suspended from the privileges of The American Kennel Club automatically shall be suspended from the privileges of this Club for a like period.

SECTION 2. *Charges.* Any member may prefer charges against a member for alleged misconduct prejudicial to the best interests of the Club. Written charges with specifications must be filed in duplicate with the Secretary together with a deposit of $10 which shall be forfeited if such charges are not sustained. The Secretary shall promptly notify the Board which shall meet and fix a date of a Board hearing not less than 3 weeks nor more than 6 weeks thereafter. The Secretary shall promptly send one copy of the charges to the accused member by registered mail together with a notice of the hearing and an assurance that the defendant may personally appear in his own defense and bring witnesses if he wishes.

SECTION 3. *Board Hearing.* The Board shall have complete authority to decide whether counsel may attend the hearing, but both complainant and defendant shall be treated uniformly in that regard. Should the charges be sustained, after hearing all the evidence and testimony presented by complainant and defendant, the Board may by a majority vote of those present suspend the defendant from all privileges of the Club for not more than six months from the date of the hearing. And, if it deems that punishment insufficient, it may also recommend to the membership that the penalty be expulsion. In such case, the suspension shall not restrict the defendant's right to appear before his fellow-members at the ensuing Club meeting which considers the Board's recommendation. Immediately after the Board has reached a decision, its findings shall be put in written form and filed with the Secretary. The Secretary, in turn, shall notify each of the parties of the Board's decision and penalty, if any.

SECTION 4. *Expulsion.* Expulsion of a member from the Club may be accomplished only at a meeting of the Club following a Board hearing and upon the Board's recommendation as provided in Section 3 of this Article. Such proceedings may occur at a regular or special meeting of the Club to be held within 60 days but not earlier than 30 days after the date of the Board's recommendation of expulsion. The defendant shall have the privilege of appearing in his own behalf, though no evidence shall be taken at this meeting. The President shall read the charges and the Board's findings and invite the defendant, if present, to speak in his own behalf if he wishes. The meeting shall then vote by secret written ballot on the proposed expulsion. A ⅔ vote of those present and voting at the meeting shall be necessary for expulsion. If expulsion is not so voted, the Board's suspension shall stand.

ARTICLE VIII

Amendments

SECTION 1. Amendments to the constitution and by-laws may be proposed by the Board of Directors or by written petition addressed to the Secretary signed by twenty percent of the membership in good standing. Amendments proposed by such petition shall be promptly considered by the Board of Directors and must be submitted to the members with recommendations of the Board by the Secretary for a vote within three months of the date when the petition was received by the Secretary.

SECTION 2. The constitution and by-laws may be amended by a ⅔ vote of the members present and voting at any regular or special meeting called for the purpose, provided the proposed amendments have been included in the notice of the meeting and mailed to each member at least two weeks prior to the date of the meeting.

ARTICLE IX

Dissolution

SECTION 1. *Dissolution.* The Club may be dissolved at any time by the written consent of not less than ⅔ of the members. In the event of the dissolution of the Club whether voluntary or involuntary or by operation of law, none of the property of the Club nor any proceeds thereof nor any assets of the Club shall be distributed to any members of the Club but after payment of the debts of the Club, its property and assets shall be given to a charitable organization for the benefit of dogs selected by the Board of Directors.

ARTICLE X

ORDER OF BUSINESS

SECTION 1. At meetings of the Club, the order of business, so far as the character and nature of the meeting may permit, shall be as follows:

> Roll Call
> Minutes of last meeting
> Report of President
> Report of Secretary
> Report of Treasurer
> Reports of Committees
> Election of Officers and Board
> (at annual meeting)
> Election of new members
> Unfinished business
> New business
> Adjournment

SECTION 2. At meetings of the Board, the order of business, unless otherwise directed by majority vote of those present, shall be as follows:

> Reading of minutes of last meeting
> Report of Secretary
> Report of Treasurer
> Reports of Committees
> Unfinished business
> Election of new members
> New business
> Adjournment

The obedience club must be democratic in nature and every member should be given the privilege of voicing his opinions in determining the club's policies. When the officers and board of directors are elected annually by the members at large, the power is controlled by all—not just by a limited few.

Most training groups will find that there are many advantages in having their own separate clubs and in holding their own specialty shows, but the cooperation of the breed clubs should also be encouraged. The pros and cons of obedience training versus breed exhibiting will not be discussed here, except to say that they can profit from one another. The obedience club may find it more satisfactory to hold its first Obedience Trial in conjunction with an all-breed show. The

Fig. 1. Rockefeller Plaza: For ten years obedience-trained dogs performed here under the author's guidance. *Courtesy: Mary Priscilla Keyes.*

show-giving club may be glad of the added interest obedience creates. To isolate one from the other shows poor judgment at the expense of the dog for obedience training and the breeding of better dogs go hand in hand.

In planning its program of operation, an obedience club should resolve to have dogs on call for the purpose of giving demonstrations and exhibitions. The club that is willing to serve for charity benefits and local events will be a popular

Fig. 2. The Stand-Stay at an outdoor show.

one. Sought-after publicity will be forthcoming and the club will gain the good will of the press, as well as the respect and admiration of the community. There are many organizations and occasions which provide excellent opportunities to gain recognition; hospitals, for example, where obedience

Fig. 3. A full dress exhibition staged during National Dog Week. *Courtesy: Mary Priscilla Keyes.*

combined with tricks appeals to both children and adults. One successful obedience specialty club in New York pays annual visits to every major hospital in the metropolitan area. The therapeutic value deriving from this type of entertainment is given high acclaim by hospital officials. Demonstrations during drives to collect money for the March of Dimes, the Heart Fund, the Community Chest, or for local S.P.C.A.'s and humane societies, with the dogs "passing the plate," have

proven popular. Schools, scout groups, camps, and orphan-
ages are especially keen for activities that have to do with
animals. Obedience training becomes part of the child's education, for a youngster will learn a lesson from training his
dog that will remain with him throughout his life.

National Dog Week, Be Kind to Animals Week, local fairs,
sportsmen's shows and society events (with the dogs dressed
for the occasion) provide additional opportunities to create
good will. A participating club will gain wide recognition for
the constructive and helpful work it is doing in the community.

Exhibitions prior to baseball games or other athletic events
will acquaint the general public with a new type of sport.
Yankee Stadium, with 70,000 in attendance, has witnessed a
demonstration of trained dogs on six separate occasions.

Television is a natural outlet for the obedience-trained dog.
Whether on film or by actual appearance in the studio, dog-
training presentations can be assured of a widespread and
appreciative audience. When presented in an amusing way,
visual education makes a lasting impression and gives diversity to work otherwise serious in nature.

The obedience club is primarily for training dogs, but the
social aspects need not be neglected. Social activities will hold
the interest of those members who, for a number of reasons,
are not able to take an active part in the training program but
whose unswerving support of the club's aims is invaluable.
Occasional get-togethers, picnics, and annual or semi-annual
dinners, with interesting speakers and the showing of slides or
films, will help a club to grow. Amateur movies taken of club
affairs and of the dogs in training, in 8 or 16 mm film, will
furnish many laughs. Such films have an educational value as
well, for there is no better way to judge one's ability as a
trainer than to see the results on the screen. One club in Texas

limits its membership to family groups. The club's monthly meetings are held in private homes and the result is a successful obedience training club with a healthy social atmosphere.

There are many advantages in having permanent training quarters, if a club is financially able to to so. Such quarters can be used as a clubroom where rehearsals for exhibitions may be held, afternoon tea or cocktails served, and the board

Fig. 4. The author presents her fifth consecutive obedience exhibition at Yankee Stadium. *Courtesy: Mary Priscilla Keyes.*

meetings held or annual dinners given. Work combined with pleasure makes for an intimate feeling of friendship between members.

To attract attention to the club and· the training classes, attractively illustrated brochures and posters may be displayed in public buildings, dog shops, stores, and veterinarians' offices. The announcements should state when training

Officers

Application for Membership in

(Name of Club) _____

Name: Mr.
      Mrs.
      Miss. _____
                        (Please Print)

Address: _____ City _____ Zone ____ State _____
              Street

Home telephone: _____ Business telephone: _____

Name of Dog: _____

Breed of Dog: _____

Sponsored by: (1) _____

              (2) _____

Dues are _____ for one person, _____ for husband and wife

I herewith enclose $ _____ for Annual Dues

The Board of Directors reserves final decision on all applications

I certify that I will abide by the by-laws, rules and decisions of _____
_____ , and will hold harmless the Club and all persons connected therewith in any
capacity whatsoever, from any and all liability, cost, and expense for any injury or damage to persons or
property caused by any dog brought by me to Training Class or other events held or sponsored by this Club.

Dated: _____ Signed: _____

Fig. 5. Sample application for membership in an obedience club.

classes are held, the time and place of meeting, and the conditions under which a dog may be enrolled. The name, address, and telephone number of the person with whom to get in touch for additional information should also be given. Brochures which fit into a business envelope will facilitate mailing and keep postage at a minimum.

Mimeographed news bulletins, whether published monthly or quarterly, and sent to each club member, to editors of dog magazines, to local newspapers, and to radio and television stations, are quite beneficial, providing the items are constructive and of general interest. The resulting publicity will be especially helpful to a newly formed club which is limited in its capacity to pay for advertising.

The relationship of the obedience club to the training classes may take one of two forms. The club may conduct a series of classes where membership in the club is not a prerequisite for attending the classes, or it may hold classes which only club members in good standing may attend. Both systems are popular. In the opinion of the author, the first appears to offer an advantage in localities where obedience training is relatively new and where there is need to increase interest and keep up enthusiasm. When the classes are restricted, the scope of the training activities is limited. A few clubs insist that the dog and owner graduate from the beginners class before the owner is eligible to become a member of the club. Whether this ruling is advisable is a question for the club to decide.

The TRAINING CLASS is a vital part of the obedience club and of the dog's education. The dog is brought into contact with other dogs and he has the opportunity to overcome his problems under supervision. The owner has the advantage of associating with those who have had experience and he gains knowledge by observation. Classroom training helps to prepare the handler and dog for participation in the Obedience Trials at dog shows. The training is stimulated and there is a competitive spirit among the owners and the attitude "let the other person's dog wear the dunce cap!"

Excluding the privately owned and professional groups, training classes may be held independently of an obedience club when sponsored by another organization. The American Society for the Prevention of Cruelty to Animals, in New York City, is one example. Every year many hundreds of dog owners attend classes endorsed by the Education Department of the Society. Other groups currently sponsoring training programs are the Elks Clubs, the Lions Clubs, boards of education, adult education centers, departments of recreation, humane societies, and community centers. In fact, any civic-minded body of persons which recognizes the advantages of teaching dogs the principles of good citizenship may approve classes for the purpose of training owners to train their dogs. The participants need not necessarily be members of the sponsoring organization.

As soon as the training class becomes a reality the details should be handled in a business-like way. The responsibility of administration should not be left to the training director (he will have enough worries of his own). Administrative problems should be placed in the hands of the sponsoring organization, or left to the judgment of a training committee appointed by the president and board of directors of the club. There will be the task of securing a place in which to hold the classes, and the problem of finding a capable instructor. The question of fees must be decided upon, what courses will be given, the number of lessons per course, and the day of the week and hours most suitable for training.

Advance publicity will demand considerable preliminary work. Advertising must be done through news items in local papers, through posters and illustrated brochures. Local radio and television stations must be advised of the forthcoming event, and application blanks prepared. The necessary correspondence, the enrolling of the dogs, and the keeping of class-books and records is a full-time job. One person should not be expected to assume all the headaches.

The public, on the whole, is becoming more broad-minded on the subject of dog training and it recognizes the benefits derived from such activity. Authorities have been persuaded to open the doors of school gymnasiums, community centers, and city halls. Park officials, YMCA's, churches, and restaurants cooperate in offering training programs. In some instances, universities permit the use of campus grounds. Armories and privately owned riding stables frequently contribute their facilities.

A big handicap is overcome when the training can be done out-of-doors. A greater number of dogs can be accommodated and there is no problem about quarters in which to work. When the training is done indoors, it is impractical to work in a room smaller than 40 or 50 feet square. However, such places are hard to find. The larger the room, the better, but the rent for a large room is often prohibitive.

The kind of floor in the training room is important. Results will be poor if the dogs slip and the owners have a hard time keeping their footing. Rubber matting will remove this hazard, though it will add to the expense. Tanbark is excellent for jumping purposes but distracting to the dogs; it also makes the teaching of retrieving and scent work difficult. A room at street level is preferable to one where it is necessary to climb stairs. Quarters with a door opening onto the street are more desirable than an inside room with long passageways. When the dogs are exercised at frequent intervals there should be little cause for complaint, but owners are reluctant to take their dogs outside when it involves a long walk. The training room with a stage or balcony has added advantages. The extra space will provide a place for the dogs to stay when they are not working and for visitors to observe the class.

Fig. 6. When held outdoors, the class size is unlimited. *Courtesy: Louise Branch.*

The recent popularity of obedience training has resulted in an abundance of trainers. Some good, some bad! Taking one dog through to the C.D. degree, or even to the U.D. title, does not qualify a person as an authority. One must have the advantage of training hundreds of dogs of *all breeds* and under *all conditions*. Nothing can take the place of experience. With the shortage of experts, however, it may be necessary to compromise and select someone who, although lacking in experience, is a good teacher and forceful leader. He should be sympathetic toward people and love and understand dogs. A professional dog person, although he may not be a trainer, has a more varied experience and a greater general knowledge of dogs than the private individual with one or two pets. There are a number of good training books and films available to aid the beginner. Occasional visits made to more experienced classes will assure the new group of success through the novice training at least.

There are two types of training classes. One is the kind where members are permitted to join at will and to come whenever they feel like attending the class. In the other type, a specific number of lessons makes up the course. For the newly formed club, the latter is the better system. When we were children, we were not permitted to enroll in school when the term was half over, nor was the matter of attendance left to our whims of the moment. A training class, especially for the beginner, is a school for dogs and must be given the same consideration.

The total number of lessons included in a training course may be from nine to twelve, at the rate of one lesson a week. Some clubs prefer to hold a beginners class which runs for twelve or thirteen weeks, but the author has found that results are just as satisfactory from the shorter course if the training is systematic and a brisk schedule is outlined. Long drawn-out periods of basic training can become boring; as a result, class members lose interest. It is better to demand hard work with extra home practice than to prolong the training and fail to hold the enthusiasm of the members. With few exceptions, a dog can learn the basic exercises in two months, even under the guidance of inexperienced owners. The owner then has the privilege of enrolling in the novice class to prepare for dog show competition or in the intermediate, if he desires to continue with the advanced training.

The fee one must pay to train a dog will depend upon the circumstances. Fees range from five to twenty-five dollars for a nine- or ten-week course. In some clubs combined classes cost as much as thirty-two dollars. Considering the professional charge in comparison, where the dog is boarded and trained by a professional trainer, these are nominal figures.

The training class receipts should cover expenses. The following must be taken into consideration. The rent of the training room, the salary paid to the instructor, an allowance for the purchase of equipment (such as rubber mats and jumps), and supplies of stationery, application blanks, printed matter and postage. There will be extras for janitor service and for advertising. At graduation time there will be an outlay for diplomas, ribbons, prizes, perhaps even a gift or flowers for the judge.

Rent for the training room will average ten to twenty-five dollars a night (unless space is given free). The instructor's fee may range from fifteen to twenty-five dollars per lesson, and up, depending upon the number of hours he contributes weekly. Some clubs prefer not to have a paid instructor; instead, the members volunteer to assist with the training. When the instructor receives remuneration for his services there is a greater feeling of responsibility and the club or sponsoring organization is entitled to a voice in all matters pertaining to the classes. The obedience club may wish to carry on classes in different localities under more than one trainer. In this case, the club may pay the instructor a percentage of the training fees received from his pupils. The financial arrangement of the training class will be different in every case and must be adjusted to meet the existing conditions.

The training courses that may be offered are as follows: beginners class, for dogs that have had no previous training; the novice class, for dogs that have graduated from the beginners and need additional training both for home behavior and competition in the novice class at dog shows; intermediate class, for the purpose of teaching jumping, retrieving, and dumbbell work; the open class, to prepare the dog for the open work at dog shows; and the utility class, for teaching the utility exercises. A special course may be given for the dogs with a particular failing that only individual coaching can overcome. The need for the problem class (as it is called) will arise when the dog becomes ring-wise or takes advantage of a situation.

In the beginners class the rate of improvement is more or less standardized. From this point on, the dog's progress is variable. This will make it necessary to choose the class, or classes, most suited to the dog's particular needs. It is at this point that two classes are sometimes combined. The owner whose dog has graduated from the beginners class may want to repeat the course for more experience, or he may want to take the novice work as well as the intermediate. Graduates from the open course may wish to continue with the open work even though the dog is ready to attempt the more advanced utility training. No dog should be allowed to combine two classes such as intermediate and utility, or open and utility, if the work in both is unfamiliar to the dog and he has had no previous training in either class. Training is progressive and the dog must be conditioned for each new experience through steady advancement. He should not be encouraged to attempt unfamiliar exercises without the fundamental instruction.

When selecting the opening and closing dates for the classes, holidays should be eliminated. The final or graduation night should not fall close to Christmas, Thanksgiving, or Easter holidays. Three or four courses may be given each year, but they should be planned to permit a winter and summer vacation. A week's grace at the completion of the scheduled time, to allow for the unexpected, may avoid confusion. Sometimes a class has to be cancelled without notice and the lessons extended.

Selection of the day and the hour will be optional. Children's classes are popular on Saturdays, or Sunday afternoons. Adult classes may be held at a daytime hour, but evening classes appear to be more popular in metropolitan areas.

An occasional youngster may be permitted to work with grown-ups, but it is advisable to separate the two groups whenever possible. Children work best with children, adults with adults. It is not that the child is unable to compete with an older person. On the contrary, a youngster will take a more serious attitude toward training and he will find time for home practice that will often place him at the head of the class, but an adult sometimes resents working with children. A special class for teen-agers will eliminate the possibility of such a reaction and, at the same time, it will encourage group exhibition work where the children can play the leading roles.

An hour of work is sufficient for the beginner, the novice, and the intermediate groups. When the classes are divided because of a large enrollment, it will require a two-hour period for each of the three groups. A club that has been in existence for some time and which meets only once a week may find it necessary to shorten the training periods in order to include all classes. When meetings are held on two different days, the training can be done in a more leisurely fashion. (Suggestions for the division of the classes are given in the chapters covering the courses.)

As has already been said, publicity should be released several weeks prior to enrollment and literature should be distributed to pet shops, veterinarians' offices, sporting-goods stores, and other public places. The application blanks with complete information should also specify the closing date for the receiving of entries and the number of dogs that will be accepted. The first night is usually spent in getting organized, so applications may be received at the second meeting. This practice, however, should not be encouraged. Progress will be retarded if new dogs enter after the class has already started. Dog training is done by gradual advancement. It is important that both owner and dog be in attendance from the beginning.

A duplicate set of books should be kept for each course that is offered. One will be for the training director and the other for the training committee. The records should list the name and address of each owner and his telephone number, the breed of dog (unless it is a specialty club), and its name, age, color, and sex. To simplify the task of checking in, the owner may be assigned a number which will serve as his identification throughout the course.

The training committee should be responsible for equipment to be used in case of an emergency. A pail, shovel, sawdust, newspapers, disinfectants, and a mop will come in handy. Dogs in the beginners class occasionally have mishaps due to the excitement and unexpectedness of working with other dogs. One or two persons may be designated as the "clean-up squad," or each member can be responsible for his own dog's mistakes.

The owner should be warned not to feed his dog for several hours before coming to class and to take extra precautions to exercise him until he has become accustomed to the routine. If the training period is long, a five or ten-minute break at the half-way mark, at which time every dog must be taken outdoors, will help to keep the training floor clean. Drinking water should be available at all times.

Visitors may be permitted and encouraged to attend, if there is room for them to sit quietly without disturbing the members while they are training. Commotion caused by people entering and leaving the room should be discouraged and unnecessary talking prohibited. It is inconsiderate to ask an instructor to teach, or to expect pupils to concentrate, during noise and confusion.

It is optional whether a club wishes to charge a visitors' fee. If guests are required to pay, there will be less outside interference. The visitors' fee ordinarily is three to five dollars for the nine weeks' period or one dollar per night for the occasional onlooker. A card issued to anyone taking the visitors' course will entitle him to the same consideration given to the owners taking an active part in the class.

Arrangements should be made to have a pet shop or supply house representative on hand the first two nights with a complete line of collars, leashes, jumping sticks, dumbbells, scent articles, and other items required for training purposes. The training director would do well to meet in advance with whomever is going to supply the class. He can thus arrange to eliminate unsuitable collars and leashes from the stock of supplies. A large dog requires a long, heavy-link chain collar. A medium-length collar should be made of medium-weight material. The very small breeds can use the small size or baby link. Owners cannot resist the temptation to buy a thin chain (thinking it will be more comfortable for the dog) and if the long thin chains are eliminated from the available stock, there will be no conflict in the owners' minds.

The leash should be six feet long and made of flat leather or strong webbing. Round leashes, chains, and the regular three-foot walking lead should be barred from the classroom. The width and weight of the leash will depend upon the size of the dog for which it is to be used.

The training equipment is so very important that the owners should be encouraged to wait until the first evening of class before purchasing it. A poorly fitting collar and a leash that is too short or one with a weak snap will get the handlers off to a bad start. If dogs are not brought to the first class meeting, the owners should be advised in advance to take a piece of string and measure the actual size of the dog's neck. Add two or three inches to this length and if the oval will slip over the dog's head, it is the length of chain collar that will be needed.

The classroom will need equipment such as floor mats (if indoors), and a fifty-foot clothesline complete with snap and pulley for the problem dogs and for teaching directed jumping. When convenient it is helpful to have a loudspeaker system and a time clock that will ring at the close of any specified period to prevent running over-time.

The training committee should appoint someone to check the dogs in each week upon arrival and to assist the training director during the training. There will be chores such as placing the mats and shifting the hurdles. The director may occasionally need help with a problem dog or with an owner who is slow to grasp the knack of handling. Able assistance will simplify the instructor's work so that the class can progress smoothly. (Assistant trainers will be discussed later in the chapter entitled *The Training Director*.)

The director and the training committee should decide upon and announce early in the course the number of times the owner and dog must be present in class and working in order to be eligible to graduate with a diploma. In a nine-week course, a dog should be required to attend at least six of the nine sessions. In a twelve-week course, he should be present at least nine times. A female in season should not be permitted to come to class, but she should be given credit for attendance if the owner comes and observes the training so that he can carry on the work at home. Noting the cause of absence in the class-book will prevent the inconsiderate owner from bringing his dog back too soon.

The requirements for graduation should be outlined and understood from the beginning. The owner should know in advance what he is expected to accomplish in the weeks that follow. For graduation some clubs prefer to score the dogs individually, as in the novice class at dog shows, but set 150 points as passing instead of the usual 170. This is usually after a twelve- or thirteen-week period of training, when the dog heels off leash. Other clubs prefer to have the dogs judged as a group and specify the following, which is a fair test after nine weeks of training:

(1) To heel on a slack leash with automatic sits; (2) To heel with the leash over the handler's shoulder; (3) To remain in the sitting, the down, and the standing position; (4) To obey the commands to lie down, to come, and to go to heel position, even though the command and signal must be used together.

The caliber of work achieved in a training class varies as much as the dogs themselves. A great deal depends upon where the classes are held, how many lessons the dogs have had, how competent the instructor is, and the purpose behind the training. When the classes are sponsored for the purpose of training pets to have good manners, stress is not placed on the finer points necessary in competition, but rather on general behavior. Probably the most backward of all classes are those held in big cities. By law, the dogs must be kept on leash, which encourages them to bark and growl and fight with one another. They come in contact with each other only at class and the result is lack of attention to the owner's commands. It may take several lessons before a dog becomes attentive to his owner and mindful of his work.

When training classes are held as part of an obedience club's activities, they move along at a more rapid pace and, from the show-ring point of view, are more successful. Such classes have experienced dogs and more individual attention can be given to show-ring procedure. Another factor, and a very important one, is that the club membership usually consists of persons who understand dogs and know how to handle them. Kennel owners, professional handlers and trainers, and the people who exhibit regularly at dog shows, anticipate a dog's reactions and will meet the situation with the requisite skill. The pet owner lacks this knowledge.

Added to these things are some other basic points that must be taken into consideration at all times: the age of the dog, his breed, his disposition, the amount of home training he receives and, most important of all, the ability of the owner. Because of these and other contributing factors, training classes will never be of equal caliber. They can all, nevertheless, maintain a high academic standard.

Detailed plans for graduation should be made when the course is about half way through. Diplomas, if secured ahead of time, can be filled out and ready for the signatures of the training director and the representative of the club or organization sponsoring the classes. The judge should be invited well in advance in order to prevent a last-minute rush to secure the right person. The judge may be licensed by the American Kennel Club to judge at Obedience Trials, but this is not necessary. He may be a local person familiar with obe-

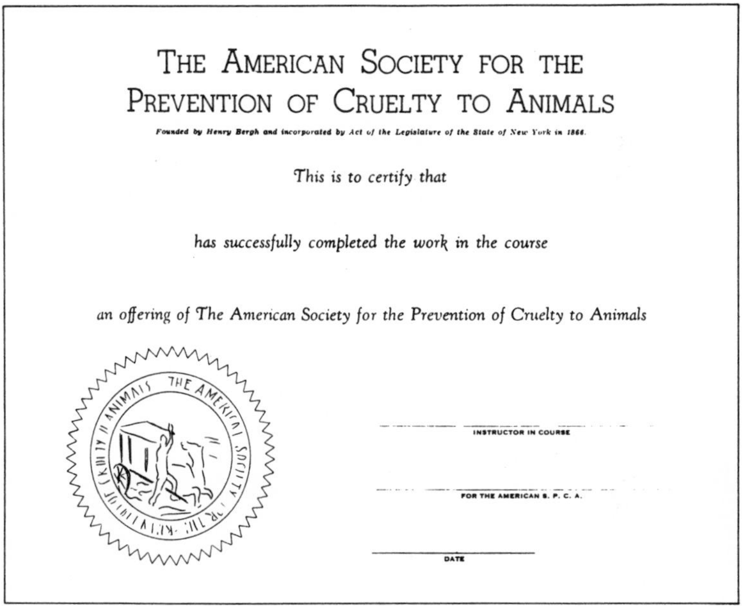

Fig. 7. A sample diploma.

dience training. If the class is unusually large, two judges will find testing the dogs less of an effort.

The programs for the graduation exercises should be prepared and ready for the printer as soon as all details have been completed. Arm bands with numbers must be obtained and an ample supply of application blanks announcing the next course should be available.

Three weeks before graduation the training director should

The American Society for the Prevention of Cruelty to Animals

presents

A   D E M O N S T R A T I O N   O F   O B E D I E N C E   T R A I N I N G

Washington Irving High School   June 9 at 8:00 P.M.

JUDGES   :   Miss Dorothy M. Bach

                   Mr. Mason Webb

INSTRUCTOR: Miss Blanche Saunders

P R O G R A M

WELCOME   :   Mr. Warren W. McSpadden,   General Manager, ASPCA

*   *   *   *   *

JUDGING OF DOGS in Beginners' Course and Advanced Course

BEST PROGRESS   :   1st, 2nd, and 3rd - Rosette and Ribbons
                                     (to be chosen by Miss Saunders)

BEST HANDLING   :   1st, 2nd, and 3rd - Rosette and Ribbons

BEST PERFORMANCE   :   1st, 2nd, and 3rd - Rosette and Ribbons

*   *   *   *   *

DEMONSTRATION of Special Advanced Obedience Training received

after beginners' work.

*   *   *   *   *

PRESENTATION OF RIBBONS   :   Miss Bach and Mr. Webb

PRESENTATION OF DIPLOMAS   :   Miss Saunders

All flowers,   corsages,   gifts, and decorations

presented by members of the classes.

Call or write to the ASPCA, 441 East 92nd Street, New York 28, N. Y..
(TRafalgar 6-7700)now, for an application blank if you wish to enter your
dog in an Obedience Class. Our fall course begins early in October.

26th Obedience Training Course

Fig. 8. Sample graduation program.

remind the class that everyone taking part in the final exercises must be present the week before graduation so that the instructor and the training committee can pass on the dogs' work. If absence is imperative, the owner should request to have his dog checked for steadiness the preceding week or on the day of graduation at an earlier pre-arranged hour. It should also be stressed that even though a dog is permitted to take part in the final exercises, this does not mean that a diploma will necessarily be forthcoming. The decision whether or not a dog passes the course should be made the final night. This prevents a let-down in training during the last week and, at the same time, provides an incentive for the owners of backward dogs to do extra home practice.

When diplomas are withheld from dogs which do not deserve to graduate, a high standard will be maintained. The dog that is permitted to slide through with inferior work is not prepared to do the more difficult advanced exercises. To forewarn the owners and to create harmony, the instructor and the training committee should arrange to meet privately with any member whose dog's work is not up to expectation. The owner should be told that his dog is on probation and encouraged to work extra hard. Owners sometimes fail to understand that certain dogs, because of their disposition or the handlers' lack of skill, cannot be expected to make the grade the first time. Participation in two beginners courses may be necessary to accomplish the same results that others achieve in a single course. The owner should realize that if he fails to graduate, it is nothing to be ashamed of, and that by repeating the course he will get better results.

To give every member of the class an equal opportunity to receive some award, it is suggested that ribbons and prizes be offered in the following categories: best performance by the dog, best handling by the owner, and greatest improvement made by both owner and dog during the course.

Graduation night, with outside judges officiating, and the awarding of prizes and diplomas, which have been inscribed with the dogs' names, establishes the training class as an essential part of dog obedience.

2

The Owner

THE OWNER who enrolls his dog in a training class assumes definite responsibilities. He has a duty to the club, to the training director, to the other members of the class, and to his dog. A training class involves not just one individual, but many persons with equal rights and privileges. Thoughtfulness and cooperation assures a congenial atmosphere in the classroom.

The first consideration is the matter of attendance. A class cannot be systematically conducted when there is a feeling of unconcern or disinterest. The schedule for a training class is worked out with the owner's best interests in mind. He should take the attitude that regularity and punctuality are imperative. When the first lesson is held without dogs, the owner should be encouraged to realize its importance, and indeed, he should make every effort to be present. An occasional day off is to be expected, but frequent absences during the course, especially in the beginning, retard the dog's progress and result in general confusion. The dog will not do as well as the other dogs and the owner will not understand the instruction.

No less important is the value of promptness. When the tardy owner dashes in while the class is in progress, it creates disturbance for all the other members. The dog does not have time to become adjusted to his surroundings before he is thrust into the training routine and he will be slow to concentrate on his work. Resolve, then, that as an owner you will attend every meeting if possible, and that you will be punctual throughout the course.

The next thought to bear in mind is that class training requires team work. Perhaps one dog will advance more quickly than some of the others, but unless the class work is done in unison, there will be chaos. The owner must accept the fact that working as a team is essential in a training class, and he must consider the rest of the group while he is training his own dog. A chain is as strong as its weakest link. To the instructor, the training class is as good as the most backward pupil!

The owner should purchase the correct training equipment and bring it to class regularly. The wrong type of collar, the lead with a snap that opens at the crucial moment, or a short walking lead are nuisances that can be easily avoided. A little home practice in putting on the slip-chain collar will avoid long delays in the classroom, where precious time will be lost making changes while the entire class stands idle.

Each owner is familiar with the habits of his dog. Forethought will avoid unpleasantness that may result in drastic action for which the entire class will have to pay the price. Accidents will happen! But the owner who permits his dog to lift his leg promiscuously, either inside the premises or against the building when entering or leaving, is thoughtless and selfish. Carelessness along these lines has caused many classes to be evicted and refused other quarters in which to train. The owner should be cautious about feeding his dog before coming to class and he should exercise him carefully. He should observe the dog's actions in class and take him out if it seems necessary.

If an accident occurs during the training, the owner should stand still and raise his hand. He should not attempt to drag the dog out of line because it will only spread the mishap over a greater area. Request that a chair be placed at the spot until arrangements can be made to have it taken care of.

The owner whose dog has a belligerent nature should tell the instructor about his problem and seek his advice before the class begins. Every precaution will be taken against dog fights, but a dog is enrolled at the owner's risk. A muzzle may be recommended or the suggestion made that the owner sit quietly in a corner the first few times until the dog becomes accustomed to the distractions and is less excited. If the owner is not able to control a dog who creates a disturbance, he cannot expect to train with the other members until he can do so without causing ill-feeling.

Owners of female dogs are usually aware of the period when she will come in season and they should be on guard for the inevitable. Don't run the risk of spoiling the lesson for everyone else by taking a bitch to class that will attract male dogs. Dismissal is inevitable but the damage will already have been done! Dogs in the beginners class have not had sufficient training to work under tempting conditions. The female should be checked weekly, and when she comes in season, the owner must resign himself to missing three or four weeks of class training. Before she is brought to class again, she should be bathed with a disinfectant solution to eliminate any lingering odors. Although the female in season must be absent, the owner should be present so that he can observe the class work and carry on the training at home. This will keep the dog at the same level of performance as the others, and the class will not be held back when she re-enters.

When the owner arrives with his dog the first time, he should be ready for the unexpected. The dog should be kept on a short leash and close to the handler. He should be kept away from other dogs and from corners of the room and pieces of furniture. Every time the dog sniffs (and this goes for the females as well), the lead should be jerked sharply and the dog warned "Be careful!"

Excessive barking can be stopped if the owner puts his hand around the dog's muzzle and orders him to behave. If that makes no impression, the leash should be held tight and the dog cuffed sharply across the end of the nose. Lunging at the other dogs should bring a more severe whack across the muzzle or under the chin. Either the hand or the end of the leash can be used for this purpose. This will give the dog something else to think about instead of trying to pick a fight. *Never*, under any circumstance, stand still and permit a dog to bark and surge forward repeatedly without discipline. Turn immediately and walk away, jerking the leash hard at the same time.

Before starting to train, the owner should play with the dog and get his attention. It will be more difficult than at home because of the many distractions, but until the owner can get his dog to look at him, little progress will be made. The dog's favorite toy or little bits of food may entice him. This does not mean that the dog will be bribed throughout the course, but a titbit now and then will help to overcome a problem.

If the dog is distracted because other members of the family are sitting on the sidelines, he should be taken into the classroom by the person who is to do the training. The others can arrive later and should remain out of sight until the end of the training period. A few lessons will encourage the dog to center his attention on his handler and with practice he will learn to obey in spite of temptations.

Still more advice: *Keep your eye on your dog while training! Concentrate on him.* This will give you the advantage of timing your corrections. *Listen to the instructor!* Do what he tells you. When you are not sure of the instruction, raise your hand and ask a question. Glance toward your neighbors occasionally to see if you are in accord with the rest of the class, and don't try to anticipate the instructor's commands. Keep your distance from the other dogs. Walk in a straight line and try to avoid crouching. Use the leash to discipline the dog, and do it with authority. Throughout the training, command first, correct second, and encourage immediately.

Women trainers are advised to wear comfortable shoes with rubber heels. Unless one's footing is secure, the dog will work badly because he will be afraid of getting stepped on. Clothing worn by the trainer should not blanket the dog and interfere with his work. Valuables should be left at home so one can concentrate on the dog instead of the pocketbook.

Distractions will be of little concern after a fair amount of training, but in the beginners class, the less noise, the better. When the time comes for you to sit on the sidelines while the other members work, be quiet and don't talk. If you have visitors, ask them to do the same. The others are trying to listen to the instructions, and a constant babble makes it hard to hear and difficult for the training director to concentrate on his teaching. You can learn a great deal by watching others train. Take advantage of the opportunity. While observing during the rest period, insist that your dog rests as well. Make him lie down at your feet. Keep him on a short leash and away from the other dogs. This will prevent a possible lunge toward those working on the floor—a very annoying habit.

If training the dog is a family affair, the owner will have to show more consideration than ever. Uncontrolled children are as disturbing as uncontrolled dogs. If youngsters attend the class, the parents should insist that they sit quietly on the sidelines. When a husband and wife, or two adult members of the family attend, it is a good policy for both to do some of the training, providing, of course, that they have attended the previous lessons and understand the instructions. To be considered a well-trained pet, the dog must obey every member of the family. He will do so only when he has the respect for each which is achieved through training.

The owner should continue with the dog's training outside as well as inside the classroom. When the dog is required to enter and leave the building or training quarters with dignity, he will learn to be obedient no matter where he is.

The dog enrolled in a training class should not be expected to make the same progress he would if he were in the hands of a professional trainer. The owner must remember that *he* is learning as well as the dog. The professional trainer already knows how to handle and how to meet the various problems that arise. The amateur lacks the knowledge which comes from experience. When a dog is trained professionally, six to eight weeks are required for basic work, and during this period the dog is given intensive instruction every day. In training class he works only one evening a week, unless the owner is conscientious and trains at home.

If the owner becomes discouraged at what he feels is lack of progress, he should stop and consider the chief advantage of the class, which is that *he* is learning how to make the dog obey. Nevertheless, the owner should realize that home training is the most important thing of all. The owner-trainer should put his dog through the training routine for at least ten to fifteen minutes twice a day. It is a waste of effort and money to attend a training class unless the dog is given the home practice that is so necessary. The poor work resulting from lack of practice will reflect on the owner, the dog, and also on the training director. *The director can only instruct a person how to train. The owner must practice to gain perfection.*

The attitude the owner takes toward his dog's training is a significant point. The diploma, although a delightful reward, is not the main objective. The important thing is that the dog is learning, under the guidance of his owner, to be a better behaved animal. No two dogs respond to training in the same way. Dispositions vary and there are the differences in age, in breed, and in the owner's ability to handle his dog. The same progress will not be made by all. If an owner fails to make the grade the first time, he should accept it gracefully. It is no discredit to him as a trainer. It may mean that it will require two or three times as long to reach the goal, but in the end this can be a brilliant one. When the instructor recommends that the beginners class be repeated he does so with all good intentions. A miracle will often occur with an additional three or four weeks of training, and the owner will accomplish his purpose of gaining a well-mannered pet.

The withholding of a diploma from a dog that is not ready to graduate is done for the dog's sake and not because of a personal grudge. If the dog is not prepared to go on to the more advanced training, his work will reflect on all concerned and will lower the standard of the class or training club. A diploma is important but only when it has real significance.

Mention should be made of the owner who, in his enthusiasm, tries to gain more knowledge of training by attending a number of classes and taking the advice of different trainers and instructors. Be loyal to your training director. A temporary set-back is sometimes necessary to overcome a specific problem. A good instructor recognizes this fact, and he is not afraid to sacrifice the quality of work temporarily if he succeeds in the long run. Only by knowing the dog's history and by watching his progress from the beginning can one decide what action to take. Nothing is more confusing to the dog than having his handler study under different teachers and take the advice of a number of people.

The mistakes most commonly made by the owner are the following:

Failure to use the correct snap on the lead.

Not holding the hands sufficiently close to the body.

Giving commands without changing the tone of voice.

Corrections not definite.

Yelling at the dog.

Becoming angry and taking it out on the dog.

Repeating a command for no apparent reason.

Saying the dog's name to cause him to break on the stays.

Not concentrating on the dog and anticipating how he will react.

Permitting the dog to lag instead of enticing him to speed up.

Motions too quick and erratic.

Grabbing at the dog and hovering over him.

Incorrect timing of the command with the correction and the correction with the praise.

Not walking in a straight line, hesitating on the turns, and stepping into the dog on the halts.

Giving indistinct commands and confused signals.

Nagging the dog.

Wagging the finger and pointing at the dog on the stays.

Pushing against the dog to make a correction (the dog will push right back).

Neglecting to review the previous lessons to keep the training progressive.

Using the same routine so the dog gets bored and works mechanically.

Too little praise.

Not giving the dog credit when he uses intelligence.

Not giving the dog sufficient play to make him like obedience training.

Every owner is guilty of making at least some of these mistakes. The owner must first train himself to handle correctly or he cannot expect to train his dog to the best advantage. What is needed is a class where the *owner* is scored on performance and on the way he conducts himself. An appropriate term—"Owner Obedience."

3

The Dog

THE DOG in training, like his master, deserves certain rights and privileges. When enrolled in a training class, the dog's good health must be the first consideration. No dog can be expected to do his best work when he is listless and low in spirits—the inevitable result of sickness or infection. Moreover, the presence of a sick dog in the classroom may spread disease to all the other dogs.

Since the dog cannot speak for himself, the owner must do the thinking for both. The dog will not be able to concentrate unless he is physically comfortable. Hunger, thirst, fatigue, or lack of exercise will prevent him from keeping his mind on the training.

The dog that is nervous or high strung may be better equipped to face the first training lessons if given an aspirin prior to coming to class. The dog should be fed lightly or nothing at all until after the close of the training period. After a few visits he will become more self-assured and will no longer need special attention.

Dogs are curious by nature and they dislike to be hurried. It is not fair to expect the inexperienced dog to give you his full attention without first letting him have an opportunity to become familiar with his surroundings. When brought to class early and given a few minutes to get acquainted with the other dogs, he will take his training more seriously.

A puppy five or six months old can be taught simple home obedience. A training class seldom accepts a dog under seven or eight months of age. The very young dog is easily distracted and his puppy ways would create too great a disturbance among the older dogs. Preliminary home training has its advantages, but the corrections should not be too severe nor the work too demanding. Simple home obedience will help the dog to adjust more easily to class training when he is older. Train the young dog by the *prevention* method. Teach him to do the right thing and avoid the wrong. Fewer corrections will be necessary and the dog will learn to enjoy obedience training.

Dogs learn by associating their act with a pleasing or displeasing result. They must be disciplined when they do wrong, but they must also be rewarded when they do right. Disposition, breed, and age will determine the degree of severity with which the dog must be handled. The instructor can only give the methods used in training and make suggestions for overcoming each dog's problems. The actual teaching will be done by the owner, so he must know what he can expect from his dog. The aggressive temperament requires authority combined with forcefulness. Shyness needs firmness in a kind way. They both need patience. The dog's disposition should be analysed and the owner must adjust his handling accordingly. Coax the shy dog. Demand from the bully. Pep up the loafer. No play for the clowns. Hold firm against the obstinate and disguise corrections from the skeptic.

The greatest obligation every owner has to his dog is to keep him happy and working in a gay and cheerful way. The dog's every mood is registered by the way he carries his tail (if he has a tail). It is the "Stop!" and "Go!" signal to be closely observed by the trainer, and the sign to either proceed with caution or to go full steam ahead. The owner will do well to heed this warning.

Females in season can be trained at home but not taken to class until they cease to attract the male dogs. In most cases this will be for a period of three weeks, or possibly longer. If the owner expects his female to come in season during the term, it would be better to wait for the next series of lessons. The training can then be continued without interruption.

There are a few dogs—not many—that are ready to pick a fight with every dog they see. Dismissal from the training class is inevitable unless the owner is willing to take precautions. If the dog is required to work while muzzled, he should wear it at home occasionally so he will get used to it and will not be annoyed when submitted to the unexpected in class. He won't enjoy wearing one at first, but he will learn to accept it, and the action will be for his own protection as well as that of the other dogs.

Dog training cannot be considered an eventful experience for the owner unless it is a sporting one for the dog. The dog's bill of rights, were he able to express his opinions on training, would probably be something like the following.

Play with me! At heart, I am a frisky fellow and always ready for a game.

Be kind, and I will do my best to please you.

Be generous with your praise. It is the best reward I can have.

Be fair. Tell me what you want before you correct me, then praise me when I do it.

Be patient. I can absorb just so much at a time.

Be consistent so I can learn right from wrong.

Give your commands clearly and make your signals distinct, so that I won't be confused.

Give me confidence and security. Even flatter my ego a little.

Don't lose your temper and hit me in anger. We will both be upset if you do.

Your voice and a jerk on the collar will tell me I have done something wrong.

Don't over-train me. Training is hard work.

Don't expect me to work after I've eaten. That's when I am sleepy and lazy.

Don't grab at my coat nor pinch my skin.

Don't point your finger in my face.

Consider my health and make allowance for the weather. Lost time can be made up under better working conditions.

Keep me from getting bored by changing the routine occasionally.

Never—never nag me. Nagging makes me miserable.

Hold me if I need correcting so I won't become hand-shy.

Never punish me unless I deserve it. Was it your fault I did wrong?

If you don't expect a miracle, I will improve if you give me time.

A spike collar will *make* me obey but you won't be proud of the way I work.

Most of all, keep me happy.

The owner should feel that if his dog could speak, he would say, "Obedience training is fun for me, too. Thank you for training me."

4

The Training Director

WHAT MAKES a good training class director? Before this can be answered, one must point out what makes a good trainer. If an individual is to judge how each and every dog is to be handled in a training class, he must be an expert. He must have experience! Not that of taking just one or two dogs through the preliminaries, but the kind of knowledge gained from working with dogs of all breeds and under all conditions. The training of dogs is not a mathematical problem which can be solved with a specific formula. The temperament and individual characteristics of each dog must be considered and the training technique varied to meet the occasion. When a trainer knows what he can expect from a dog and what his reaction will be, he has the advantage. The trainer automatically anticipates the dog's next move and decides whether to force the issue or to lessen his demands.

Knowledge of dog psychology doesn't come easily. It is a field so specialized that we have only scratched the surface. There is an art in knowing when to be gentle, when to be firm, when to rebuke, and when to encourage. We are not all artists, but we can learn through experience.

The good trainer is born with the essential qualities that give him the natural ability to coordinate his body motions with every move the dog makes. The result is perfect timing. That is why some trainers succeed where others fail. When the trainer is definite in his actions because he knows what he is doing, the dog *knows* that he knows, and the result is— *respect!* Respect gained through admiration and not through fear will bring a happy response that is proof of one's training personality.

A dog can be forced to *be* obedient, but he cannot be forced to *like* obedience! Therefore, the expert is not a bully. He recognizes the fact that all training is progressive and that each new step becomes easy if the preceding lessons have been thoroughly understood. He is not afraid to retrace his steps momentarily if in so doing it will give the dog confidence.

Because of his experience and understanding, the proficient trainer is aware of the disastrous effects caused by nagging and he will avoid it at all costs. Because he is patient, he doesn't become exasperated if results are slow in coming. He doesn't expect a miracle. The clever trainer succeeds in making the dog feel responsible for the correction. He is kind, yet firm, and above all will make obedience fun for the dog.

A good trainer, however, does not necessarily make a good training class instructor. Some people may train at home and give private instruction with success, but when faced with a large group they lack the necessary qualities of leadership. In the training class it is not a question of working out a single problem, but of solving fifty different problems all at the same time.

In addition to the qualities of forceful leadership and the ability to take the initiative, the training director must be a likeable person and have the admiration and respect of his pupils. He must have diplomacy and be patient and tolerant of others. It is not always easy to teach someone else how to accomplish what one is able to do oneself.

The good training director never permits the class to be held up for a long period of time while he discusses one dog's problem with the owner, nor does he hold back the group for one or two backward dogs. The owners with special problems should be asked to come early or to stay after class for personal instruction.

The respected director starts his classes on time and demands attention throughout the training period. He insists that the training room be quiet except for the necessary commands. The training room is not the place for idle chatter. The instructor's responsibility does not end with the calling out of the commands. Through the use of words he must create a mental picture of each exercise. He must patiently repeat each step over and over until even the most backward pupil grasps the idea. Most training classes are made up of adults whose school days are a thing of the past and some are not quick to learn the technique of training.

When it is possible, the class director should divide the beginners' group into two parts. This will allow for a rest period at which time the owners may watch the others and see how they train. Knowledge can be gained from watching— if only to learn what *not* to do!

The vigilant director should not dismiss his class without introducing a new exercise or a variation of the class routine in order to encourage home practice. The egotist who thinks his dog is good and needs no training between sessions can be made to understand that there is always room for improvement.

The initial meeting of a training class should be held without dogs unless it is a club affair and the dogs have had previous training. The confusion that results when a group of untrained dogs and inexperienced handlers comes together for the first time is too much to cope with and little training would be accomplished. A quiet get-together, where problems can be discussed calmly and the various steps demonstrated without noise and excitement, is more enlightening.

After the announcements about the class procedure and the club sponsoring the classes, the showing of training films makes an excellent introduction to the evening's program. This will give the beginner an over-all picture of what he

Fig. 9. The first training class should be held without the confusion of dogs.
Courtesy: Mary Priscilla Keyes.

is expected to accomplish during the weeks that follow. After the films, the director would do well to demonstrate the basic steps with two or three untrained dogs brought to the class for this purpose. When this is followed by a short exhibition with dogs that are already trained, the group can see by comparison how quickly results may be achieved.

A question-and-answer session will benefit the entire class. The questions should be repeated clearly by the instructor and his answers given so that everyone in the class can hear. Usually one person's questions are relevant to the problems

REGULATIONS

ASPCA OBEDIENCE TRAINING COURSE
Manhattan

VISITORS:

1. Visitors must report attendance at the desk before each session.
2. Visitors must remain on the balcony at all times.
3. Visitors must refrain from loud conversation while the classes are in session.

CLASS MEMBERS:

1. Do not feed your dog before class. Feed your dog in the morning or after class.
2. Make sure that the dog has been walked before classes to prevent accidents.
3. Keep dog on tight lead when going up and down stairs to avoid accidents and prevent dogs from clashing.
4. The attendance desk is in the basement, at the head of the gymnasium stairs. Be sure to call your number to registrar each class night.
5. When your dog is in heat, do not bring her to class. This will necessitate the dog's absence for two weeks. Before returning for further training, the dog should be bathed.
6. When the dog is in heat, the owner should inform the registrar, so that she may record it. However, the owner's attendance is important so that the lessons may be practiced at home, and imperative if the dog is to be credited for attendance.
7. More than three absences will automatically eliminate the dog from receiving a diploma.
8. Eligibility for taking part in the graduation exercises are:
     1. Attendance.
     2. Dog's ability to do the work.
     3. Improvement.
9. Qualifications for a diploma are:
     1. Attendance.
     2. Dog's ability to do the work.
10. Miss Henley reserves the right to drop any dog or switch him to another class if it is to the dog's advantage.
11. Please keep dogs quiet and on short leads at all times unless you are working on the floor.
12. The best shoes for training are low ones with rubber heels. Please wear them whenever possible.
13. Women cannot train dogs when holding pocketbooks. Please do not bring them onto the floor.
14. Dogs are not allowed on the balcony at any time.
15. Water for dogs will be placed at the end of the training hall near the elevator.
16. When in doubt about proper equipment, please consult Miss Henley.
17. The weekly lesson is not sufficient for training your dog. It is important to practice lessons at home daily, for 15 minutes, morning and night.
18. Women's and men's lavatories will be found on the balcony of the gymnasium. Please inquire.
19. All classes begin promptly, so please be on time.

Fig. 10. A sample copy of regulations for class members.

of other members of the group. A general discussion will thus avoid time-consuming repetitions of the subject.

Members should be warned what to expect the following week when they arrive with their dogs. They should be shown how to stop uncontrolled barking by keeping the dog on a short leash and placing the hand around his muzzle, and how to handle the situation if a dog fight develops. It must be impressed upon the handler never to stand still while his dog lunges forward toward another dog. The good handler must turn away and jerk hard on the leash. A demonstration should be given of the proper way to control an obstreperous dog by pulling the collar tight and rapping him across the nose. This technique can be used to prevent fights and to stop excessive noise.

It would be well to remind the owners not to feed their dogs for several hours before coming to class and to see that they are exercised. Request the owners to keep their dogs on a short lead when entering and leaving the building, to walk in the center of all passageways, and to keep the dogs (particularly the males) away from corners and posts. A dog that deliberately misbehaves inside the building should be barred from the classroom. The trained dog is expected to do more than just obey a few simple obedience commands. He must have good manners as well.

The owners of female dogs should be instructed to check them carefully each week. One that shows signs of coming in season must not be brought to class. Recommend that the owner attend and observe the training so that he can carry on with the lessons outside the classroom and the dog will not get behind in her work. Before she is brought to class again at the end of the three- or four-week period, suggest that she be bathed in a disinfectant solution to remove any lingering odors. The cause of absence should be noted in the records.

Women handlers should be advised to wear low, comfortable shoes with rubber heels and to leave valuables at home so that pocketbooks may be safely left on the sidelines. They should dress sensibly and select clothes that will not interfere with the dog while he is being trained.

The training director should inform the class at the first meeting what the requirements will be for graduation. Even though the dog and his handler attend the class regularly, they must, in order to receive a diploma, meet the demands for performance agreed upon by the director and the training committee. A dog should not be permitted to graduate until he is under complete control, heels on a slack leash, remains in the standing, sitting, and down positions, and obeys commands to lie down and to come, even though the response is slow. A beginners graduation should be judged more leniently than the novice class at a regular Obedience Trial.

When the training is done out-of-doors, the instructor can teach as many as 30 or 40 owners and dogs at a time. When working indoors, a training area 40 by 40 feet can accommodate about 12 dogs if they work in a circle. A room 60 by 80 feet will take about 25 dogs. If the class must be divided because of the large enrollment, it should be done at the first meeting so that the instructor will be able to start his classes promptly the following week. The division may be done in one of two ways. The first group may work the full 45 minutes to one hour and then be permitted to leave; or the group may work 20 to 30 minutes, then have a rest period while the second group trains. The latter method is preferable when the room is a good size and accommodates a large number of people. If the space is small, the onlookers will cause too much confusion and the classroom should be cleared during the instruction. The group may further be divided according to the size of the dogs so that the small breeds will not be overwhelmed by the larger ones and will make a better showing.

At the initial session, before the owners are permitted to purchase their training equipment, the instructor should discuss the training collar and review the method of putting it on. He should explain how to hold the leash and the use of the jumping stick. (Jumping sticks will not be brought to class until later in the course.) The lesson for the following week should be demonstrated. It will consist of heeling with about-turns, sitting at heel, and the sit-stay on leash. Before leaving, owners are permitted to purchase their training equipment. They will have a full week to practice before the dogs are brought to class the first time.

It is wise for the training director to prepare a list of the subject matter on which he will speak the first night. One is inclined to forget certain points which should be fully understood from the beginning. A sample copy for the notebook may be as follows:

Welcome.

Responsibility of owner:
   (a) Feeding and exercising of dog.
   (b) Promptness and regular attendance.
   (c) Attitude of owner toward training.
   (d) Home training.
   (e) Females in season.
   (f) Women's suitable apparel and shoes. Leave valuables at
        home.

Division of classes.

What to expect the following week:
   (a) Keep dogs on short leash.
   (b) Keep away from other dogs.
   (c) Watch dog's manners in entrance hall and training room.
   (d) Be responsible for dog's mistakes.

Show training films if available.

Discuss:

  (a) Equipment (collar, leash, jumping stick).
  (b) Requirements for graduation:
      1. Attendance.
      2. Dog's ability to do the required work (not every dog will graduate).

Demonstrate:

  (a) Use of collar and how to hold the leash.
  (b) How to prevent fights and stop barking.
  (c) Following week's lesson—heeling and sitting and the sit-stay.

Stress importance of:

  (a) Timing the command with the correction and the correction with the praise.
  (b) Intonation of voice commands.
  (c) Proper snap of leash so collar will click.
  (d) Home practice—15 minutes morning and night.

Hold an open question-and-answer session.

When the owners arrive the first evening with their dogs there will be a great deal of confusion until the dogs quiet down and the owners understand the instructor's commands. The group may work abreast in a single line or it may work in a circle. The method used depends upon the size and shape of the room and the number of trainees present. A circle will accommodate a larger number of dogs. (Four markers, such as chairs or posts outside of which the members must pass, should be used to maintain the size of the circle.) By alternating from one system to the other, the handlers and dogs will receive a more varied experience.

When the circle method is used, the owners should be called onto the floor and told to take their positions with their dogs sitting at heel on the inside of the circle. They should be advised to stay at least six feet from the person ahead. If each handler will drop back to a distance of six feet after an about-turn, the other handlers will drop back automatically and the spacing will be kept even.

When working abreast in a single line, the point should be stressed that the about-turn must be done together. Handlers with large dogs or those who walk quickly must slow up at each side of the room and wait until the command is given to make the turn. Otherwise everybody will be going in a differ-

Fig. 11. One method of working in a group—the circle. *Courtesy: Louise Branch.*

ent direction and further commands from the instructor will be impossible.

Before starting the lesson, the instructor should check the collars and explain that thereafter each owner must be responsible for seeing that his dog's collar is on correctly. The instructor should see that the handler has the right kind of training lead and that he is holding it in the proper way. A few moments should be taken to demonstrate the day's lesson. This should be done for each new step as the training progresses, but long speeches and discussions should be avoided, since they will bore the members. Demonstrating a technique at frequent intervals helps the beginner to grasp an idea more easily; it also keeps the class alert.

This brings up the question of whether a training director should handle dogs that belong to members of the class or use their dogs to demonstrate an exercise. The answer is yes. This practice will serve two purposes. Unless the instructor can handle the leash of a problem dog to judge the dog's reaction to training, he cannot advise the owner what precautions to take. The other advantage is that the owner will see by comparison how quickly, with the right kind of handling, a difficult dog can be brought under control. Every owner feels his own dog is different and when he sees the instructor overcome a handicap, he will be less inclined to take the attitude that "It's easy to make some dogs do it, but I would like to see him get *my* dog to obey!"

The class should perform the exercises in unison. This will enable the instructor to watch every dog. Owners frequently attempt to train in class as they would at home, with no thought of the other members. They will have to be reminded to wait for the commands, not to anticipate the action. When each step is done simultaneously the instructor, by quickly glancing about the room, will note the handlers who are having trouble. Suggestions may then be made and assistance given.

The instructor's commands should be stated clearly and distinctly. The success of the training depends upon timing the voice with the correction, and the correction with praise. Therefore, the director must give a verbal picture throughout his teaching. For example, the command "Forward" is followed by "Say Heel! Jerk! Praise!" When the command "About turn" is given, the instructor again repeats "About turn, say Heel! Jerk! Praise!" When the class is given the command to halt and the dogs are supposed to sit, the instructor advises: "Halt! Pull up with your right hand, push down with your left, say Sit! Don't forget the praise." The action will correspond to the word picture as it forms in the owner's mind. The routine will become a habit and before long the members will do the right thing without stopping to think "What comes next?"

The advantage of training a pure-bred dog over a mixed breed is that the trainer knows what to expect from the pure-bred and how he will react to training. A breed that is pure for generations has taken on certain temperamental characteristics that will run true to form. The difference between instructing an all-breed class and a specialty club is that the training director will encounter in the former the temperamental characteristics of all breeds, not merely those which are typical of one.

The training director must be prepared to instruct the owners according to the breed of dog they are handling and at the same time maintain a system of training that will apply throughout the instruction. For example, the owners of Boxers must be warned: "Use voice authority. Make definite corrections but handle quietly. Don't nag your dog or he will retaliate." Poodle owners should be encouraged: "Be liberal with praise to flatter the dog's ego." Poodles are show-offs and they enjoy working in their effort to please when they are made the center of attention. The Irish Setter gives the impression that obedience training is beneath his dignity as a sporting dog. Setters, as well as certain members of the working group, take a happy-go-lucky attitude where they will bite and grab at the owner's arm or hand in play. In this case the owner must be told: "Don't pull your hand away! Hold it still and close to your body. When the dog tries to nip, slap him once, good and hard, and tell him in no uncertain terms to stop his nonsense!"

Some terrier breeds are so flighty and inattentive that the owners may lose faith in dog training. The instructor can only forewarn the owner that until he can get his dog's attention he will make little progress. The corrections must be severe enough to make the dog forget outside distractions. Every time the dog turns away, tell the owner: "Smack him on the rear to make him look at you." If the owner still can't get the dog's attention while heeling, suggest that he carry a small switch in his right hand. When the dog forges ahead, the owner should demand "Heel!" and whack the dog under the chin once to make him draw back by himself. This suggestion may be made to every owner whose dog lunges forward repeatedly and will not respond to leash corrections. Recommendation should further be made that the heeling be done close to a wall or fence to keep the dog from ducking away. The owner should take special precaution not to use the switch any more than is necessary so that the dog will not become hand shy. Two or three good rebuffs when properly done will cure even the most determined dog of darting ahead.

There are dogs in every training class that are pathetically scared and those who get stage fright when they appear in public. The instructor must encourage the owners: "Be firm in a kind way! If your dog won't walk on leash, don't jerk it—instead, pull the leash tight and slowly drag the dog along the floor until he feels for secure footing. When he takes a few steps by himself, slacken the leash and give him a great deal of praise." The timid dog will gain confidence in time if he is not jerked severely and if the owner does not let him have his way.

Every dog can be lazy at times. Many dogs are clowns. All

dogs are suspicious. The owner must pep up the loafer the best way he can. Suggest the use of titbits and the giving of encouragement. The clowning must be stopped by bringing the training to an immediate halt, while the voice demands that the dog behave. Corrections must be disguised at all times to avoid the dog's distrust of either the owner or the instructor.

The training director may occasionally have to demonstrate the knack of throwing a dog off balance if he insists upon standing on his hind legs and pawing at his owner. Quickly pulling the leash to one side and then to the other will give the dog insecure footing and teach him to keep all four feet on the floor. A quick kick backward with the right foot to rap a dog on the rear, will help to bring him around more quickly on the about turn. This is especially true of large strong breeds. Praise should immediately follow such a correction.

Throughout the training the instructor must stress the importance of giving the first command in a friendly tone and then resorting to a *demanding* tone of voice if the dog disobeys. He must emphasize the value of increasing the severity of the corrections when the dog is reprimanded more than once for the same misdemeanor.

The director must observe the action to see if the voice command is given *before* the leash is used and that praise is given with the correction. The training will be successful only if the timing is accurate. He must watch for hand signals that might confuse the dog or conflict with those that will be used later in the advanced work.

A vicious dog—one that repeatedly and without provocation attacks either humans or other dogs—should be barred from attending the training class and the owner's money refunded by the club or sponsoring organization. The director may, at his discretion, recommend the use of a muzzle for a dog that has an over-aggressive manner, especially if the other dogs are disturbed by his attitude. Precaution should be taken to prevent fights and possible injury, but the owner entering a training class must be given to understand that he does so at his own risk. Instructing a large number of owners with different breeds of dogs under the difficult conditions that exist in a training class is quite an undertaking. The responsibility rests on the shoulders of the training director. The burden is not a light one.

The question of assistant trainers is not a pressing one unless there are several classes in different stages of training. One person can handle a large group with only occasional help for such things as holding the leash of a dog that breaks consistently, or helping an owner gain control over an obstreperous animal. The need for assistant trainers will come with the introduction of the more advanced courses, for by this time each dog will have reached a different point in the training.

A person who assists in the training program should follow whatever system is used by the head training director (if there is such a person) or that agreed upon by the club trainers. Perhaps an improved technique is desirable, but those who volunteer to help in the teaching must work in harmony with the instructor. Consistent training will avoid confusing the dogs. It will prevent criticism of the various methods of instruction, and the class will progress more rapidly in the advanced training that follows. The biggest handicap an instructor can have comes from those owners who attend a number of classes and work under different teachers. One instructor may force the dog at a point in his training where the other instructor would recommend leniency. Or he may suggest letting up at the crucial moment. It is possible to tell what action to take only when the instructor knows the dog's history and has watched his progress from the beginning. It is natural for an owner to seek knowledge elsewhere if he feels he has gained all he can from a given source, but the mixing of instructions during the teaching period is not satisfactory. The success of the training class depends on the training director and his assistants. The instruction will be more easily understood and carried through when there is continuity.

The latest trend in dog obedience is to hold classes where those who are interested in obedience can learn to become training class instructors. As in any profession, there is always need for capable leaders and for uniformity in teaching.

Instructors classes, under the direction of the author, were previously conducted in New York City under the auspices of the Association of Obedience Clubs and Judges. The class for beginners was held in conjunction with the ASPCA all-breed training classes, and was limited to 12 representatives from local training clubs. The advanced instructors (they must have taken the nine-week beginners course before being eligible for the advanced group) studied the open and utility training at a specialty training club, where they learned how to teach the open and utility exercises and how to overcome the individual problems.

At such a meeting, the student instructors observe the teaching of a beginners class of 75 dogs, broken down into 3 one-hour sessions. They also observe 1 to 1½ hours instruction of an intermediate group (this includes jumping and dumbbell work). At the close of the training period the instructors meet for an additional hour to hold an open discussion to clarify controversial points and to unify training methods.

The procedure for the next two weeks remains the same except that the owners of some of the most difficult dogs from the classes are asked to cooperate by remaining with their dogs for an additional hour and permitting the instructors to handle them. This serves two purposes: the dogs that need the most training receive extra practice and the instructors, by changing dogs frequently, learn how to handle the different breeds.

During the fourth or fifth week the student instructors take over the teaching of the volunteer group after observing the instruction of the beginners classes under the regular instructor. This acquaints the members with classroom teaching and gives them the experience of using a loud speaker (which is used in this particular class).

Halfway through the course the instructors are permitted to conduct the regular classes for a 10 or 15 minute interval. They follow the routine that has been used throughout the training and make suggestions on how to handle the problem dogs.

The advanced instructors, who meet on another evening, observe for three hours the teaching of the specialty club's open and utility classes. At the close of the training period each instructor brings his own dog into the classroom and suggestions are made on how to overcome problems. The students do not actually teach in the advanced course, but comments and personal opinions are encouraged. Suggestions, if they meet with general approval, are put into effect.

This may not be the ideal set-up for teaching instructors to conduct obedience classes, but it is a step in the right direction. The next few years should show significant progress along these lines and a standardized program may soon be available to all people interested in becoming obedience instructors.

SUGGESTIONS FOR INSTRUCTORS

Be prompt. Start the classes on time.
Maintain an orderly classroom.

Insist upon the owners having the correct training equipment.

Limit preliminary lectures. The instruction will be more thoroughly understood after the owners have had some training experience.

Demonstrate each exercise when introducing it to the class.

Demand the attention of every member of the class during demonstrations.

Instruct in a loud clear voice so that everyone will hear the commands.

Repeat the instructions over and over.

If a loud speaker system is used, cultivate a microphone voice; speak slowly, enunciate distinctly, and keep the tone low and on a level keel.

Keep the class active. Idleness leads to boredom.

Request that all members perform the exercises together.

Observe the class as a unit. Correct the owners at the time a mistake is made so the instruction will be more effective.

Give a word picture of each exercise, especially in the beginners class. Calling out the commands such as "Forward" and "Halt" will not teach the owners how to get results.

Explain the reasons why the hand signals and the leash corrections are made the way they are.

Judge how a dog will react to a situation and advise the owners what they can expect from the dogs.

Insist that the owners walk briskly while heeling, especially on the about-turns.

Stress the importance of using a series of jerks on the leash to make an inattentive dog watchful of his owner, and to jerk the lead parallel to the floor.

Observe the owner's posture while training and how he carries the leash.

Watch for incorrect timing. The command must be given first, followed by the correction *and the praise* together.

Don't burden the owners with the finer points of training until the dogs are under control. They will be too busy to concentrate on little things.

Change the class routine; avoid following a set pattern. This will prevent the dogs from anticipating.

Follow an outlined schedule so the necessary progress will be made.

Credit an individual owner when he gives a good correction and compliment the class as a whole when it does good work. Praise is as important to the owners as to the dogs.

5

The Beginners Course

Beginners Course: For dogs with no previous training.
Length of Course: Nine weeks.
Training Period: 1½ to 2 hours.
Purpose: To teach the basic exercises.
Training consists of:

Heeling with about-turns (the right-about and left-U).
Sitting and sit-stay.
Come-fore and going to heel position.
Coming when called.
Lying down and the down-stay.
Sitting from a down position.
Standing at heel, stand-stay, stand for examination.
Stick jumping.
Heeling with leash over shoulder.
(*Note:* All work done on leash.)

Lesson 1 (Dogs to be left at home):

Welcoming speeches by the officers and training director of
the club or sponsoring organization.
General announcements pertaining to the training classes (see
p. 52).
Show films, if available, on obedience training.
Demonstrate the obedience routine with both trained and untrained dogs.

Hold a question-and-answer session.

Discuss the training equipment and its correct use.

Preview Lesson 2, which consists of heeling with about-turns, sitting, and the sit-stay.

Assist the owners with the purchase of their training equipment.

Remind the class to practice at home.

Lesson 2:

New exercises:

Heeling with about-turns.

Sitting and the sit-stay.

The owners are called onto the floor and the dogs made to sit on the left side of the trainer. The leash is held short in *both* hands. If working abreast, the owners face the instructor. If working in a circle, the dogs sit at heel position on the inside of the circle and the instructor stands in the center.

Check all collars to see that they are the right weight, length, and correctly placed on the dog.

Review the method of holding the leash in both hands so the dogs will be kept under control and the six-foot length will not seem awkward.

Start the lesson with heeling and sitting. Make right-about and left U-turns every few feet so that the dogs will be more attentive and less interested in the other dogs.

Warn the owners to keep their spacing and not to hesitate on the about turns. Urge them to *keep moving* and to jerk the lead *after* they turn in the opposite direction.

The commands will sound something like the following: "Forward! Say heel! Jerk! Praise! About turn! Say heel! Jerk! Praise! *Keep moving* on the about-turn! Halt! Command Sit! Up with the right hand, down with the left! Don't forget the praise!" Large dogs can be brought around on the about-turn more quickly if the owner kicks backward with the right foot to rap the dog unexpectedly on the rear. Praise should follow immediately.

Fig. 12. The correct way for novices to hold the leash while heeling.
Courtesy: Mary Priscilla Keyes.

The class will have to be reminded: "Transfer the lead from the left to the right hand when you hear the command halt and before you tell the dog to sit. This will shorten the lead so that you will have control over the dog and can make him sit straight. When you prevent mistakes, you won't have to correct them later. The dog that sits at an angle must be

Fig. 13. The dog is corrected for sitting too far ahead. *Courtesy: Mary Priscilla Keyes.*

slapped on the off-side hip! Hold the lead tight when you do it. Cuff him before he sits down—don't wait until he is already sitting! If he continues to sit crooked, cuff him harder. Forward! About turn! Jerk! Praise! *Keep moving.* Walk briskly, especially on the about-turn! Use a series of short, snappy jerks to make the dog forget outside distractions!

Halt! Forward! Jerk the lead in the direction of travel. Not up in the air! That lifts the dog from the floor. When you make an about-turn, pivot sharply to the right and snap the lead parallel to the floor *after* you are headed in the opposite direction. *Keep moving!* When you make a left U-turn, bump into the dog to make him draw back by himself. Carry the leash comfortably in both hands. Keep it short but slack, and have your dog under control. Tighten the lead to make a correction, but don't drag or hold it tight. When you snap the lead the right way, you will hear the collar click. Pat your side after you jerk the leash to reassure the dog, and coax him to come in close.

"While heeling, carry your left arm straight and hold it close to your body. When the dog forges ahead, jerk backward! When he lags, jerk forward! Don't exaggerate hand motions. Use a wrist action as well as bending the elbow and snap the leash short and hard. Throughout the training, *command* first, *correct* second, *praise* third! Pat your left leg and tousle the dog's head after each correction to overcome hurt feelings. *This is done without taking your hand from the leash.*"

When the owners halt, the dogs must sit square and close to the side. Remind the class: "*Don't* step into your dog! It will make him move away from you. If he sits wide, pull him in close and hold the lead tight until he sits down the way he should. When he goes too far ahead, hold the leash in back of your body in the left hand and jerk backward *before* you stop moving! If he persists in sitting too far ahead, step across in front of him and block him with your left leg. At the same time, pull the lead tight across your left hip. Your dog must learn never to pass your left knee when either heeling or sitting, and not to sit at an angle. If he does, take up the slack in the lead with the right hand and use your left hand to cuff him on the off-side hip! Praise your dog immediately after the correction so his feelings won't be hurt."

(The class member whose dog is being exhibited in breed, and who brings the dog to training class primarily for the experience of seeing other dogs, may request the privilege of

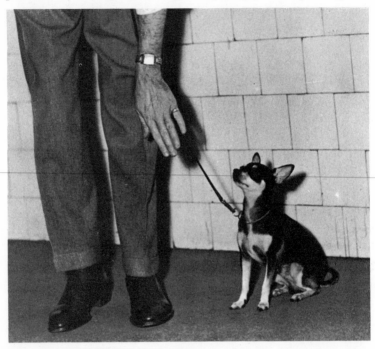

Fig. 14. When the dog is at heel position, the signal to stay is given before the handler moves away. *Courtesy: Mary Priscilla Keyes.*

having the dog stand at heel instead of sitting. When the dog has had more training, he will learn to distinguish between the sit and the stand-at-heel and will not be confused.)

The sit-stay is the next exercise. (*Note:* If the dogs are working in a circle, the director asks everyone to face the center of the circle with their dogs sitting at heel position. This will allow the handlers to back away from their dogs during the sit-stay without stepping on the other dogs in the class.)

The instructions may be as follows: "Hold your left hand, palm back, close to the dog's nose and command 'Stay!' Step out with your right foot and turn and face your dog. Stay

Fig. 15. Correct signal to make a dog stay when in front of the handler.
Courtesy: Mary Priscilla Keyes.

close to him at first! Pivot back on your left foot to heel position without circling your dog. Again, tell your dog to stay! Signal back with your left hand and move out on your right foot. Keep your leash slack, but be ready to make a quick correction if your dog shifts position! Now, with the dog facing you, hold your *right* hand in front of his nose and say 'Stay!' and back away to the full length of the lead."

Fig. 16. The leash is held on the dog's right whenever the owner circles back to heel position. *Courtesy: Mary Priscilla Keyes.*

At this point the instructor should explain that when the dog is at the handler's side in heel position, the stay signal is given with the left hand held in front of the dog, palm back. When the dog is sitting and facing the owner, the stay signal is given with the right hand. It is held with the palm toward the dog and the fingers pointing to the ground. This is the signal that will later be used to make the dog sit from the down position. It should be put into effect at the start of training.

The director's instructions may continue as follows: "With your dog facing you at the full length of the leash, circle slowly to the right and pass in back of your dog to heel position. As you move around, take up the slack in the lead with the left hand and hold it on the right side of the dog. If he moves, *stand still* and repeat the command 'Stay!' as you jerk him back to a sitting position. Hold the dog with both hands, if necessary, while you circle around him, but don't let him move from that spot until you give him permission! Stand quietly at his side. *Pat and praise him while he is still sitting.* Now release him from training and play with him just as you do at home!"

The director continues: "Next, tell your dog to stay and stand in back of him. Stay close at first and be ready to correct him if he moves! The dog is permitted to turn his head but not his body. Correct him if he does! Step back to heel position. Don't praise him yet. Tell him to stay once more. Step in back of him to the full length of the lead. Return to heel position. Say 'Stay!' and face him. Go to the right of the dog and stand in back of him! Walk past him and face him again! Return to heel position. *Don't* keep saying, 'stay, stay, stay!' Repeat the command if the dog breaks, but otherwise don't say anything. Move slowly in the sit-stay exercise until the dog becomes accustomed to staying by himself. If the dog breaks position, move quickly! Allow as little time as possible between the actual mistake and the ensuing correction!

"With dogs in heel position, say 'Stay!' Back with your left hand, out on your right foot, and go to the end of the lead.

Lean over and put the lead quietly on the floor. Say 'Stay!' as you do so. Pick up your lead. Say 'Stay!' at the same time. Drop it again without leaning over. Pick it up. Circle back to heel position."

Fig. 17. The leash is used to correct the dog that breaks on the sit-stay. *Courtesy: Mary Priscilla Keyes.*

The owners must be reminded: "Whenever your dog moves forward to break the sitting position bounce the palm of your hand against his nose, or lift the lead sharply to throw him back again into position. Keep your lead slack when you step out from your dog! Use a firm tone of voice when you give a command the first time—a demanding voice if the dog disobeys. *Don't keep repeating your dog's name!* Stress the command. *Don't keep talking to the dog!* If he is sitting, let him alone. Repeat the command if your dog is disobedient; otherwise, keep quiet!"

Frequent variations in the way each exercise is done keeps the owners active, the dogs alert, and makes the class interesting. The owners will have to be warned: ."Don't hover over your dogs! Stand up straight! Keep your hands off your dog! Use your leash to make the correction! Don't put your leash down until you are told! You must be ready to correct your dog every time he moves! Let's try another sit-stay. Leave your dogs! Give the command and the signal simultaneously! Watch your dog closely! Concentrate on him! Correct him at the start of each mistake; don't wait until he has already made it! Circle around your dog and stop at heel position. Once more, command him to 'Stay!' Back with your left hand, out with your right foot, and go to the full length of the lead. Face your dog! If he moves, hold the lead above his head and snap it away from you to throw the dog back on his haunches! Repeat the command 'Stay!' in a demanding tone. Return to heel position. Circle around in back of your dog but hold the leash on the dog's right. Don't praise or pat him yet, or he will become unsteady and break before he should. Exercise finished! Now praise your dog and play with him! Release him from training for a few moments so he will learn to enjoy his work."

Near the close of the hour the instructor should demonstrate the next week's lesson, which will consist of the comefore, going to heel position, and coming when called. The heeling will also include the fast and the slow.

Lesson 3:

New exercises:
    Come-fore.
    Going to heel position.
    Coming when called.
    Heeling in a fast and slow pace.

Review:
    Heeling with about-turns (right-about and left-U).
    Sitting at heel.
    Sit-stay with leash on the floor and the handler at a greater
        distance.

The come-fore teaches the dog to sit and face his handler instead of sitting at his left side. When teaching the exercise, the instruction may be:

"Forward! Keep your lead slack. Command 'Come-fore' and walk backward without moving the position of your hands on the lead. As the dog is coming in front, gradually gather the lead up and coax him in close! Hold the lead tight and tell the dog to sit! Praise him immediately! Tell him to stay! Step back to heel position without circling. (This will speed up the exercise.) Forward! Walk backward, keep your lead slack, command 'Come-fore' with emphasis on the *come!* Don't drag your dog around on a tight lead! The lead is used to bring the dog in close and to make him sit squarely in front. Step back to heel position! Forward! Command the come-fore! Remember, the dog does the turning! All you do is walk backward two or three steps. When the dog turns around, gather the lead up and tell him to sit. Praise at once!"

The instructor will have to remind the owners: "Stand up straight! Don't lean over your dog! Hold your hands low and close to your body! Pull up on the lead to make the dog sit! If he doesn't obey immediately, lean over and slap him quickly on the rear, but hold the leash tight at the same time.

Insist that your dog sit straight and squarely on both hips. If he sits at an angle, hold the leash tight and cuff him on whichever hip is out of line."

Every obedience exercise includes the come-fore position. It is therefore important that the dog learn to do it correctly from the very start of his training so he will not get into the habit of doing sloppy work.

The going-to-heel exercise is teaching the dog to go to the handler's left side from the come-fore position. The instructions are:

"With your dog in the come-fore position, take hold of the lead the same as you do when heeling. When you hear the command 'Forward!' say 'Heel!' walk to the *right* of your dog, and keep going! The dog will swing around to your left side automatically. Halt! Tell your dog to sit, then praise him! Tell him to 'Stay!' and step in front of him again! Up close! You should be as near your dog as possible. Again, Forward! Command 'Heel!' Walk past your dog and keep going! The left hand guides the dog around into place at your left side. Halt! Make your dog sit! Tell him to stay and face him again. This time, to make your dog go to heel position, step backward with your left foot *after* you command 'Heel!' and jerk the lead with a snap! This will bring the dog to all four feet. Now walk forward. Guide the dog around into place with your left hand. Halt! Make him sit immediately! Now let's do the two exercises together. First the come-fore. Forward! Command 'Come-fore!' Walk backward with little motion of your body. Stand up straight! Keep your lead slack while the dog is making the turn! Gather up the lead as the dog comes in front, and hold—hold—hold the lead *tight* until he sits. Praise and pat him! Next, command 'Heel!' Now jerk the lead hard as you take a step backward with the left foot. Praise the dog at once as he swings around to heel position.

You may have to walk backward two or three steps at the beginning, but soon your dog will get the idea of going around to your left side by himself whenever he hears the command 'Heel!' "

In practicing the going-to-heel exercise, the owner must be

Fig. 18. The owner must stand erect when teaching the dog to come.
Courtesy: Mary Priscilla Keyes.

reminded: "Give the command without moving the leash, then snap it hard when you step back with your left foot. Praise him immediately. Move your feet less each time so that the dog must do most of the work. Snap the lead in a series of jerks if the dog is stubborn, but never drag him around on his tail end."

The instructor may prefer to have the dog go to heel position by going to the right and circling in back of the owner. This method does not give as snappy an appearance as the left side finish and it involves changing the leash from one hand to the other, but either type of finish is permissible. The training procedure remains the same. The command is given first, followed by the correction (with the right hand in this case), and then immediate praise.

Perfection in going to heel position will not come in the third lesson, nor even in the fourth or fifth. There will be a gradual improvement throughout the course.

Coming when called, or the recall exercise, is the next step in the dog's training. If the class is working in a circle, it is done the first time *toward* the center of the circle and the second time *away* from the center toward the outside walls. To teach the recall in class, the instructor tells the group: "Handlers face the center of the room with dogs sitting at heel position. Command your dog to stay. Face him to the full length of the leash. Hold the leash in your left hand. Stand up straight with your feet spaced apart to prevent the dog from darting off to one side! Call your dog by name! 'Bozo, come!' Gather the lead up with both hands and when he is close, command 'Sit!' Praise and pat him immediately! Say 'Stay!' and move back again to the end of the lead. Call your dog! Keep your voice happy! Coax your dog to come! When he obeys, tell him with more authority to sit! Praise him! If the dog doesn't respond the moment he hears his name and the command to come, snap the lead quickly, but loosen it at once. It is done with a motion similar to snapping a whip. You will hear the collar click when you do it correctly. Don't pull or drag your dog to you or he will never want to come! Use a cajoling tone of voice after the command and after each correction. Use the lead to make the dog sit square and as close as possible, and to prevent a dash in the opposite direction. Next, make your dog go to heel position! (The handlers will now have their backs to one another, ready to call their dogs in the opposite direction.) Tell your dog to stay and face him to the full length of the lead! Now circle back to heel position. We'll alternate the recall with the sit-stay exercise. This will teach your dog not to anticipate your

Fig. 19. Praise is most important of all. *Courtesy: Mary Priscilla Keyes.*

command by coming *before* he is called. Tell your dog to stay and face him again. Stand up straight! If you lean over, the dog will crawl in instead of coming gaily. Call your dog! *Use his name!* If your dog doesn't come on your first command, snap the lead hard and then coax him in the rest of the way! Keep your hands low and in front of your body. Gather up the leash in a hand-over-hand motion."

The instructor should watch to see that the command to come is given first, followed, if necessary, by a sharp snap on the lead, which is loosened immediately. The dog must want to come of his own free will. Remind the owners: "Stand erect with your feet apart to discourage the dog from darting off the one side. Gather up the leash as the dog comes forward. Command 'Sit!' when the dog comes in front and correct him if he sits crooked. Don't forget to pat him."

Near the close of the hour, the instructor should demonstrate Lesson 4. This will consist of lying down on command, the down-stay, and sitting from the down position.

Lesson 4:

New exercises:

Lying down on command.
Down-stay.
Sitting from a down position.

Review:

Heeling with turns.
Sitting at heel.
Sit-stay with leash on floor—owners at distance.
Come-fore.
Going to heel position.
Coming when called.

To teach the class how to make their dogs lie down on command is perhaps a little more difficult than the exercises learned up to this point. Every dog will react in a different way, but the method of teaching remains the same. The director should advise the class:

"Face your dog—not to the full length of the lead, but half way. Transfer the lead to your *left* hand. Hold the left arm straight down close to your left side. Keep your elbow straight. Take up the slack in the lead until it just clears the floor. Step on the lead with your *right* foot so the lead will

Fig. 20. A stubborn dog is made to lie down. *Courtesy: Mary Priscilla Keyes.*

slide under your instep. Raise your right hand and hold it upright. Stand up straight! Command 'Down!' Pull up on the lead with your *left* hand but keep it close to the body! Hold the lead tight until the dog obeys. When he does, say a quiet 'Good boy' and release the pressure on the collar. It may be necessary to use both hands on the lead and hold—hold—

hold until the dog lies down. The full weight of the body is placed on the right foot to avoid being thrown. The hand signal can be given later. Don't praise or pat your dog too much when he is in the down position. It will tempt him to get up before he is told. Hold the lead tight until the dog lowers his body to the floor! Don't fail to slacken the lead the

Fig. 21. Pressure applied to the shoulder will help force the dog down.
Courtesy: Mary Priscilla Keyes.

moment the dog obeys! Keep the left elbow straight at the start of the exercise so there will be room to pull the lead upward. Don't lean over except to push on the dog's back to force him down if he is stubborn. Hold your right hand at shoulder height for the down signal. Drop it quickly and cuff the dog's nose if he creeps forward. Use a forehanded motion when he creeps to your right. A backhanded motion when he darts to the left."

A dog will occasionally jump at his owner or growl in retaliation when he is forced to lie down. In such cases the instructor should tell the owner:

"Use the end of your lead to flip the dog sharply across his

Fig. 22. The down signal is indicated by the raising of the hand. *Courtesy: Mary Priscilla Keyes.*

nose but pull the lead tight under your instep at the same time so the dog can't lunge at you. Under these circumstances, hold the right hand waist high and close to the body. After you sting the dog's nose with the end of the lead, hold your hand in position and repeat the command more forcefully until the dog obeys. Avoid nagging by slapping at the dog repeatedly."

Fig. 23. The dog that shows defiance is rapped across the muzzle with the end of the leash. *Courtesy: Mary Priscilla Keyes.*

The down-stay is done in the same way as the sit-stay. If the class is working in a circle, the owners face the center of the circle with their dogs at heel. The instructor tells the class:

"Your dog must first learn to lie down from a sitting position on your left side. Place your left hand on the collar and leash under the dog's neck. Pull his head slowly to the floor as

Fig. 24a. The dog is made to lie down at heel position. *Courtesy: Mary Priscilla Keyes.*

you command 'Down!' and hold him tight until he obeys. Or you may run the lead under the *left* instep and pull steadily until the dog goes down. When he does, say 'Stay!' and resume an upright position while the dog remains down. Wait a few moments, give the command 'Sit!' then jerk the dog to a sitting position and pat him immediately. Let us repeat this exercise. Down at heel! Now sit!

Fig. 24b. The signal to make the dog lie down at heel is given with the left hand. *Courtesy: Mary Priscilla Keyes.*

"With your dog in the down position, tell him to stay. The command and signal for the down-stay is the same as for the sit-stay. Command 'Stay!' Back with your left hand, out on your right foot. Keep the lead slack so you won't pull your dog forward. Move slowly. Use a demanding tone of voice when you step forward. Go back to heel position without circling. Command 'Stay!' and face your dog again. Circle around in back of him. Don't say your dog's name—it will tempt him to get up. Stress the *command!* Leave him again. Circle back to heel position, but hold the leash slack on the dog's right side. Wait a moment . . . ! Now praise your dog while he is still in the down position, then release him from training. Put your dog in the down position once more. Say 'Stay!' If he gets up, move quickly! Jerk him down again as fast as you can and repeat the command with more authority. If he creeps forward, bounce the palm of your hand against his nose. You must draw an imaginary circle around the spot where you left your dog—and this goes for the sit-stay as well. If the dog moves out of this circle, he must be corrected. Each time a correction is necessary, do it with more severity. Leave your dog again! Face him the full length of the lead. Circle around, but this time step over his back to heel position. Hold him down if he tries to get up. Tell him to stay! Face him again. Drop your lead. Circle back to heel position. Wait a moment . . . ! *Praise your dog while he is still down.* Exercise finished! Now praise your dog again and make a fuss over him!"

When the dogs are facing their owners, they are made to sit from the down position in the following way. The instructor orders:

"Stand up straight! Hold your lead in your left hand. Command 'Sit!' Run the right hand along the lead and jerk it up sharply *after* you give the command. At the same time, tap the dog's front paws with your right foot. Praise him the moment he jumps up to a sitting position. Remember to give the command 'Sit!' then jerk the leash, then give praise! Keep your dog from crowding your body.

"If he creeps forward, raise your knee and bump against him to push him away from you. Make your dog lie down! Make him sit! Command first, use the leash second, praise third.

Fig. 25. The right way to correct a dog who lies down during the sit-stay and to teach the dog to sit from the down position. *Courtesy: Mary Priscilla Keyes.*

Again, command the down! Give the command to sit! Move in slightly toward your dog as you give the command to make him keep his distance! If he doesn't, jump to a sitting position at once, snap the lead hard!"

The instructor should explain that a dog can take a sharp correction providing he is praised at the same time. The class routine will now combine all the exercises which have been learned up to this point. The instructor's commands may sound something like this:

"Forward! Jerk forward! About turn! Halt! Jerk backward! Forward! Fast! (This should be a fast walk or a slow running pace.) About turn in a fast! Slow! Left U-turn in a slow! Halt! Jerk backward! Forward! Come-fore! Walk backward and make your dog sit in front. Make him go to heel position! Give the command first, jerk the lead, then praise immediately! Ready for a sit-stay! Face the center of the circle with your dog at heel position. Tell your dog to stay! Face him. Drop your lead and move back two paces. Everybody, clap your hands lightly. Correct your dog if he moves! Walk quickly past your dog and stand behind him! Walk past him and face him again! Circle back to heel position. Give praise and pick up your lead. Command your dog to stay! and face him at full length of the lead. Call him! Make him sit at once. Praise him! Make him go to heel position. Praise again! Command him to stay and face him at full length of the lead! Call him! Make him sit! Praise him! Make him go to heel position! Tell him to stay and face him once more at full length of the lead. Circle back to heel position, but hold the leash on the dog's right side. Tell him to stay and face him at half the lead's length. Command and signal him to lie down! When he obeys, say 'Stay!' Now make him sit! Command first, jerk second, praise third! Command the down! Make him sit! Make him lie down! Tell him 'Stay!' and circle back to heel position. Keep him in the down position! Leave him once more and face him at the full length of the lead! Command the sit! Circle back to heel position!"

When the class routine is performed in this manner the dog will have no idea of what is coming next and he will learn to wait for all commands. It makes him steady and he will not anticipate. The methods of teaching remain the same and only the customary procedure is varied.

A demonstration should be given of the exercises in the fifth lesson. This is standing at heel position and the stand-stay. The homework for the following week should include these two exercises along with the regular training routine.

Lesson 5:
  New exercises:
    Standing at heel position.
    Stand-stay.
  Review:
    Heeling with automatic sits on the halt.
    Sit-stay.
    Come-fore.
    Going to heel position.
    Coming when called.
    Lying down.
    Down-stay.
    Sitting from a down position.

To teach the dog to stand at heel position, the owners are told: "Hold the lead short in the *right* hand. Don't jerk the lead when you come to a halt or the dog will sit down! Take up the slack in the lead by pulling it forward with your right hand. Give the command 'Stand!' while you are still moving and at the same time touch your dog gently underneath his tummy or scratch him along his back. The hand motions are similar to those used when stretching an elastic band. The right hand reaches forward, the left hand pulls backward. Forward! Stand your dog! Forward! Stand him again! *Don't* pull on your dog's tail! *Don't* yank his hair and *don't* grab his skin! The corrections come from underneath. Forward! Stand your dog! Tap your dog under his tummy or in front

Fig. 26. The right hand signals the stand-stay; the left lifts the dog to a
standing position. *Courtesy: Mary Priscilla Keyes.*

of his right back leg. Perhaps he will stand if you scratch his
back! If he swings his rear end away from you, reach over his
back and touch him in front of the left back leg."

The instructor should explain that the left hand is gradually brought forward, first to the dog's side, then to his shoulder, and finally to a point in front of his nose, so that he will

learn to recognize the stand signal, which is really the signal to stay. When the dog is given the signal while he is standing, he will learn to hold that position just as he did in the sit or down.

The owners of small dogs (or large dogs for that matter) may be instructed to loop the end of the lead under their dog's stomach to keep them in a standing position until they learn the meaning of the word. The right hand holds the leash to control the pull on the collar. The left hand lifts the dog to a standing position when he attempts to sit down.

If the dog snaps or bites when he is touched underneath, the owner should be advised: "Take up all slack in the lead and pull it forward so the dog cannot turn his head! Support him against your body in a standing position until he is no longer resentful. When he stops growling and snapping, quietly stroke his back and praise him."

Tell the handlers: "Take an extra long step forward on your right foot so the dog will be able to see the hand signal more clearly, or use the right hand instead of the left to cut across in front of the dog if he appears to respond to the right hand signal." Stress the point: It is easier to keep the dog standing than to lift him from the sitting position!

The stand-stay is done in the same way as the sit and down-stay. The owners are reminded:

"With your dog standing at heel, command 'Stay!' Back with your left hand, out on your right foot! Keep the lead slack when you move away from your dog. Bounce his nose with the palm of your hand if he takes a step forward! Step back to heel position without circling. Say 'Stay!' Now face your dog to the full length of the lead. Keep the lead in your hand, but hold it slack! Circle back to heel position. Hold the leash straight up with the left hand as you move around to heel position. Leave your dog and stand in back of him. Walk past him and face him full length of the lead. Return to heel position. Keep the dog standing. Wait a moment . . . ! Leave him again. Return to heel position. *Praise him while he is still standing*. Exercise finished! Now praise your dog again and make a fuss over him."

At this half-way mark in the beginners course, the dogs should be heeling on a slack lead with only occasional corrections. They should make about-turns and change their pace from a fast to a slow and to a normal on voice command. If they don't, the corrections have not been properly timed or as severe as they should be. When the voice command gives *warning*, and the lead is used to make the correction, the dog will learn to heel close to the owner's side no matter how fast or slowly he moves nor in what direction he turns.

When the owner halts, the dog should sit quickly. If he is slow or inattentive, tell the owner:

"Spank your dog on the rump to make him sit faster! Hold the lead tight at the same time so he can't duck away. If he sits at an angle, spank him on the off-side hip! Pat and praise him at the same time. Your dog can take a firm correction if it is accompanied by praise. Jerk hard! Praise enthusiastically!"

The leash is now transferred to the *left* hand. It is wadded up so it will not dangle in the dog's face. The arm is held close to the side with the elbow straight. The instructor commands: "Forward! Jerk forward! Halt! Jerk backward! Keep the dog close and make him sit squarely by snapping the leash in back of your body before you stop moving. Forward! Jerk forward! About turn! Pivot sharply and snap the lead close to, and in front of your body. Halt! Jerk backward! Except when making corrections, keep your left arm straight and close to your side!"

The lead is transferred to the left hand to get perfection in heeling. It cannot be used at the start of training when handling an unruly dog or the owner would have little control. For finished work, the leash carried in the left hand will overcome crooked sits and prevent the dog from passing the owner's left knee.

By this time the come-fore should be done smoothly, but watch for poor sits. The hand that is nearest to whichever hip is out of line makes the correction by slapping the dog sharply. The opposite hand holds the lead, which is pulled tight when the correction is made. The foot may be used for the same purpose and in the same manner, but *never* without holding the lead taut to keep the dog from ducking away.

By now the dog should have a fair idea of going to heel position by himself. He should at least start when he hears the command "Heel!" He may need assistance for a complete finish. The instructor advises the class:

"Jerk the lead to your left side with both hands immediately *after* you give the command! This will make your dog start promptly. Use a series of snaps and reach as far back as you can so your dog will have room to make a complete turn. As the dog circles around, bring your left hand forward and pat your knee to coax him to come and sit close." Advise the owner: "Give the command without moving the hands. Keep the lead slack except for the jerk that follows the command, and possibly a second jerk if the dog goes too far without turning around. Success in this exercise depends on your timing. Command 'Heel!' then jerk the lead and praise at the same time!"

At this point in the dog's training he should respond immediately to the command "Come!" He will have to be corrected occasionally for lack of attention and be made to sit straight and close when he comes in. To overcome the tendency to sit crooked, tell the owners: "Walk backward slowly for ten or fifteen feet and make the dog follow closely in front! When you halt, tell him to sit!" This exercise, if repeated consistently, will teach the dog not to fear the motion of the feet and to snuggle up close to his owner when he is called.

To get a more rapid response to the command "Down!" the instructor should remind the handler to raise his right hand quickly and command the dog to lie down. It is the *coming-up* motion of the hand that should cause the dog to drop. If the voice and signal are ignored, the handler should stamp sharply on the lead in mid-air to get the dog down at once. The right hand is still held at shoulder height. A quiet "Good fellow" will assure the dog that all is well. Every time a correction is made, it should become progressively more severe. Remind the class: "Until your dog will work perfectly on lead, he will never work without it! For instance, in the down exercise, if the dog hasn't started to go down the moment you raise your right hand, snap out the command insistently and follow immediately by stamping on the lead with the foot! A quiet word of praise will prevent ill feeling." The same principle applies when making the dog sit from the down position. The important factor is the timing! The right hand is lifted with a snap which is the signal to sit. Next comes the command "Sit!" followed by a quick upward jerk on the lead with either the right or the left hand. The dog is praised along with the correction. The timing of the action is first the signal or the command, then the jerk and praise together.

The foregoing instructions apply to all training. It will be used repeatedly during the beginners class. The members must have these essential features pointed out to them at regular intervals throughout the course. When an owner concentrates on a new exercise he is inclined to forget the previous rules of training. This is why the training director must repeat again and again a word picture of each step until the owner acts automatically.

Training can be considered successful only when the dog is happy in his work. Each handler must be reminded: "Watch the reactions of your dog! If one that is normally gay works with his tail down, the training is too severe! Keep the following rule in mind:

"If, for instance, your dog ignores your command and signal to lie down and continues movement toward you, move toward him and make him carry out your order; but if he shies away from you, let up in your training and make your demands less urgent! To keep your dog happy you must be liberal with praise that is timed to correspond with the correction! Never let the dog blame *you* for unpleasantness! *He* is the one who should feel guilty if he makes a mistake."

Before the class is dismissed, explain that Lesson 6 will include the stand for examination and alternating the sit with the down and the stand-at-heel position. Furthermore, the heeling exercises will be done with the leash hanging over the shoulder.

Lesson 6:

New exercises:

Stand for examination.
Alternating the sit with the down and the stand-at-heel position.
Heeling exercises with the leash over shoulder.

Review:

Heeling and sitting.
Sit-stay.
Come-fore.
Going to heel position.
Coming when called.

Lying down.
Down-stay.
Sitting from a down position.
Standing at heel position.
Stand-stay.

When the training for the stand for examination is done individually in the classroom, it consumes a great deal of the training period. To lead up to this particular exercise without wasting time, the instructor should get the dogs accustomed to the approach of a stranger by doing the sit-, the down-, and the stand-stays in the following way:

The owner is instructed: "Tell your dog to sit-stay and circle your neighbor's dog to your right. Return to your dog. Tell him to stay and circle your neighbor's dog to your left. Return to your dog. Watch your own dog as closely as you can. Make a correction if he moves! At the same time, if your neighbor's dog acts uncertain when you approach him, reassure him by telling him to stay as you walk around him, and step on the leash if he tries to dart away."

Other variations are: "Everybody, tell your dog to stay, take two steps forward and circle the room clockwise (or counter-clockwise) and return to your dog. Tell him 'Stay!' cross to the opposite side of the room and circle the dog opposite yours. Return to your dog." This routine is repeated with the dogs left in the down and stand positions. It accustoms the dogs to having a stranger approach and breaks the ground for the stand for examination.

In the stand for examination, the training director orders: "Stand your dog and face him the full length of the leash! Drop your leash. Move one dog to the right and stand in front of him. Slowly circle around him without touching him. Face him again. Circle around once more and while you are walking past him, drop your left hand and run it along his back. Keep moving as you circle around him. Face the dog again. Go up to him and this time come to a stop and gently touch his head, back, and tail. If he starts to move or shy away, say 'Stay!' Return to your own dog and stand in front of him. Pick up your lead and circle back to heel position. Hold the lead on the dog's right side! Don't gather the lead up tight. It will tempt your dog to sit and he must remain standing. Leave him again. Face him. Drop your lead. Move one dog to the left and stand in front of him. Circle around without touching him. Face him again. Circle around, drop your left hand and run it along his back as you go past. Face the dog again. This time, gently examine his head, back, and tail. Say 'Stay!' if he starts to move! Go back and face your own dog. Pick up your lead. Circle around to heel position. Hold your hands still and your leash quiet. Wait a few moments and keep your dog standing! Now, *while he is still standing*, praise him and make a fuss over him!"

When the above procedure is practiced in the sit- and down-stays as well as in the stand-stay, the dogs will become steadier in performance and less resentful or fearful of the unexpected. It will avoid long delays and consuming a great deal of classroom time doing individual examinations.

This will be as good a time as any to alternate the three positions, *e.g.*, sitting, lying down, and standing at heel. The dogs can easily learn the difference between them if the commands and signals are given distinctly. The training director will give the following instructions:

"Forward! Halt! That means *sit!* Forward! Stand your dog! Give the signal and the command together! Forward! Down your dog! To make your dog lie down at heel position, pull your lead upward with your right hand, place your left hand on the collar and leash under the dog's throat, and pull his head to the floor. After his head goes down, he will lower his body. Or else use your left foot on the lead to get your dog down. When he obeys, say 'Stay!' and stand up straight! Forward! Say 'Heel!' Step out quickly and give the leash a jerk! Your dog will catch up with you, but you must give the command 'Heel!' as you move forward. Down your dog at heel! To make the dog drop more quickly, lower your left hand onto the leash with a snap! Tell him to stay! Stand up straight after your dog goes down. Forward! Halt! Your dog should sit immediately! If he doesn't, sting him on the rear! He should sit automatically the moment you stop moving unless you give him a command to stand or lie down."

As the weeks go by and the owners reach the point where they begin to work with the leash thrown over the shoulder, remind them that it should not be too slack, nor should it be too tight. Otherwise they will not have the necessary control over the dog. Caution them as follows:

"From now on, your voice is the most important factor! Since you will only use your leash occasionally, you must learn to control your dog by voice. Use commands in every part of the exercise until your dog gets into the habit of working accurately. Later these commands can be eliminated. Say the word 'Heel' every time you make a turn and at every change of pace, and say it with authority! When you start, motion forward with the left hand. When you halt, say 'Sit!' while the dog is still moving and motion backward. Keep your dog under control from the start. Correct with the leash when necessary and praise at the same time, but after a correction let go of the leash at once."

The down exercise, the recall, and the finish (or going-to-heel-position) should be practiced with the leash lying on the floor. If the dog doesn't respond instantly to the command "Down," tell the owner: "Start to bend your right knee when you give the command and signal to lie down! This will remind the dog of his early training, when you used your foot on the lead, and he should go down immediately. If he still doesn't obey, lean over and cuff him lightly on the nose! After the correction, hold your hand in place and repeat the command with more authority."

When called, the dog should start the moment he hears his name and the command "Come!" If he doesn't, tell the owner: "Pick up your lead and snap it hard! Keep your hands on your knees until the dog is close enough to touch him, then take hold of his collar and pull up to make him sit."

An excellent way to get a dog to come more reliably in a group of dogs is to have the owners form a circle with their dogs sitting at heel position. The leash is held in both hands. Give the command "Forward!" As the owners and dogs move toward the center of the circle, tell the owners: "Step back from your dog quickly! Let go of the lead with your left hand to give the dog freedom! Snap out the command 'Come!' Then jerk the lead hard and continue to walk backward to the outside of the circle. Make your dog follow, sit in front, then send him to heel position."

As the dogs approach one another in the center of the circle, they immediately become interested in one another and are less attentive to their owners. When the command to come is followed by a quick snap of the leash at the moment the dog is *not paying attention*, he will take the blame for the ensuing correction and the next time will turn quickly when he hears the command.

Before the class is dismissed at the close of the 6th lesson, the instructor should demonstrate stick jumping and tell the owners to bring their jumping sticks to class for the rest of the course.

Lessons 7 *and* 8:

  New exercise:

   Stick jumping.

  Review:

   Heeling and sitting.
   Sit-stay (handlers at a distance).
   Come-fore.
   Going to heel position.
   Coming when called.
   Lying down.
   Down-stay (handlers at a distance).
   Sitting from a down position.
   Standing at heel.
   Stand-stay.
   Stand for examination.
   Alternating the sit with the down and the stand-at-heel position.
   Heeling exercises with leash over shoulder.

From this point on, class work will consist of repeating the exercises with variations while striving for ever greater perfection. The only new lesson will be stick jumping. Class progress will vary considerably, depending on the dogs and the handlers. One group of dogs may be well behaved and accomplish more with the same amount of training than another group made up of difficult dogs or poor handlers. The rate of achievement will depend upon the circumstances.

Variation of the class routine is essential if the dogs are to become steady in performance. Changing the order of the exercises will prevent the dog from anticipating and will keep the owner active and interested in the training program. The routine will be a review of all the exercises and will include the following:

"Forward! Halt! Forward! About turn! Fast! About turn in a fast! Slow! About turn in a slow! Fast! Left U-turn in a fast! Slow! Left U-turn in a slow! Normal! Come-fore! Face your dog the full length of the lead. Call him! Make him go to heel! Tell him to stay and face him the full length of the lead. Return to heel position. Face him again. Call him! Step back to heel position without circling. Face him. Make him lie down! Make him sit! Circle back to heel position. Now praise!"

After a brief pause, the instruction may continue with further variations:

"Forward! Halt! (That means Sit!) Forward! Down your dog at heel position! Forward! Stand your dog! Tell him to stay and face him full length of the lead! Circle back to heel position. Face him again. Make him lie down! Call him! Now send him to heel!"

On the stays, the procedure may again be varied:

"Tell your dog to sit and stay! Drop the lead. Leave him. Face your dog. Return to heel position. Leave him and circle your neighbor's dog to the right! Return to heel position. Circle your neighbor's dog to the left! Stand in front of your own dog. Run past him and stand in back of him! Run past him and face him! Clap your hands! Return to heel position." This routine can also be used while the dog is in the down and stand positions.

When the owner is kept busy with a varying routine, the time flies quickly and the dog doesn't learn an exact procedure that will tend to make him anticipate his owner's commands.

Stick jumping, which is introduced at this point in the course, offers diversity from the usual basic work. The owner and the dog will be glad of the change. Aside from its practical home value, jumping conditions the dog for the advanced training which includes leaping over hurdles.

Stick jumping in the classroom may be speeded up by divid-

ing the class in half and making two columns work down
each side of the room at the same time. The owner then goes
to the end of his respective line by circling either to the left or
to the right of the room to be ready for the next time around.
The instructions are:

"Wad up your leash and hold it entirely in your left hand.

Fig. 27. Stick jumping. *Courtesy: Mary Priscilla Keyes.*

Carry the jumping stick in your right hand. Your dog must
jump and then walk at heel on a slack leash before he is permitted to jump a second time!" The majority of owners are
tempted to let the dog jump without controlling him in between.

When jumping is first tried, it will make it easier if the
instructor or training committee members place a number of
benches or chairs down the center or sides of the room ten to

fifteen feet apart, against which the owners may place their sticks. The instruction will then continue:

"Throw your left arm forward over the stick and command 'Hup!' or 'Over!' If your dog has never tried this before, step over with your left foot and hold the stick low until the dog learns to jump. If he refuses, hold the lead tight and slowly pull—pull—pull him across the first time. Don't give up until your dog jumps or walks over the stick, even if you have to place it on the ground! If you do, he'll balk more than ever the next time. Don't string the dog up in the air! Pull him *forward*. Hold the stick level. Drop your left arm toward the floor after the dog jumps so that the leash will be slack when he lands on the opposite side. Come to a halt, command 'Heel!' the moment the dog lands, and jerk the leash backward with a snap so he will learn to return to heel position immediately! The timing of the action will be: Command 'Hup!' Jerk your left arm forward! Command 'Heel!' and jerk your left arm backward! Give praise immediately!"

When the benches and chairs are removed, the stick jumping is performed in the same way. The instructor takes one owner and dog at a time (or two if there are two columns working) and makes the dog first heel, then jump, then heel for ten or twelve feet before letting him jump again. More heeling, then more jumping. It will simplify the instruction if the director will call out: "Heel! Jump! Heel! Jump!" or if he will designate the exact places on the floor at which the dog is to jump over the stick.

Since jumping is a little more exciting than the usual routine, the training director will have to remind the class not to spend the entire time at home practicing stick jumping. This is a minor part of the dog's training and owners should not neglect the other exercises.

During the sixth or seventh lesson, the training director

should call attention to those dogs whose work is not up to standard and request that their owners do a little more home training. This will serve to warn them that graduation is not far away. The class should be reminded of the requirements for graduation and of what each dog will be expected to do in order to receive a diploma.

At the seventh meeting (of a nine-week course) the instructor should ask if everyone intends to be present the following week. He should mention that the dogs will be passed on at that time (the week before graduation) and that no dog will be permitted on the floor graduation night unless the instructor has approved him and feels that he is ready to participate. If an owner does not expect to be present at the pre-graduation meeting, arrangements should be made to have the dog passed on at some other time.

A dog that has not been able to make the grade should be eliminated the week before graduation. The instructor and the training committee should meet with the member to discuss the circumstances of the case. Usually an owner will understand that the dog's lack of progress was not due to any one thing, but to a combination of factors. Perhaps the dog was an unusually difficult one to train. Possibly the owner was slow to grasp the technique of handling. A number of lessons may have been missed. In any case, it is better to have all unpleasantness taken care of in privacy instead of permitting the owner to attend the final lesson and then to have the disappointing experience of "flunking" the course in the presence of family and friends.

At this time the training director should forewarn the class that approval to take part in the graduation exercises does not necessarily mean that the dog will receive a diploma. The final decision will be made on graduation night. (*Note:* The improvement during the last week will be miraculous!)

Lesson 9: GRADUATION.

As each owner arrives with his dog, he should be given a number either on an arm-band or on a string to be hung about his neck. He should be requested to take his seat without indulging in last-moment practice. The dignity of the graduation ceremony should be maintained. However, it is suggested that the owner try to find an isolated place where he can work without attracting attention in order to give his dog a preliminary warm-up.

There are two ways to test the dogs on the final night. They may work individually (except for the sit- and down-stay exercises), or the class may work as a unit as they have been doing throughout the course. If the class is small the individual test is all right, but when the dogs are worked separately it is time-consuming and commotion results because of the long delays. The author prefers the method where the usual routine is performed and the judge picks the best working dogs by the process of elimination. One must remember that the beginners class is made up of inexperienced handlers and dogs. The owners are not yet conscious of show-ring procedure and if they are asked to do something out of the ordinary it will affect the dogs' work. The instructor should calm the class with: "Handle your dogs tonight just as you have been doing for the past few weeks! Try not to be self-conscious or your dogs will react unfavorably. Don't worry about the judging. Be natural and do the best you can!" Instilling this attitude in the class will ease the tension and relieve taut nerves.

If the dogs are judged separately, the scoring sheet form for the novice classes at dog shows may be used (providing the dogs have had off-leash training as well as the Figure-8). More leniency should be shown in the scoring than at an official A.K.C. Trial. It would be unreasonable to expect the owner to meet the rules and regulations for novice class work after only eight lessons.

If the dogs are tested as a group, the judge or judges should be supplied with a clip-board and paper on which to make notes. Prizes may be offered for best performance, best handling, and greatest improvement. For obvious reasons, the instructor makes the award for greatest improvement, but the judge will make the selection for best performance and handling. Ribbons and prizes offered in these three categories will give everyone in the class an equal chance. A very difficult dog may not do well in actual performance, but his owner may receive a first prize for the skillful way in which he handled him. The purpose of the training class is to teach the owner to do the training, so the handling award is one of the most important.

The instructor should put the owners and their dogs through the entire routine while the judge (or judges) makes notes. If the class has been divided throughout the course, the first group should work in its entirety, after which the second group is put through the same exercises. The best working dogs from each of these groups will then be called to the floor again to work a second time for placings in the ribbons. If the elimination method is favored, the dogs that make the greatest number of mistakes are called upon to drop out of line. The other dogs continue working until the judge reaches a decision. The first dogs should not be eliminated until the instructor has made an effort to put the class through the complete routine at least once. Otherwise the dogs will not be given a fair test. The same procedure is followed for selecting the best handlers.

The ribbons and prizes should not be awarded immediately after the judge has made his decision. The instructor should first hand out diplomas to the owners whose dogs have done passing work, and any scheduled exhibition of advanced training given. To assure an orderly and well-planned final meeting, the announcement of the winning dogs (which usually creates excitement) should be withheld until the other graduating dogs in the class have been honored. Graduation will thus conclude happily for the members of the class, for the instructor, and for the club or organization responsible for the classes.

6

The Novice Course

Novice Course:	For dogs that have graduated from the beginners course.
Length of Course:	Nine weeks.
Training Period:	1 to 2 hours.
Purpose:	To continue the dogs' basic training and to prepare them for novice class work at dog shows.

Training consists of:

Heeling on leash, including Figure-8.

Stand for examination (as required in the show ring).

Heeling off leash.

Recall off leash.

Sit-stay (1 minute).

Down-stay (3 minutes).

Drop from a distance.

Lessons 1, 2, and 3:

A thirty- to forty-minute review *on leash* with the dogs working as a group. This will include heeling, about-turns, fast, slow, sitting at heel, come-fore, going to heel position, recall, lying down, sitting from the down position, and stand for examination. Object: To gain perfection for the show ring and to see how seldom the leash need be used to make corrections.

Each exercise is done first by command, then by signal, alternating from one to the other. The instruction may sound like this:

"Forward! If your dog doesn't start, jerk the lead with a snap, then give praise! Halt! If your dog is slow to sit, spank him on the rear without saying anything. The dog should sit automatically every time you stop. Forward! Come-fore! Make your dog sit straight! By *voice* only, make your dog go to heel position. The dog's name may be used with the command. Give one command and if the dog doesn't move when he hears the word 'Heel,' follow with a snap on the lead, but praise him immediately. Forward! Come-fore! By *signal* only, make your dog go to heel. Don't use the dog's name when you use the signal. The signal is the left hand dropped to the side with force. If the dog ignores the signal, jerk the leash hard and give praise at the same time. If the dog moves on the first signal, avoid jerking the lead and use praise instead as the dog comes around to sit at your left side. Forward! Halt! Your dog should sit at once.

"Tell your dog to stay! Face him the full length of the leash. By *voice* only, tell your dog to come. Remember to use his name. Keep your voice happy. Give one command and follow with praise. Stand up straight and hold your elbows close to your ribs. Use a hand-over-hand motion to gather up the lead as the dog comes in. If he doesn't sit immediately, don't say anything but reach over and cuff him sharply on the rear to make him sit promptly. Then praise him. Say 'Stay!' and move back to the end of the lead. By voice only, call your dog! If he doesn't move on the command, follow with a sharp snap on the lead without repeating the command. *Praise the dog when he starts toward you.* He should sit close and square. By signal only, make your dog go to heel position. Praise him as he moves around into place.

"Forward! Come-fore! Your job is to make the dog sit straight in front of you. Tell him to stay and step back to half the length of the lead. By *voice* only, tell your dog to lie down. If he obeys immediately, reassure him with a quiet 'Good fellow.' By voice alone, tell him to sit! Praise him when he jumps to a sitting position. *Signal* him to lie down. Stand up straight. If the dog ignores the signal, follow by stamping on the lead. Arch your back and reach out with the right foot and drop it quickly on the lead. Signal the sit. If the dog doesn't jump up at once, jerk the lead upward and tap his front paws without saying anything. Praise him when he is sitting!"

Throughout the review on leash the essential points to keep in mind are: When the dog doesn't obey the *first* command, the correction is made with the lead without repeating the command. After the dog has been corrected, the owner should give praise and encouragement to create good will. When signals are used, the corrections follow without using the voice except to reassure the dog that there are no ill feelings. Remind the class: "Give only *one* command, then make the correction. Give only *one* signal, then make the correction. Give *praise* at all times."

The sit-stay and the down-stay are done as a group. Tell the class: "Leads off! Tell your dog to sit (or down) stay! Give the command and signal together! Handlers cross to the opposite side of the room. If your dog moves, don't yell at him. Go back quickly, gently take hold of his collar, and jerk him back to the spot where he was left. Snap the collar hard and repeat your command to stay in a more demanding voice. Give the command and signal to stay and leave him again. Return to your dog. Tell him to stay! Face him across the room. Move toward the exit but stay where your dog can see you. If he is still sitting, step out of sight but return after a few moments to where he can see you. Go out of sight again. Return to your dog. Leave him once more! Go and sit down some place. This may tempt the dog to break and you can bring in a good correction. A dog doesn't like to have his owner relax when he has to sit at attention."

The stand for examination can be practiced together. The instructor tells the class:

"When I tell you to pose or stand your dog for examination, take one step forward to bring your dog to a standing position. Pose him, give the signal and command to stay, and face him the full length of the lead. Keep the lead slack. If the dog takes a step forward, cuff his muzzle with the palm of your hand. Repeat the command but hold your hand in position. Then slowly back away. Return to heel position, but don't gather up the lead. Keep your hands still and hold them close to your body. Leave your dog again. Return to heel position. Exercise finished! Praise and pat your dog *while he is standing* and then release him from training. Again now, everybody, pose or stand your dog for examination! Don't wait to be told what to do! Take a step forward to get your dog on his feet! Pose him. Tell him to stay and face him to the full length of the lead! Carry out these four steps one after the other without waiting."

At this point, the instructor and his assistants walk down the line and touch each dog in turn. This will prepare the dog for the stand for examination as performed at obedience trials. The instructor reminds the owners: "If your dog starts to move from position, say 'Stay!' in a demanding tone of voice. Your dog must realize that he has more to fear from disobeying your command than from a stranger who approaches."

For best results, the Figure-8 must be done individually. Two or three dogs may work at the same time in different parts of the room. Instruct the owners as follows:

"Hold your leash in both hands, low and in front of your body. When you circle the post to the right with the dog on the outside, speed up and use a series of quick snaps on the lead. When you circle to the left with the dog on the inside, slow down a bit and if he crowds you bump him with your left knee! Circle to the right again—speed up! Give a series of jerks! Circle to the left—slow down! To the right again. Don't jerk this time. Use praise instead! This will teach your dog to change pace and stay close as he makes the Figure-8."

The Figure-8 may be practiced as a group while doing the heeling exercises. The instructor commands: "Forward! Everybody circle to the right!" The entire class makes one complete circle in the designated direction around an imaginary post and then continues in the original direction. When the instructor commands "Circle to the left!" the class does the same thing in the opposite direction. The handlers must remember to speed up when the dog is on the outside of the circle and to slow down when he is on the inside. The series of jerks alternating with no jerks at all, but praise, will teach the dog to stay close.

Approximately half to three-quarters of an hour will be consumed for the group work. The balance of the period may be used for more practice on individual recalls, the sit- and down-stays, or divided among the total number of dogs present for the solution of individual problems. These may be poor heeling, crooked sits, wide about-turns, or sloppy finishes. The owner should select the exercise on which he wants special assistance, while the instructor and the other members of the class help to overcome the specific problem.

Lessons 4, 5, and 6:

Use twenty minutes for a review on lead of the work as outlined in the first three lessons; object: To get close heeling and immediate response to one command or signal. To gain perfection, advise the class: "Wad your lead up and carry it entirely in your left hand! Jerk forward when you start. Jerk backward when you halt. Give quick short snaps! Praise with each correction." This accustoms the dog to heeling with the lead held in either hand and the corrections can be made with less body motion. Carrying the leash in the left hand will prepare the dog for more accurate heeling and sitting when the leash has been taken off.

If the class is working in a circle, the instructor should explain how the members can help one another during the heeling exercises. If the dog ahead lags, tell the owner who is walking behind: " 'Accidentally' touch the dog in front of you to perk him up a bit. This will make him feel that he is safe only when close to his owner." Members of the class are cautioned: "Be careful not to frighten the dog. If the dog thinks the touch in the rear was accidental, he will take the blame for the unpleasantness and look to his owner for protection." After this type of correction the owner should make more fuss over his dog than ever.

Introduce the left-about-turn at this time. Although the left-about-turn is no longer required for the show ring, it has its advantages in training.

The leashes are then removed. Remind the class: "Your dog will work off leash only if he has worked satisfactorily on leash!" Tell the handlers: "When you start say 'Heel!' Motion forward with your left hand! If your dog forges ahead, *demand* 'Heel' and motion backward! The dog will remember the leash corrections and will respond accordingly. Every time your dog steps out of perfect heel position, snap out the command 'Heel!' in a demanding tone of voice! Whenever you make an about-turn, say 'Heel!' You can drop the voice command later when the dog is reliable."

The members must be reminded: "When the dog is off leash you must control him entirely by voice and signals. If you timed your corrections accurately from the beginning, your voice will keep the dog's attention and the signal will help him to carry out the action. When the dog is heeling well, give him a confidential 'Good fellow,' or tousle his head occasionally, to let him know you are pleased with his work. On the halt, snap out the command 'Sit!' while the dog is still moving and signal back with the left hand. This will prevent him from passing your knee and sitting too far in front. When your dog does the right thing and avoids the wrong, he won't have to be corrected so often and will enjoy obedience training."

Heeling, either on or off leash, can be performed in the classroom by having the owners do the heeling routine in group formation. Four dogs abreast and four or five dogs deep, working as a drill team, will make the owners familiar with the right and left angle turns used in the show ring and does not consume a great deal of time or space.

The recall off leash is done individually with the group again working in a line. The person on the end and the one in the center are told: "Leave your dog! Call him! Keep your voice happy. Give one command and follow with praise to encourage the dog to come. If he fails to respond to the first command, change your tone of voice to a demanding one. The command 'Come,' even though stern, if followed by 'Good boy!' will overcome uncertainty. If your dog still fails to respond, kneel down and coax him in to you. If he runs away, *don't run after him!* Turn and walk away in the opposite direction as you call the dog's name. As he starts toward you—and nine times out of ten he will—praise him enthusiastically." Tell the handlers: "Point to the floor directly in front of where you are standing and insist that the dog come and sit there. When he does, pat him and make a fuss over him, but keep him sitting there." The next two owners in line then leave their dogs and the same procedure is repeated until all the dogs have been called individually and are sitting in front of their handlers. The dogs are made to go to heel position by either command or signal. By making them wait and do the finish together, the dogs will become steady and not go to heel position before they are told.

In the recall exercise the majority of dogs do not wait to hear their name, but start on the sound of the handler's voice. To overcome anticipation suggest: "Before you call your dog, use several imaginary dog names with the command to come, such as Bozo, come! Rover, come! . . . then . . . *Mike!* Come! (Mike of course being the actual name of the dog.) If the dog breaks on hearing the imaginary names, follow the command by the word *Stay!* Bozo, come-*Stay!* Rover, come-*Stay!* And finally, *Mike!* Come!" This teaches the dog to wait for his name and he will not be confused if he hears a voice similar to that of his owner. This preliminary training is especially valuable for demonstration work, where all the dogs are left sitting in line, and called one at a time.

The novice class is made up of dogs who probably do not have their C.D. title, so the drop on recall should not be practiced. The novice group can do the drop in the distance with no ill effects. This preliminary training will avoid an unhappy attitude when the dog is later required to do the drop on recall in the open class.

If a dog will lie down on signal or command when the owner is in front of him, the distance should be gradually increased until he obeys when the owner is across the room. Instead of having the owner call the dog after he lies down, tell him: "Walk back to your dog and reward him with praise or a titbit while he is in the down position." The routine for the novice group will be approximately the following:

"Tell your dog to stay and face him half way across the room. Return to heel position. Face him again at the same distance. Signal (or command) him to lie down! Return to heel position. Leave him in the down. Face him all the way across the room. Call him! Make him go to heel! Now praise!" If the signal is used to make the dog lie down, the voice becomes the correction when the dog doesn't obey. When the command is ignored, the voice and signal are repeated with more authority.

As already suggested, the balance of the time may be divided so as to allow each handler as much individual work as possible. The handler may select the exercise on which he wants special help. If a dog is lagging on the Fast, the owner should be advised: "Hold your lead rather short in both hands, low, and in front of your body. When you change speed, use a series of quick snaps on the lead just as you did in the Figure-8, but *praise when you do it!*" Heeling should be done in a Fast (a long, continuous run), a Slow, a Fast, a Slow, one after the other until the dog will remain close to the owner in spite of every change of pace. The running motion should be smooth and the owner should glide from one speed into the other and not dart away from his dog to leave him behind. Although the owner must jerk the lead occasionally when the dog neglects to change speed, he must be reminded: "Use praise as well when you change to a Fast to assure the dog that he is doing the right thing when he stays close to your side. When the leash is used continuously, the dog will hold back from fear."

The sit- and down-stays are performed with the owners in view and later out of sight. The novice class at dog shows requires the owner to stay where the dog can see him, but practice in leaving the dog entirely by himself is excellent training even in the early stages. The stays and the individual problems, allowing five or six minutes for each dog, will use up the balance of the training period.

Lessons 7 and 8:

To prepare for graduation and for competition in Obedience Trials, each dog should be worked individually in the required routine. The owner should be given a complete run-through of the novice class exercises. The sit- and down-stays will be done together. Special precaution should be taken to observe the rules and regulations of the American Kennel Club which apply to obedience trial competition. The instructor must remind the class: "Only one signal or command may be used except where the rules state otherwise. A dog that anticipates a command, such as coming before he is called, or that fails to do the principal part of the exercise, must receive less than 50 per cent of the total number of points and does not qualify."

Lesson 9: GRADUATION.

The dogs should be scored individually. The judging should meet the rules and regulations for obedience trial competition and each owner and his dog given the same consideration. The dogs graduating from the novice class will have had eighteen weeks of training and they should work accurately.

The amateur exhibitor will often cause his dog to receive penalties for which he himself is to blame. Working individually in the novice class should eliminate the giving of double commands and signals which the owner usually does unconsciously. It will make the handler aware of how important he is in relation to his dog's performance and acquaint him with show-ring procedure so that Obedience Trials will not be so strange or different from what the owner and dog are accustomed to in training class.

It is for the club to decide whether diplomas will be issued to the dogs taking the novice course. When the dogs are judged with the same strict ruling as in the novice class at shows, it would seem reasonable to award a diploma to all dogs that receive a qualifying score. The novice diploma would certify that the dog is ready to compete in the novice class at trials and to continue with advanced training. Failure to receive a diploma may discourage an exhibitor from entering a dog that is not prepared to meet the test. Unless a dog is well-grounded in his novice work, he will encounter many problems in the open and utility classes.

7

The Intermediate Course

Intermediate Course:	For dogs that have graduated from the beginners or novice class.
Length of Course:	Nine weeks.
Training Period:	1 to 2 hours.
Purpose:	To train the dog to jump and to retrieve on command.

Training consists of:
  Review of basic work.
  Carrying and retrieving assorted articles.
  Carrying and retrieving the dumbbell.
  Jumping the solid, the bar, and the broad jump while carrying.

Lesson 1:
  Review:
    Heeling on leash with about-turns, fast and slow.
    Sitting at heel.
    Heeling off leash.
    Sit-stay.
    Come-fore.
    Going to ·heel position.
    Coming when called.
    Lying down.
    Down-stay.
    Stand for examination.

Stand-stay.

Drop in the distance.

Note: In all the review exercises one command or signal is given, followed immediately by a correction if the dog doesn't obey (as outlined in the Novice Course). Give praise at all times.

The instructor should take the last twenty minutes of the period to demonstrate with different dogs how to make them

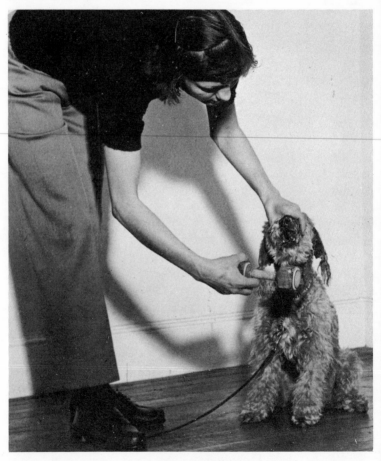

Fig. 28. A dog is taught to hold the dumbbell (note foot on leash). *Courtesy: Mary Priscilla Keyes.*

hold the dumbbell and assorted articles, how to get the dogs into a standing position with the dumbbell or article in their mouths, and how to make them carry while walking. Explain to the class as follows:

"Make your dog sit while you partially face him. Drop your lead to the floor, stretch it tight, and step on it with your right foot. This will keep your dog from backing away. Press his jaws apart with your left hand, gently command 'Take it!' and slip the dumbbell or article into his mouth with your right hand. Hold the dog's head high to keep it in place. Stroke his head or scratch his back and praise him. After the dog has held the object for a few moments, say 'Out!' and quietly take it away. If you practice with an assortment of articles, your dog will become more reliable in the retrieving exercises."

The class must realize the importance of keeping the article in the dog's mouth after it is placed there. Tell the owners: "If the dog resists, hold out until he gives in. From then on, it will be easy."

By demonstrating the exercise with different dogs, the class will see that the reaction is not always the same. Some dogs will accept the article meekly. Others will struggle and growl and try to claw it out with their front paws. By hooking the left hand underneath the collar and grasping the flap of skin under the dog's throat, the instructor will have complete control. Tell the class:

"Every time your dog drops the article, hold him tight while you cuff him across the nose. Say 'Phooey!' in a displeased tone of voice. A lot of feeling can be put into this expression to make the dog realize that by dropping the article he has done wrong. Pick up the article and give it to him again. Each time he drops it, the correction becomes more severe. However, a dog will usually indicate his intentions of

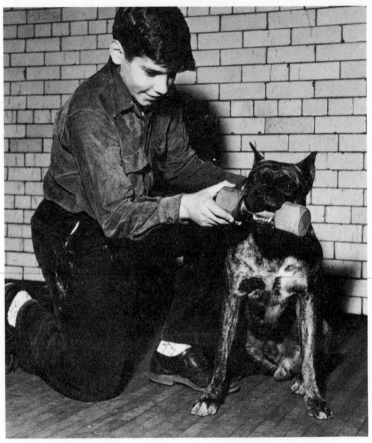

Fig. 29. Patience is rewarded. *Courtesy: Mary Priscilla Keyes.*

dropping whatever he is holding. The owner can prevent this from happening by tapping the dog under the chin and telling him to hold it! An ounce of prevention is worth a pound of cure. And remember, ten or fifteen minutes of practice night and morning will teach your dog to hold anything you give him."

To get the dog into a standing position when he is holding something in his mouth, the instructor should support the dog's head by holding the collar and grasping the skin under his throat. Place the other hand on top of his head and dip it quickly toward the floor to make him lose his balance. This will bring him to a standing position. The instructor then walks slowly backward to encourage the dog to follow. If the dog cooperates, the instructor can then move to the full

Fig. 30. The dog is coaxed while carrying the dumbbell. *Courtesy: Mary Priscilla Keyes.*

length of the lead to give him more freedom while carrying. Advise the owners: "Keep the leash slack and praise the dog in a high-pitched voice. Pat him and make a fuss over him while he is holding the dumbbell."

In the week between the first and second lessons, the owner should succeed in teaching his dog to hold the dumbbell, a block of wood, or a leather glove, and to carry them while heeling. The dog should also do the sit-stay while holding an article. This will be in preparation for Lesson 2 and the homework for the week. Tell the members: "Bring an assortment of articles as well as the dumbbell to class each time."

Lesson 2:

New exercises:

Holding the dumbbell or article on command.
Carrying while heeling.
Holding an article while doing the sit-stay.

Note: While teaching the dumbbell work, the classroom training will be more successful if the group works in a line instead of in a circle.

The owner who has not been able to teach his dog the three exercises that make up this lesson should request the help of an assistant trainer or more experienced member of the club. The class will otherwise be retarded because the group must work under the following commands:

"Dogs on leash! Have your dog sitting at heel position. Command 'Take it!' and give him the leather glove. (Most dogs prefer a glove to anything else. If they have a favorite bedroom slipper, use that.) Wait a moment—tell him 'Out!' Praise immediately. Give it to him again. Command 'Out!' Tell him 'Take it!' Forward! Keep your leash slack! Praise the dog in a high tone of voice as you walk along! About turn! Halt! Say the word 'Sit!' but don't pull up on the leash. If you do, the dog will drop the article. Forward! Halt! Tell him 'Out!' Take the article and praise your dog!"

Remind the class: "While your dog is carrying, talk to him, fuss over him and give him a lot of praise and encouragement. Make him proud of his accomplishments! If he drops the article at any time, cuff him on the nose and say 'Phooey!' before you take it from the floor and give it to him again. Make your corrections more severe each time so he would rather hold the article than be corrected for dropping it!"

To practice holding the dumbbell on the sit-stay, tell the class: "Take the lead off! Give your dog the dumbbell. Leave him and cross to the opposite side of the room. If he drops the dumbbell, go back quietly, take hold of his collar, slap him once across the nose and say 'Phooey!' Put the dumbbell back in his mouth and leave him again. Everybody, return to heel position. Say 'Out!' and take the dumbbell. Now praise and pat your dog and make a fuss over him."

The dumbbells crashing to the floor on the first night will make the training-room sound like a bowling alley. Dogs that have been carrying perfectly at home become excited when working with the other dogs. It is not surprising that even the best of them will occasionally drop his dumbbell, or whatever else he is carrying, in the classroom. For this reason it is preferable to use leather gloves or blocks of wood for the first lesson. There will be less noise and confusion.

Carrying is the basis of all advanced training. Once learned, the class work can continue, but until each owner can get his dog to perform this exercise creditably well, the entire group will be held back. It is suggested the instructor dismiss the class early the second week and give extra time to the problem dogs so that the class will be able to continue working together as a group.

Before dismissing the class, the training director should demonstrate the part of Lesson 3 where the dog must reach to take the dumbbell or article from the owner's hand. Different dogs should again be used to illustrate the point. The dog is made to sit at heel position and is held close to the left knee. The collar is pulled around on his neck so that the leash is on top. It is held short in the left hand. The object is held in the right hand and close to the dog's jaws. The instructor commands "Take it!" After the command, the leash is *slowly* tightened until the dog opens his mouth to swallow. The article is slipped in quickly and the pressure released immediately. The dog is praised and patted at once. Remind the class:

"Give the command first, then tighten the lead. Praise the dog the moment he opens his mouth to receive the article. Support the dog against your left knee so he cannot duck away. When the dog shows signs of opening his mouth by himself, give the lead a snap instead of pulling it tight. This will make the dog obey more quickly." The purpose of this lesson is to encourage the dog to *reach* for the article instead of passively waiting to have it placed in his mouth. He will soon learn if the trainer jerks the lead sharply after each command and praises the dog when he obeys. Until a dog will reach out to take an object from the hand on command, he will not reach out to take it from the floor, nor will he be dependable in the advanced work, which includes retrieving, scent discrimination, seeking a lost article, and tracking.

Lesson 3:

New exercises:

Carrying the dumbbell and assorted articles while reviewing basic exercises.

Carrying on the recall.

Reaching for the dumbbell and assorted articles on command.

Review:

Holding the dumbbell and assorted articles on command.

Carrying while heeling.

Holding an article while doing the sit-stay.

The class is called to order with the dogs on leash and sitting at heel position. After the review exercises, the instructor commands: "Give your dog the leather glove! Out! Give it to him again! Forward! Halt! Forward! Come-fore! Move back to the full length of the leash. Call your dog! Tell him 'Out!' Make him go to heel position! Don't forget to praise! This time, give him the dumbbell! Face him at the full length of the lead! Circle back to heel position! Tell him to 'Stay!' Face your dog! Make him lie down while he still holds the dumbbell! If he drops it, correct him! Call him! Make him sit in front of you! Tell him 'Out!' Make him go to heel! Leads off! Give your dog the block of wood. Tell him to stay! Face him across the room. Return to heel position. The dog should still be holding the article. Tell him 'Out!' Praise him! Starting with the dog on the end of the line, give him the dumbbell. Face him across the room! Tell him to 'Come!' When he is in close to you, tell him 'Sit-stay!' The sit-stay command will help to keep the dumbbell in his mouth. Now take the dumbbell, praise him, and make him go to heel position. Next dog!" (And so on down the line until every dog has been called in from the sit-stay while carrying his dumbbell or some other article. This exercise can be repeated several times.)

The leads are put on the dogs again and the owners are told: "Swing the collar around so the leash is on top. Hold it in your left hand and close to the collar. Hold the dumbbell in the right hand close to the dog's muzzle. Command 'Take it!' Follow by slowly pulling the leash tight. Praise the dog the moment he opens his mouth. Wait a moment—command 'Out!' Good fellow! Take it! Out! Good fellow! Your dog must reach for the dumbbell in the air before he will reach for it when it is lying on the ground! If he ignores your command, each succeeding jerk must be a little harder than the previous one in order to get the results you are after. Time your praise so the dog will not dislike the dumbbell nor resent the training. Never force the dog to open his mouth by pressing the dumbbell against his teeth. If he is stubborn, insert the middle finger of your right hand behind his canine teeth and pry open his jaws. Then slip the dumbbell in quietly. Again now, command 'Take it!' Jerk! Praise! Tell him 'Out!' "

The exercise is repeated while the owner faces the dog instead of standing at his side. The lead is brought up over the dog's head between his ears and held taut. The dumbbell or glove is held low in front of the dog. He is commanded to "Take it!" and the lead is pulled upward and forward with a snap. The entire class can do this in unison. They must be reminded that if the dog reaches forward to take the dumbbell when he hears the command, he should not be jerked, but praised. If he ignores the command, a quick snap on the lead should follow.

Before dismissing the class, the instructor should outline the work for the following week. This will consist of having the dog take the dumbbell while walking. Each new step when teaching dumbbell work depends upon the success of the previous lesson. If the owner fails in a particular exercise, it is a waste of time to go on to the next. That is why retrieving is difficult, though not impossible, to teach in a group. The dogs reach various stages of training where it requires individual instruction to overcome problems.

To demonstrate taking the dumbbell while heeling, the instructor should select a dog that will reach out to take the dumbbell on command. The lead is wadded up and carried in the left hand. The dumbbell is carried in the right. The instructor walks with the dog at heel position, then lowers the dumbbell in front of the dog and close to his mouth. He gives the command "Take it!" and jerks the lead forward in a series of short snaps. Remind the class: *"Don't stand still! Keep walking! Repeat the command if the dog does not reach for the dumbbell and tug the leash harder each time. When the dog takes it, continue with the heeling and while you are still walking, reach for the dumbbell and command 'Out!' Success in this exercise depends on the continuous movement, that is, giving the dog the dumbbell and taking it from him while both you and he are steadily moving forward."*

Lesson 4:

New exercises:

Taking the dumbbell or article from the owner's hand while heeling.

Taking the dumbbell or article from the owner's hand while the owner walks backward.

Jumping the solid, the bar, and the broad jumps while heeling.

Review:

Holding an article on command.

Carrying while heeling.

Holding an article while doing the sit-stay.

Carrying an article while reviewing all basic exercises.

Carrying on the recall.

Reaching for an article on command.

With the class called to order, the instructor reviews the previous lessons. He then commands: "Give your dog the glove! Praise him! Command 'Out!' Give it to him again! Forward! While walking, command 'Out!' " When doing this exercise the instructor should suggest that when the owners reach the opposite side of the room they do an about-turn and halt to wait for the other members of the class. With everyone in line again, the instruction continues:

"Forward! While walking, give your dog the dumbbell! *Keep moving!* Don't stop until you reach the opposite side of the room. Then do an about-turn and halt. With your dog still holding the dumbbell, Forward! While walking, reach for the dumbbell and say 'Out!' Continue to the other side of the room, about turn, and halt!"

When the class procedure follows this pattern, the line will be kept more or less even. Some dogs will be slower than others but everyone will be going in the same direction. The owners are next told:

"Face your dog about two steps in front of him. Hold your

lead in your left hand and wad it up so it doesn't dangle in the
dog's face. Hold your dumbbell in your right hand. Now,
walk *backward* and command 'Take it!' Keep moving and
when the dog reaches for the dumbbell, permit him to have
it. Halt! Remove the dumbbell! Tell your dog to stay and
step away from him. Command 'Take it!' Repeat the command as often as necessary and follow it with a series of little
short snaps on the lead. (The lead may come over the dog's

Fig. 31. For better control, hold the leash in both hands. *Courtesy: Mary
Priscilla Keyes.*

head or underneath his chin, or to the side; it makes little difference so long as the owner gets the results he is after.) When you reach the opposite side of the room, halt and make your dog sit in front of you. Take the dumbbell from him and then have him go to heel position. Face your dog again. Not too close! Walk backward. Command 'Take it!' Keep moving and give little tugs on the leash until the dog obeys. Praise him every time he reaches to take the dumbbell."

The final twenty minutes of the period can be spent in teaching the dogs to jump. The hurdles should be low to accommodate the smaller dogs. When there is a great variation in size, it is advisable to have two complete sets of jumps, one for the small dogs and one for the larger breeds. The purpose of the exercise, however, is to teach correct jumping form rather than to see how high the dogs can jump. The solid, bar, and broad jumps should be lined up in a row, ten to fifteen feet apart. (When the space is small, one jump may be placed on each of the three sides of the room and the jumping done in a circle.) Tell the owners to line up at one end of the room in front of the solid hurdle. The instruction then is:

"Take your leash exactly as you do for heeling. Hold it short, walk up to the hurdle, and step over with your dog. Don't change the position of your hands on the leash. Command 'Hup!' and pull the dog forward with your *left* hand. When the dog jumps, snap out the command 'Heel!' and jerk the lead backward with the left hand. Continue to the bar jump and do the same thing and then to the broad jump."

When the dog learns to jump freely and no longer hesitates, the owner may step to the side of the jump while the dog goes over by himself. Watch the position of the owner's left arm. It should be held out from the body and pointing toward the center of the jump with the leash sufficiently tight to keep the dog under control. The commands are "Hup! Heel! Hup! Heel!"

There will have to be constant reminders: "If your dog balks, don't slacken the leash. Pull steadily until he goes over. If the dog is permitted to have his way, he may refuse the hurdle at a future time. Keep the lead slack while the dog is jumping so he will not be thrown off balance. Snap out the command 'Heel!' the moment he lands to keep him under control. If the dog lunges forward after he jumps, say 'Heel!' in a demanding tone and snap the lead harder. At the same time flip the end of the lead across his nose to make him draw back of his own free will, or come to a halt and do an abrupt about-turn and jerk the lead hard in the opposite direction."

Before dismissing the class, the members should be warned that the following week the dogs will be expected to carry their dumbbells or other articles over the three jumps. Members should be urged to practice at home so the dogs will carry such articles as blocks of wood, leather gloves, or wallets. Advise them to bring an assortment of such articles to class. If the owner does not have a set of standard jumps on which to practice, a broom stick laid across the rungs of two chairs, over which a cloth is draped, will give the appearance of a solid barrier. A board placed in a doorway will serve the same purpose.

Lesson 5:

New exercises:

Concentrated work on the "Take it" to prepare the dog for picking up the dumbell from the floor.

Carrying the dumbbell and other articles over the three jumps.

Review:

Holding an article on command.

Carrying while heeling.

Holding an article while doing the sit-stay.

Carrying an article while doing all basic exercises.

Carrying on the recall.

Reaching for an article on command.

Taking the dumbbell or article from the owner's hand while heeling.

Taking the dumbbell or article from the hand while the owner walks backward.

Jumping the solid, the bar, and the broad jump while heeling.

To get the dog to the point where he will take an object from the floor on command, each step of the "Take it" exer-

Fig. 32. Note the position of the hands when teaching the dog to take the dumbbell from the floor. *Courtesy: Mary Priscilla Keyes.*

cise must become a little more advanced. Much will depend upon the progress the class as a whole has made thus far. If the dog is taking the dumbbell while heeling, the next step is to lower it closer to the floor. Finally it is dragged along the floor or "accidentally" dropped in play. The director will have to adjust his instruction to his particular group of dogs. When the usual training routine is varied to include jumping and carrying objects over the hurdles, the dog may take the attitude that retrieving is fun, and he will learn to enjoy the dumbbell work instead of resenting it as so many dogs do.

To encourage home training it should be announced that no dog will receive a diploma from the intermediate course (if diplomas are to be awarded) unless he picks up his dumbbell from the floor on command. This will leave a balance of four or five weeks in which to accomplish the training. As a word of warning, the home training should not be too severe, or damage may be done which cannot be overcome in the classroom.

Lessons 6, 7, and 8:
New exercises:
Taking articles from the floor on command (retrieving).
Jumping combined with carrying until the dogs will "Hup-Heel" over the three hurdles without the lead.

Review:
Holding an article on command.
Carrying while heeling.
Holding an article while doing the sit-stay.
Carrying an article while doing all the basic exercises.
Carrying on the recall.
Reaching for an article on command.
Taking the dumbbell or article from the owner's hand while heeling.
Taking the dumbbell or article from the hand while the owner walks backward.
Jumping the solid, the bar, and the broad jump while heeling.
Concentrated work on the "Take it" to prepare the dog for picking up the dumbbell from the floor.
Carrying the dumbbell and other articles over the three jumps.

The intensity of the struggle to teach some dogs to retrieve on command will serve to warn the owner and the instructor of the dangers inherent in using too much force. Patience, repetition, encouragement and praise with each step made progressively difficult will insure satisfactory results. A dog will not take an article from the floor until he will take it from the hand. He may in play, but not in real obedience. When play is used to entice the dog, it should be combined with obedience to make him associate the act of picking up the article with serious training. For example, tell the owner: "Keep the dog on leash and toss the article out in fun! Give the command 'Take it!' and follow with a tug on the leash, even though slight. Keep your voice happy! When the dog picks up the article, grab it from him and toss it out again!"

The many methods used to teach the dog to retrieve are given in *Training You to Train Your Dog** and need not be discussed here except to say that one must use ingenuity. The first lessons of holding, carrying, and reaching to take the dumbbell from the hand should be straight obedience. From this point on, play in one form or another should be used to encourage the dog so he will learn to enjoy his work and retrieve willingly. The trainer must then resort to straight obedience again to make the dog reliable under all conditions.

The purpose of this manual is to outline classroom procedure. It is therefore suggested that the instructor take ten or fifteen minutes at the close of Lessons 6, 7, and 8 to give special help to those owners who have been unable to reach the last rung of the ladder where the dog will pick up an article from the floor on command.

The jumping and carrying over the three hurdles should improve to the point where the dog jumps on command and stays at heel position after he jumps. The class must be reminded: "If a dog does not perform this exercise creditably well when the lead is on, he certainly won't when the lead has been taken off. Until the dog is able to jump the three hurdles on a slack leash and stay at heel position after he jumps, it is a waste of time to try it without the lead."

* Saunders, Blanche, New York: Doubleday & Co., 1946.

If the majority of the class members have been successful in getting their dogs to pick up the dumbbell or articles by the seventh or eighth lesson, the class can still work as a group, but the retrieves should be done individually. The instructor would advise: "Starting with the first dog in line, Forward! Toss your dumbbell on the floor ahead of your dog and command 'Take it!' After you give the command, flick the lead sharply as you walk past the dumbbell. *Don't* let the dog pass the dumbbell without taking it. The dog must learn never to ignore an article when he has been told to pick it up. Continue to the opposite side of the room, do an about-turn, and halt. Next dog the same thing!" After each dog has retrieved individually, the entire line-up can do it together, but the dogs must be kept on leash to prevent fights. In this exercise, other articles may be substituted for the dumbbell.

Next, have the owner toss the dumbbell out while the dog is heeling, but instead of continuing to move forward, tell him: "Walk backward! Make the dog return with the dumbbell and sit in front. Tell him 'Out!' and make him go to heel."

When the dogs reach the point where the retrieve can be tried without the leash, it should be done one at a time. Dogs are jealous of their possessions and a scrap may result if two dogs run out simultaneously after their dumbbells. Encourage each member: "Let your dog go after the dumbbell while it is still moving! This is where play can be introduced to encourage the dog to work quickly and gaily. He can be made to wait for commands later on." Tell the owner: "As soon as your dog picks up his dumbbell turn and run away from him. This will make him think he is being left behind and he will hurry to catch up with you."

A dog that will not retrieve on the flat will not retrieve over the hurdle. It is a waste of time to permit an owner to attempt the retrieve over an obstacle unless he has been suc-

cessful with the preliminary training. In the meantime, however, the owner can train the dog to jump the hurdle while
carrying and to jump back over the hurdle and sit in front.
The dumbbell is removed and the dog is made to complete
the exercise in the usual way. This will make the dog familiar
with the retrieve over the obstacle routine even though he
does not actually take the dumbbell from the floor.

When the dog reaches the point where he will retrieve by
himself, advise the owner: "Let the dog jump over the hurdle
to get his dumbbell in play. He can be steadied down later on.
If he gets too excited, voice commands will keep him under
control. Say 'Stay!' then throw the dumbbell. Command
'Hup!' Point to the dumbbell and say 'Take it!' then 'Come!
Sit! Out!' and finally 'Heel!' Continue to give these commands
until the dog is reliable. If he refuses at any time to pick up
the dumbbell, keep pointing at it and change the tone of your
voice to make it more demanding. If the dog becomes sullen,
revert to play again."

The intermediate course, as outlined here, is to prepare the
dog for the open class work, where he must retrieve on the
flat and over the hurdle. If time permits, there should be a
short review of the novice work every week to include heeling, the sit- and down-stays, coming when called, and the drop
in the distance to pave the way for the drop on recall. The
owner may be successful in teaching the retrieving exercises,
but he should not become careless and neglect the basic training.

Lesson 9: GRADUATION (Note: The dogs to work as a group).
   Heeling off leash with automatic sits.
   Individual recalls.
   Individual drops in the distance.
   Sit-stay.
   Down-stay.

Heeling while carrying.
Individual recalls while carrying.
Taking an article from the floor while heeling.
Individual retrieves on flat.
Hup-heel over the solid, the bar, and the broad jumps while
    carrying (both on and off leash).
Individual retrieves over the hurdle.

It will not be difficult for the judge to select the most obedient dogs in the intermediate course, for which ribbons and prizes may be awarded for the best performance. Diplomas may be issued to those dogs that will pick up an article from the floor on command and carry while doing the Hup-heel over the three jumps, but the author feels that by not offering diplomas, over-anxiety at this crucial point in the dog's training may be prevented. Too much pressure applied at this time (which may result from the owner's eagerness to receive a signed certificate) will react badly on the dog and affect his future training. A longer period of time and a little more patience may avoid the situation where the dog will work unhappily throughout the rest of his obedience training career. The instructor should encourage the owner to consider the intermediate course as a stepping stone to the open work that will follow.

8

The Open Course

Open Course:	For dogs that have graduated from the intermediate course or retrieve on command.
Length of Course:	Nine weeks.
Training Period:	1½ to 2½ hours.
Purpose:	To prepare the dog for the open class at Obedience Trials.

Training consists of:

Heeling (including the Figure-8) off leash.
Drop on recall.
Retrieve on flat.
Retrieve over the solid jump.
Broad jump.
Long sit (3 minutes, handlers out of sight).
Long down (5 minutes, handlers out of sight).

It would not be practical to outline a series of weekly lessons for the open course. Except for a general review of the novice and intermediate work, the training must be done individually. At this point the dogs will excel in one exercise and falter in others. But with practice the mistakes will gradually be eliminated and the dog will show improvement throughout the nine weeks of instruction.

It is suggested that the open course be divided into two parts. Section A will be for dogs that have graduated from the intermediate course and are entering open for the first time. Section B will be for dogs that have their C.D.X. title, or one or more legs toward it, and for those dogs with previous advanced training enrolled in the course for the purpose of gaining perfection.

A two or two-and-a-half hour training period would allow fifty to sixty minutes for each section with an additional twenty minutes or more at the half-way mark for the two groups to work together. Section A would come early and leave immediately after the group work. Section B would arrive in time for the combined training and would remain until the close of the period. With this schedule, the classroom will not be overcrowded.

The time allotted to each section (other than for group work when Section A and B work together) may be divided equally between the number of enrollees. The owner would be free to select the exercises on which he and his dog need the most practice. This would include the drop on recall, the retrieve, either on the flat or over the hurdle, or the correct procedure for doing the broad jump.

Ten or fifteen minutes before the close of the first period the two sections would be called on the floor to review the heeling exercises, both on and off leash, to practice drops in the distance, recalls, the drop on recall, the sit- and down-stays, or, in fact, any part of the training that can be done together. The heeling can be done in group formation, with several dogs abreast and deep, to conserve space and practice all turns. The dogs would work about twenty minutes to half an hour, at which time the second period would begin.

This proposed system is recommended when the training room is small and there is not enough space for more than one dog to work at a time. If a club is fortunate enough to have a large area in which to train, and if club members are able to assist the instructor, the training need not be so restricted. During the instruction of each group, the solid jump can be set up in one corner of the room and the broad jump in another. The drop on recall and retrieve on the flat can be practiced in still a different part of the classroom. Training during distractions will help to make the dogs more reliable. The instructor would constantly make the rounds to see how the dogs are progressing and give suggestions for improvement. He would lend assistance at such times when a second person is needed to make a correction, or he would temporarily hold up all training to overcome a dog's disobedience, such as running away, where the entire class can be of help. It would be the instructor's responsibility to see that the dogs do not interfere with one another and that the owners are not inconvenienced in their training.

During the individual instruction, if the problem is that of heeling off leash and the dog lags or is wide on the turns, the owner should be advised: "Try bribing the dog with food. Carry a titbit in the left hand to encourage the dog to snuggle up close. If this does not seem to help, put the dog back on leash. Keep it slack. Every time the dog drops back from heel position or goes wide on a turn, say 'Heel!' in a demanding voice!" An outside correction can be made surreptitiously by tossing something at the dog's heels, after which the owner must pat and praise the dog enthusiastically to reassure him and give him the protection he will seek. No outside correction should be made unless the leash is on so that if the dog becomes frightened he will not be able to dart away at the time he is corrected.

The leash is then removed and the owner is told: "Resort to voice control. Keep the heeling command gay and happy but the first time the dog steps out of line, *demand* obedience by using the word 'Heel!' in a forceful manner, followed by quick praise. When the dog is doing good heel work, whisper a confidential 'Good fellow' occasionally to keep his spirits high and to let him know he is doing the right thing."

Advise the owner: "When you do a Fast, avoid starting off with a rush. Swing into the Fast with a smooth action, *giving praise at the same time*. Glide into the Slow in the same way."

The majority of dogs will slow up on the recall when the drop is introduced. Suggest: "Let the dog get into the habit of dropping in the distance from either the sitting or the standing positions. Alternate voice with signal. Return to your dog each time after he lies down and reward him with food and praise. This may prevent him from feeling he is being punished when he is made to go down on command and he will be less resentful of the drop on recall. During practice, if the signal is ignored, follow immediately with the voice command. When the command goes unheeded, give the signal and the voice together. Don't yell at the dog, but make the command authoritative. In every case, if the dog continues to move forward after you have told him to drop, there should be some form of noise to startle the dog sufficiently to make him go down at once. The leash dropped to the floor or the heel stamped with a loud bang will usually have the desired effect."

At other times, the instructor may stand directly behind the owner with some article in his hand. When the dog ignores the signal or command to drop, the instructor tosses the article over the owner's head so that it lands on the floor directly in front of the dog. When he drops to the ground, the owner should praise him immediately. The owner can make the correction himself by holding the object in whichever hand is used to give the signal.

In obstinate cases, have the owner put the dog back on leash. Tell him: "Face your dog at the full length. Call him and run backward. As the dog gains speed, give the command or the signal to drop. If either one is ignored, quickly drop your hand and cuff the dog on the nose." The leash will prevent the dog from ducking away and the owner can get in a well-timed correction. The exercise should be repeated until the dog instantly obeys either the signal or the command to lie down.

The owner whose dog follows him in when left for the recall, the drop on recall, or the sit- and down-stays should be advised: "Carry your leash wadded up into a ball in your left hand. When I say 'Throw it!' toss the leash backward without looking at the dog so that it will either hit him or land in front of him. Then take your dog back to position and repeat the correction if necessary."

There is no definite rule to follow when giving instructions for the retrieve on the flat. Each dog may have to be corrected in different ways, but the instructor must watch for ill effects. Tell the owner: "Play is an extremely important factor, but it must be combined with actual obedience if the dog is to become dependable. Take care not to make the dog develop an aversion to the dumbbell and fear the sound of the retrieve command. At first, the dog is forced to hold and carry an object through a series of regular obedience lessons, and he is corrected if he is reluctant to do as he is told. The picking up of an object off the floor is accomplished through play if the dog is interested in playing and if he has the desire to chase anything that is thrown."

It has been suggested that an assortment of articles be used when the dog is taught to retrieve. There will be times when force must be combined with play and the dog should be made to understand and accept the discipline as part of his training and not associate it entirely with the dumbbell. Advise the owners: "With your dog on leash get his interest, and then toss the article out in front of him. He may bound away after it. If he does, give the command 'Take it' in a happy voice and jerk the lead lightly, just before the dog picks the object off the floor. The snap on the collar will remind the dog of his early training when he was forced to take and hold the dumbbell. The act of picking it off the floor, even though a playful one, is immediately established as one of obedience." The dog with no playfulness in his make-up can only be given straight obedience with the training gradually becoming more forceful.

Hesitation, slowness and uncertainty may be overcome in the early stages by telling the owner: "Whenever the dog takes the dumbbell or article from the floor, turn and run away. In the excitement, the dog will chase after you while still holding the article. He will forget for the moment he is obeying an obedience command and in the meantime, you will accomplish your objective, which is to have your dog pick up the dumbbell on the first command and retrieve with speed."

When the time comes—and it will—when the dog's attitude distinctly says he has finished for the day, the owner must be advised: "Resort strictly to obedience. The first command is given in a happy voice. The demanding tone is used when the dog is disobedient and ignores the order to retrieve. Use the collar, quietly but firmly, to make the dog do what you tell him." Force applied at this point does not have the ill effect the same force would have in the beginning. When the dog knows what he is expected to do and is corrected for not doing it, he will not be indignant except for the moment.

The retrieve over the jump will be successful if the dog is dependable when retrieving on the flat. Remind the owner:

"Your dog will not retrieve over the hurdle unless he will do a straight retrieve. He might once or twice, but you will not be able to rely on him." Advise the owner: "Walk toward the jump with the dog *on leash*. Get him excited and playful and then toss the dumbbell over the hurdle ahead of him and let him chase it immediately. Always give the command to take it and snap the leash lightly just before the dog picks up the dumbbell from the floor. Circle around the training room and do the same thing again, or instead, make the dog jump back over the hurdle. When leash corrections are no longer necessary, the leash may be removed, but the voice commands must be used in all parts of the exercise to aid and encourage the dog."

The owner whose dog retrieves in slow motion, or hesitates about jumping back over the hurdle, should be advised: "Toss the dumbbell and when the dog picks it up, turn and run! When the dog jumps back, don't make him sit but grab the dumbbell from him and throw it again!" As in the retrieve on the flat, this rule applies when the dog is learning to retrieve over the hurdle so he will enjoy his work. It will make the exercise take on the appearance of play and the dog will be less suspicious of the fact he is being trained. He can be steadied down later.

If anticipation is evident and the dog so keen he goes for the dumbbell before he should, tell the owner: "Throw the dumbbell but don't let the dog go after it!" The instructor then picks up the dumbbell and hands it to the owner to throw again; or after the owner throws the dumbbell, have him command "Heel!" *do an about-turn, and walk in the opposite direction.* When this is repeated until the dog no longer starts unless commanded, he is permitted to retrieve occasionally.

The owner whose dog consistently drops the dumbbell on

the return is told: "Do an about-turn and halt with the dog sitting at heel. Pat him while he is holding the dumbbell. If he anticipates the finish, take the dumbbell but prevent the dog from going to heel. Instead, step back to heel position yourself. Do this several times until the dog learns to hold the dumbbell until you tell him 'Out' and waits for the command to finish."

One problem is that of running around the hurdle instead of jumping it. To overcome this habit, an assistant stands on one side of the hurdle several feet from the jump, and the trainer stands on the other side. If the dog attempts to dart around, a leash is thrown on the floor by either the trainer or the assistant, to check the dog's actions. If he tries to do the same thing on the return, advise the owner: "Wad up your leash and hold it in your hand so you can make the correction yourself."

The dog that refuses to go out for the dumbbell on the first command is corrected by the instructor, who stands behind the dog and tosses an article in back of him; or the owner should tap the dog's hindquarters by kicking back with his *right* foot after he gives the command.

If the dog picks up the dumbbell but does not return at once, he is corrected by the trainer or his assistant who tosses the leash or some other article at the dog's heels *when he is not looking*. When the dog jumps back after the correction, the owner makes a big fuss over him to ease hurt feelings.

A dog can be made to pick up his feet and clear the top board of the jump more freely by the following method: The assistant stands on one side of the hurdle to prevent the dog from going around the end. The trainer stands on the opposite side with a light aluminum rod or piece of dowling in his hand. The rod is held along the edge of the top board so the dog cannot see it. When the dog is in mid-air, the rod is lifted to rap his paws and make him tuck his feet up close to his body.

The owner, throughout the training for the retrieve over the hurdle, must be reminded of several things: "Give the first retrieve command in a *happy* tone of voice. Use the demanding tone only when the dog disobeys or hesitates about picking up the dumbbell! Keep pointing at the dumbbell without moving your hand from position until the dog does what he is told! Gauge the distance you must stand from the hurdle so the dog will have room to correct himself and sit straight on the return! Use voice commands throughout until the dog performs accurately! The commands are Stay! Hup! Take it! Come! Sit! Out! Heel! The extra commands can be dropped later. After every correction, no matter how it was brought about, make a fuss over the dog to prevent ill feelings."

The broad jump problems usually include anticipation, refusal to jump on the first command and not clearing the hurdle. To overcome the first fault tell the owner: "Leave your dog and go to the side of the jump. Wait a moment and return to him. Repeat this as often as necessary to teach the dog to wait for the command. If you alternate the sit-stay with the jumping command, the dog will become steady."

The dog that refuses to jump on the first command or signal is put back on leash. The over-all distance of the jump is shortened. The owner is told: "Hold the leash slack. Give the signal or the command to jump without moving your body. Follow immediately by a severe jerk on the leash to pull the dog over the jump. Don't bother to finish the exercise, praise the dog, circle around and do the same thing again." An alternate method is for the instructor to stand behind the dog and if he continues to sit after he has been told to jump, startle him by tossing an object on the floor. The leash will prevent the dog from darting away and if the owner gives the necessary encouragement, the dog will be assured that all is well.

If the dog doesn't clear the full jump or walks on top of
the hurdle, he is corrected the same way as in the high jump.
Tell the owner: "Put your dog on leash and assume the jumping position." The instructor kneels directly behind the handler with the light rod resting on top of one of the hurdles.
If the dog is lazy about picking up his feet, the rod is lifted to
rap his paws. In the meantime, remind the owner: "Be generous with your praise. Pat the dog and convince him it was
his own fault!" This correction is not made unless the dog is
on leash and under control.

There is the dog that cuts the corners and the one that
circles wide on the return. The first problem is overcome by
telling the owner: "Lift your knee and bump the dog hard
just before he lands. If he is thrown off balance in mid-air, he
will keep his distance and jump in a straight line the next
time." To make the dog return faster, advise the owner: "Put
the dog on leash. Hold it slack. Give the signal or command
to jump and the moment the dog lands on the opposite side,
call out 'Come!' in a demanding tone of voice and immediately
snap the leash hard. After you do this two or three times,
take the leash off. Repeat the exercise but use the command
'Come' just the same. The voice can later be eliminated."

To avoid anticipating the finish, remind the owner: "Don't
let your dog go to heel position every time. Occasionally step
back to heel position yourself."

The sit-stay and down-stay problems are not so numerous,
but they can be very annoying. There is the dog that lies
down on the long sit and the one that sits up on the long
down. Certain breeds of dogs, when left by themselves, are
specialists when it comes to whining. (Have you ever listened
to a group of Poodles on the long sit and down?) There is

the dog that will cheat by creeping! If he is not permitted to walk toward his owner he will get there by crawling on his tummy.

One way to correct the dog that lies down on the long sit is for the instructor or his assistant to walk nonchalantly toward the dog then quickly step on his front paws to make him jump to a sitting position. This may make the dog think he will be corrected at future times by the judge or the ring stewards if he lies down in the obedience ring at a dog show.

To cure the habit of whining, sitting up on the long down, or creeping from position, the instructor or his assistant should startle the dog at the moment he does wrong. This may be done by tossing a chain or wadded-up leash near him. Be sure, however, that this correction comes from a hidden source. In more desperate cases a water pistol or a BB air rifle may be used to sting the dog on the rear so he will associate his act of disobedience with something unpleasant. Remember, *the dog should not know the source of the correction.* Tell the owner: "After your dog is corrected, reprimand him from the distance, return him to position, and leave him again." When the training is done in a classroom, care must be taken not to frighten the other dogs that are behaving as they should. This is why individual problems are more satisfactorily solved when each is worked on separately.

The week before graduation the training quarters should be set up to resemble an obedience ring. The owner and his dog are given a complete run-through of the open class exercises. If the dog fails to do the principal part of the exercise or anticipates a command and goes before he should, the instructor reminds the owner: "Your dog would receive a zero or less than fifty per cent on this exercise at a regular show. Please practice this week so the same thing will not happen at graduation."

GRADUATION

The judging of the open course should follow the same procedure as in the open class at Obedience Trials. Each dog works individually and the sit- and down-stays are done together. If the class has been divided into two groups throughout the training, each should be scored separately and more leniency shown in Section A, where the dogs are learning the

Fig. 33. Graduation day—the dogs receive their diplomas. *Courtesy: Mary Priscilla Keyes.*

open work and are performing for the first time. Section B would be required to meet with the rules and regulations of the American Kennel Club and the same standard of judging should be strictly enforced. Separate ribbons and prizes can be offered to the winning dogs in each of the two groups, and diplomas awarded to every dog that receives a qualifying score, whether in Section A or B. The diploma would testify to the calibre of the dog's work and certify that he is ready to compete in the open class at Obedience Trials.

9

The Utility Course

Utility Course:	For dogs that have graduated from the open course, and those that have their C.D.X. or U.D. title.
Length of Course:	Nine weeks.
Training Period:	1½ to 2 hours.
Purpose:	To teach the utility exercises and to prepare the dog for the utility class at Obedience Trials.

Training consists of:

Scent discrimination.
Directed Retrieve.
Signal exercise.
Directed jump.
Group stand for examination.

It would appear that training in the utility course requires individual instruction. With a little planning and forethought, however, the work can be done as a group in the training class and satisfactory results achieved.

A weekly schedule will not be outlined here; rather, suggestions will be made for a break-down of the classroom training during the hour and a half or two-hour period. It is recommended that the utility course be divided into two

155

parts: Utility A will be for those dogs just graduated from
the open course and enrolling for the first time; Utility B
will be for dogs having their U.D. title or one or more legs
thereon, and for dogs with previous utility training.

At the beginning of the period, the two sections work together on the signal exercise and the group stand for examination. Advise the owners: "Put your dogs on leash and use
signals for all parts of the training. Signal with the left hand
as you move forward. Jerk the lead with the right hand if the
dog is slow to start. If the dog doesn't sit when you halt, cuff
him sharply on the rear. Don't tell him to sit but praise him
when he is already sitting. Signal the forward! Halt! Signal
the forward! Halt!" (If there is room to make right and left
turns as well as about-turns, these should be included in the
heeling routine.)

"Forward! Give the signal to stand! Don't touch your
dog. Drop your left hand (or right, if you prefer) in front
of your dog's muzzle while you are still moving. If your
signal is ignored and the dog continues to move forward,
bounce the palm of your hand against his nose to make him
draw back. If the dog does not know how to stand on signal
use the voice with the signal, then gradually eliminate the
voice command and use hand motions entirely. Forward!
Give the signal to stand. Signal the dog to stay." The signal
to stay is similar to that of the stand, but the owner must be
advised: "Give the signal *before* you move away to face your
dog. Otherwise the dog will follow. Circle back to heel position! Forward! Signal the stand! Signal the stay! Give the
signal first and then step out with your right foot. Face your
dog the full length of the lead! Signal him to lie down!"

The signal to lie down is given while the dog is standing.
This may be the first time the dog is made to lie down from
the standing position, but the owner will have little trouble

if the dog responded to the signal when he was sitting. Advise the class: "If your dog hasn't started to drop by the time your hand is in an upright position, don't wait! Stamp on the leash with your foot and snap him down without saying anything! Praise him when he obeys. You must give the signal, make the correction, if necessary, then follow with praise!"

The signal to sit from the down position is the same as that used throughout the dog's training. It is the forward-upward motion given with the right hand. Tell the class members: "Give the signal to sit and follow at once by jerking the dog up to a sitting position with the lead held in the left hand. Don't raise your hand any higher than the waist. Hold it as near the dog's eye level as possible. Bring it forward with force so the dog can see the palm of your hand."

The signal to come is made by motioning across the body with either arm. Some owners prefer to use the left arm for the come signal because they feel it will not confuse the dog. During the training, the leash is held in one hand and away from the body. The free hand motions across the body and lands on the leash to snap the dog forward. Since the dog will not be familiar with this signal, the owner is advised: "Give the verbal command in this case immediately after you jerk the leash." The instructor should further explain: "Let your hand pause momentarily when it reaches the leash until you see if your dog is going to respond to the 'Come' signal. If he does, gather the leash up without jerking, but if he remains sitting after he has observed the signal, continue the hand motion and snap the leash quickly toward your body. Follow the jerk with the command 'Come!' and praise your dog to reassure him."

The signal to go to heel position is the same as in basic training. The owners are advised: "Give the signal by drop-

ping the left hand quickly to the side. If the dog remains sitting, take hold of the leash and jerk hard. Don't say anything
except to praise the dog as he moves around to the left side.
Hold the left arm in back of your body until the dog makes
the complete turn. This will assure a more accurate finish and
the dog will sit straight and square."

The signal exercise will not be difficult if the dog has received the correct basic training. If the corrections were
timed right and the proper technique used all through the
beginners course, the signal exercise will need only a little
polishing to prepare the dog for competition work in the
utility class.

The instructor should stress the following points: "Each
signal must be clear and distinct. Avoid confusing the dog by
using signals that look alike. See that the dog responds immediately to the *first* signal. Use the voice command if necessary, but don't move the hand from position until the dog
obeys. Praise throughout the exercise to encourage the dog
and give him confidence."

To keep the dog from learning a patterned routine, the
class work, with the dogs working on leash, will approximate
the following: "Forward! Give the signal to stand! Forward!
Give the signal to stand! Give the signal to stay! Face your
dog! Return to heel position. Give the signal to stay! Face
your dog again! Give the signal to lie down! Circle back to
heel position! Give the signal to stay! Face your dog!
Give the signal to sit! Return to heel position! Leave him
again! Give the signal to come! The signal to finish!" This
will teach the dog to recognize the different signals and will
prevent him from anticipating a set routine.

The dogs are next taken off leash and the signal exercise is
done two dogs at a time. The instructor starts with the one on
the end of the line and the one in the center and commands:

"Forward! Give the signal to stand! Give the signal to stay! Leave your dog and face him across the room! Give the signal to lie down! The signal to sit! The signal to come! The signal to finish!" And so on down the line until all dogs have done the exercise.

During this exercise leash corrections are impossible, so the owners must be reminded: "Your voice becomes the correction. If, for instance, your dog doesn't obey the signal to lie down from the distance, *demand* the down by voice command without moving the hand from the signal position. If you give the signal to sit and the dog ignores it, *demand* that he sit while the hand is still held in place. Follow each signal with praise!"

The signal exercise, done individually, can be repeated several times during the class period.

The group stand for examination will naturally be done in unison. As the instructor goes down the line to examine each dog in turn, tell the owner: "If your dog starts to move, call out 'Stay!' in a demanding tone. Your dog must feel that he has more to fear from disobeying your command than he has from any stranger who comes near."

Approximately fifteen or twenty minutes will be spent on the signal exercise and the stand for examination. A time-clock will indicate the end of the allotted period.

Scent discrimination comes next. It goes without saying a dog must be reliable in retrieving before scent work is even attempted. On command, the dog should retrieve all types of articles made of leather and metal. At this point in the training period, Utility A and B are divided. Group A will work under the direction of the training instructor since the members will be learning how to teach their dogs the exercise. Group B is primarily for practice under distracting conditions such as may occur at dog shows. This group will work in a separate part of the room with a member of the club or an assistant trainer to help in placing the scent articles. The members of the B Group will perform the exercise as required in regular competition, but they should be advised: "Make the necessary corrections while you have the opportunity. Convince the dog he is here to work and not to make mistakes!"

Group A, under the instruction of the training director, will form a small circle with the dogs sitting at heel position. The dumbbell is the first article used for scent work. The owners toss their dumbbells into the center of the circle. One dog at a time retrieves his own from among those on the floor. After he retrieves, the dumbbell is tossed back into the circle. As each dog goes out to pick up his dumbbell he will naturally be interested in the others. He may sniff them and be curious, but he will recognize his own because it has a familiar smell and should bring it back immediately. The instructor should tell the owner: "Let the dog see the dumbbell when you throw it, and permit him to chase it without waiting too long. This will encourage him to work faster. Next, cover your dog's eyes when you throw the dumbbell, then give him the command to take it. He will hear the dumbbell when it hits the floor, but he will have to use his nose to find it. Don't discourage the dog when he sniffs the other dumbbells. Wait and see if he picks up the wrong one before you correct him." If a dog becomes confused or uncertain all the dumbbells except one or two should be taken away. When the dog gains confidence and becomes proficient, more dumbbells can be added.

The next step is to substitute leather gloves and the regular scent articles for the dumbbell. If the dog is encouraged to retrieve different articles from among similar ones belonging to other members of the class, he will quickly learn to distinguish all items by smell. Without realizing it, the owner will have taught the dog the difference between retrieving on the flat and a retrieve where scent discrimination must be used. *When a dog has trouble with scent work, it is usually due to faulty retrieving.* In this case, the owner should work by himself and accomplish accurate retrieving before he attempts to work with the other members of the class.

Ten or fifteen minutes practice in class plus work at home should have the dogs doing scent discrimination creditably well by graduation.

The only new thing about the Directed Retrieve is the directional part. The retrieve is the same basic Retrieve on the Flat as in the Open exercise.

If the owner has not taught the dog to retrieve a glove, this should be done now at home. Until she will retrieve the glove, there is no point in proceeding. If she shows no interest in the glove, put it in her mouth with praise. Take it from her, and toss it on the ground and encourage her to get it. Since she is already retrieving the dumbbell, she will soon learn.

The instructor should see that the owner gives the proper signal for the Directed Retrieve. The left hand should be moved ALONG THE FLOOR past the dog's shoulder and nose toward the glove, NOT UP IN THE AIR. The knees may be bent to bring the hand on a level with the dog's eyes, but the feet must not move.

In practise, the instructor first places the three gloves with the two outside gloves at 60-degree angles (left and right), and the third glove directly in front. Have the owner send the dog for the center glove. Have the center glove replaced. Now have the owner send her for one of the side gloves. If she retrieves the proper glove, the owner praises her. If she starts toward the wrong glove, the instructor, standing behind the center glove, points toward the proper glove, and the

handler encourages her with "Good girl!" When she is retrieving the proper glove each time, the gloves are placed in
their Obedience ring position, the outer gloves at a 45-degree
angle, and the third glove in the center.

Where the dog continues to veer away from retrieve of the
proper glove, here's a suggestion. A 15-foot rope, fastened to
the dog's collar, is held by the instructor, who stands halfway
between the dog and the handler, but to the outside of the
path travelled by the dog. The rope is jerked only if the dog
starts toward the wrong glove. The handler repeats the command with praise. For the center glove, the instructor would
stand behind the glove.

The Directed Retrieve should not be practised too long at
a time, lest the dog get bored. Stop after a good performance.
Or, if corrections have been necessary throughout the practise session, do an exercise she does well and praise her for her
good work before ending the training session.

At the half-way mark of the training period, the directed
jump is introduced. The dogs in Utility B are given preference. They are already familiar with the exercise or they
would not have the U.D. title or legs thereon. Their training
will be to overcome problems and to gain perfection.

The dog may need assistance on the "Go" or more training
in taking the designated jump. Whatever the problem is, the
instructor must advise accordingly.

If the dog will not go a substantial distance on the first
command, he should be put on the line immediately. A fifty-
foot clothesline inserted through a ring or pulley attached to
one end of the room and placed five or six feet above the
floor, is probably the most satisfactory method of teaching
the directed jump and of overcoming problems. The instructor holds one end of the line close to the pulley and the other

end is fastened to the dog's collar. The owner commands the dog to "Go" and gives the signal with the left hand (or the right, if preferred). The slack line is taken up by the instructor as he walks in the opposite direction from the one in which the dog is moving. If the dog stops before he should, tell the owner: "Repeat the command in a demanding tone!" The instructor follows by giving the line a sharp pull to make the correction. When the dog has gone far enough, the owner calls him by name and gives the command "Sit!" If the dog does not obey, another jerk on the line will quickly put him in a sitting position.

The dog is walked back to the starting point and the "Go" is repeated. The instructor alternately pulls the dog forward or snaps the line sharply when the dog stops moving, depending on how he reacts to the training. When he leaves his owner on the first command and continues to move outward until he is told to sit, the exercise is tried off leash. The trainer stands at the inside corner of one hurdle and his assistant stands at the other hurdle. When the dog is told to "Go" the trainer and his assistant point along with the owner in the direction the dog is to take. If he doesn't sit when commanded, all three close in on him, giving the sit-stay signal. This is the palm of the hand toward the dog with fingers pointing toward the floor. As the dog becomes more reliable, the trainer and his assistant move to the outside corners of the hurdles and finally step completely out of the ring, to give the dog more freedom.

The dog is not always permitted to jump the hurdles after he is sent out. The owner should occasionally walk to where the dog is sitting and send him in the opposite direction. This will make the dog more reliable on the "Go" and teach him to wait for the signal to jump.

When the dog does not jump as directed, the instructor

should stand in the center between the two jumps. He points along with the owner, to the jump the dog is to take. The fact the instructor is standing there will make the dog hesitate before returning without jumping, and he will circle to keep his distance. When the wrong jump is taken on signal, the instructor stands at the inside corner of the jump not being used and discourages the dog from making a mistake. If others move forward to check the dog's movements when he makes an error, he will soon learn to watch for directions and will recognize the owner's signal as his clue for jumping.

If the dog goes out and sits on command but does not wait for the signal, the owner should call "Stay" immediately after he gives the command to sit, such as "Bozo! Sit-stay!" The extra command can later be eliminated.

Perhaps the dog does not start when he is given the signal to jump. In this case the instructor stands in the center between the two jumps and an assistant stays behind the dog. If the dog doesn't move when he sees the signal, the assistant should drop a wadded-up leash or a chain in back of the dog to startle him. The instructor, by standing where he is, will discourage the dog from running directly to the owner after he is startled. The dog will circle around and jump as directed if the opposite hurdle is covered by still a third person to prevent him from taking the wrong one.

Advise the owner: "Signal first! Command second! Don't use the dog's name! When you give the signal, point to the jump with a forceful gesture and keep your arm in place until the dog obeys! Give several commands if necessary, but only *one* signal! Praise your dog when it is evident he will take the designated jump!" The instructor should stress the point: "*Never* permit your dog to return to you by passing between the two hurdles. Block him immediately by running forward and literally push him over."

After the Utility B dogs have had practice on the directed jump, the Utility A dogs can be put on the line so they will learn to leave their owners on command. This is the first time in the dog's training when he is required to go away from his owner for no apparent reason. The inexperienced dog should be kept on the line for two or three weeks until he forms the habit of working accurately. When a dog will leave on the first command with no help from the line, and will continue to move outward until told to sit, the exercise may be tried off leash. The trainer and his assistant should again stand at the inside corners of the hurdles and point along with the owner in the direction the dog is to take. When the dog is sitting at the opposite end of the room, the owner walks to his dog and the dog is sent in the reverse direction.

One after the other the Utility A dogs may start the jumping, but the instructor should stand in the center of the room and block the dog from taking the wrong hurdle or from returning to the owner without jumping. When a dog is in the process of mastering a new exercise he will progress faster if he learns to do the right thing by avoiding the wrong. At this stage, frequent corrections would confuse and discourage the dog. The time to make the test difficult is when the lesson is thoroughly understood.

When the dog is learning to recognize the signal for the directed jump, he is left sitting at one end of the room almost directly in front of one of the hurdles. The handler crosses to the other side of the room and stands opposite the dog. If the dog is to take the left jump, the owner uses the left arm to give the signal and the arm is brought out from the body with force. Immediately after the signal, he gives the command "Hup!" or "Over!" in a loud clear voice. The owner must be reminded to run forward if necessary and tap the hurdle to encourage the dog to obey. At the same time, the instructor moves slowly in the direction of the designated jump with his arm outstretched. When it is evident the dog is going to leap the hurdle, he is praised enthusiastically.

The dog is left in a sitting position again and the owner crosses to the opposite side and the directional jump is reversed. This time, the signal is given with the right arm. The owner must remember to give the signal first and to follow immediately with the command. He must hold the arm in position until the dog obeys and under no circumstances should he permit the dog to return without jumping. If he attempts to do so, both the owner and the instructor must block him completely in order to make him go over the jump.

The distance is gradually increased until the dog will recognize the signal and respond accordingly from any part of the room. The instructor gradually moves outward from between the jumps to leave the center space clear and to give the dog more freedom. The first attempt to return without jumping should bring a correction from the owner who tosses a leash on the floor in front of the dog. When the dog misinterprets the direction he is to go, the instructor or his assistants move in from the side of the ring to check the dog from taking the wrong hurdle.

From this point on, all suggestions to overcome problems on the directional jump are followed during the instruction. Prevent mistakes when possible. Make the test easy at first and gradually increase the distance the dog must travel.

When the dog becomes proficient and will infallibly recognize the signal as his clue for jumping, the "Go" is included to complete the exercise.

Throughout the training in both the open and the utility classes, it is not wise to use a set routine where one exercise always follows another. If the training is varied the dog will learn to distinguish accurately between the many signals and commands. He will be more attentive and less inclined to anticipate.

One or two weeks before the close of the utility course, the training room should be set up to resemble an obedience ring. With graduation not far away, the class routine should be the same as at a regular Obedience Trial to familiarize the owner with ring procedure.

GRADUATION

The utility course should be conducted the same as at an Obedience Trial. The dogs work separately except for the group examination. The ribbons and prizes should be divided between Sections A and B, with more leniency shown the beginner. Section B would be judged with the same degree of severity as in the utility class at dog shows. Diplomas should be awarded to every dog (even in Utility A) if he receives a qualifying score. The diploma would serve to certify the dog is ready to compete in the utility class at a regular Obedience Trial.

10

The Combined Courses

Combined Courses: For dogs in all stages of training.
Length of Course: Nine weeks.
Training Period: 3½ to 4 hours.
Purpose: To conserve time when the training period is limited.

When a training club is able to hold practice sessions twice a week, the breakdown of the class-work is simplified. The courses may be divided to include beginners, novice, and intermediate one day, and open and utility another. Combined courses will be necessary when the training occurs only once a week and all five classes must convene during one training period. This will include the beginners course, the combined novice and intermediate, and the combined open and utility.

Training consists of:
    Beginners:
        1 to 1½ hours (depending upon whether the class is divided) as outlined in the beginners course.
    Novice and Intermediate (1 hour):
        The novice work as outlined in the novice course.
        Holding and carrying the dumbell (retrieving if possible).

168

Jumping the solid, the bar, and the broad jump, and carrying
the dumbbell over the three hurdles.

Sit-stay and down-stay with owners òut of sight.

Open and Utility (1½ to 2 hours):

The open work as required at Obedience Trials.

Teaching the utility exercises.

The utility work as required at Obedience Trials.

The first group, the beginners, is given the training as outlined in the beginners course.

The novice-intermediate group first reviews all the basic
exercises as outlined in the novice course. The instructor
stresses the importance of giving only one command or signal,
followed by an immediate correction if the dog doesn't obey.
The work is done off leash as well as on, and includes heeling
(with the Figure-8 done separately), the stand for examination, the recall, the drop in the distance, the sit-stay and the
down-stay.

The dogs in the novice-intermediate group are also taught
to hold and carry the dumbbell and to take it from the
owner's hand while walking at heel (as outlined in the intermediate course). Whether the actual retrieve on the flat will
be successful will depend upon the individual dogs and the
amount of home training accomplished. The dogs should
learn to jump the solid, the bar, and the broad jump while
heeling and to carry the dumbbell over the jumps without
dropping it.

The sit- and down-stays should be performed with the
owners out of sight to prepare the dogs for the open-utility
course to follow.

The final group, made up of the open and utility dogs,
works together for about twenty minutes. The basic exercises
are quickly reviewed on leash and the instructor watches to
see that only one command or signal is given, followed by a

correction if the dog does not obey. The signal exercise and the stand for examination are done as outlined in the utility course. The drop in the distance is given more attention to prepare the dogs for the drop on recall as required at obedience trials.

The stays are practiced with the handlers out of sight.

At the end of the group work (twenty minutes or half an hour), the remaining time of the open-utility period is divided equally among the dogs present to overcome problems. Alternating from week to week, the ring is set up for open work, then utility, just as it would be at an Obedience Trial. The dogs working for their C.D.X. title are taken one after the other (if it is the week for the open dogs to work first) and each owner may use his allotted time on whatever exercise he feels his dog needs the most training. This may be the drop on recall, the retrieve on the flat, the retrieve over the hurdle, or the broad jump. In some cases, there will be time for a complete run-through of all the exercises. If the dog is already familiar with the work, the owner and instructor should make each test as difficult instead of as easy as possible. This will permit corrections not allowed in the obedience ring and will make the dog reliable under conditions of stress.

In the retrieve over obstacle, for instance, the dumbbell should be thrown a short distance, then a greater one, and finally it should be tossed off to one side to tempt the dog to go around the jump. The owner must be alert to make the necessary corrections. In the drop on recall, the dog should be made to lie down just as he starts toward his owner, then half way, and finally only a few feet from the owner. This prepares the dog for the unexpected at dog shows and he will not be distracted by various routines of different judges.

At the completion of the open class problem period, the

ring is set up for utility and the U.D. dogs, or those working toward the U.D. title, receive their allotted time. The instruction usually includes scent discrimination, and practice on the seek back and the directed jump. (The signal exercise and the group examination were practised earlier.)

The instructor should again keep the thought in mind that when a dog is learning an exercise, the test should be made easy to avoid mistakes. If an experienced dog performs with few errors, the instructor should distract the dog's attention while he is working and thus introduce conditions likely to arise at dog shows. Applause, the banging of a door, loud talking, and people sitting close to the ringside, will create a dog-show atmosphere which gives the owner the opportunity to correct the dog when he is disobedient. The suggestions for instruction of the open and utility courses apply to the combined course as well.

To assure each member of the class an equal amount of training, someone should be appointed as official time-keeper. He should be given a clock that will ring out at the close of each problem period. This will discourage owners from asking for extra time and will avoid unfairness to the other members of the class.

One or two weeks before graduation the training room can be set up to simulate an obedience ring. The dogs that are working for their C.D.X. titles can be put through the regular open routine. The dogs that already have their C.D.X. and are working for their U.D. would be put through the utility exercises as well as the open. The instructor should call the owner's attention to any part of the performance in either class where the dog would receive a non-qualifying score. This will encourage the owner to concentrate on the dog's particular failing and do extra home practice.

GRADUATION:

Beginners:

> To work as a group. Review all basic training as outlined in the beginners course.
>
> Awards to be made for Performance, for Handling and for Greatest Improvement.
>
> Diplomas to be issued to all dogs that meet the stipulated requirements.

Novice-Intermediate:

> Dogs may work individually as in the novice class at Obedience Trials, or in a group as in the beginners class.
>
> The dogs to be tested on all basic exercises, holding and carrying the dumbbell while heeling and carrying while jumping the three hurdles.
>
> Awards to be made for Performance and for Handling.
>
> No diplomas to be issued unless the dog receives a qualifying score in the novice work.

Open-Utility:

> Dogs without their C.D.X. title to work as in the open class at Obedience Trials.
>
> Dogs with their C.D.X. to do both the open and utility exercises as required at dog shows.
>
> Awards to be made for Performance only (these may be broken down to comply with whatever titles the dog may have and may include a club trophy).
>
> Diplomas to be issued to all dogs who receive a qualifying score in either the open or utility exercises.

A club may prefer to offer ribbons and prizes to those dogs in the open-utility course that have not yet gained their C.D.X. or U.D. titles. Those with titles may compete for a club trophy, or give a demonstration of the utility exercises to encourage the beginner and intermediate trainees to continue with their advanced training. An interesting demonstration will renew enthusiasm and inspire activity among the club members.

11

Tracking

Tracking Course: For dogs with some training, preferably those with experience in utility work.

Length of Time: Four months and up.

Training Period: 1 to 2 hours (daily when possible).

Purpose: To make the dog eligible to compete in a tracking test.

Training consists of:

Teaching the dog to track the scent of a stranger on a trail not less than half an hour old.

Equipment:

A tracking harness.
A 20-40 foot line.
A training collar.
Six or more stakes.
An assortment of articles.

If it were possible to be transformed into a dog for even a short period of time, the instructor would be better equipped to teach others the art of tracking. Tracking is a subject on which the average person has had little or no experience and one about which few words have been written. Scent work involves a great deal of guesswork on the instructor's part, which frequently results in unjustified criticism of the dog's behavior.

It is true that inexperienced persons have been able to gain their dogs' tracking degrees. This is evident from the number of T.D. titles awarded by the American Kennel Club. With little or no assistance, owners have ventured forth by themselves to train their dogs sufficiently well to pass an official tracking test. Whether these dogs can be considered expert trailers and capable of finding escaped criminals and lost persons is another story.

In the opinion of the author (experience plus theory), teaching a dog to track or trail a scent is encouraging the dog to use his natural abilities with limitations (as restricted by the tracking line). One must be able to distinguish between a dog that is working and one that is not, and possess sufficient knowledge of weather conditions to determine how much it influences the dog's work.

There are certain facts on which experienced handlers all agree. The amateur would do well to remember them. Scent is more penetrating after sundown when atmospheric conditions cause odors to cling more closely to the ground. A cloudy day with heavy weather is preferable to one that is hot, dry, and windy. Although wind may enhance the dog's scenting ability, it changes the tracking act to one of trailing because the air-borne scents overpower those given off by the ground.

Moving objects, such as running water or shifting leaves, break the line of scent which must be recovered on stationary objects. There is a difference of opinion as to whether or not a dog can follow the track of a person wearing rubber footwear with its own overpowering scent and non-porous qualities. The author feels that some dogs can and do under favorable conditions, but strong odors such as tar or gasoline will interfere with the dog's ability to do his best scent work.

It is agreed that dogs vary in their innate ability to use their nose. Some breeds seem to be made for work of this kind, being endowed with the type of nostril that retains scent for a long period of time and possessing ears of a shape that helps to concentrate the odor into a given area.

We sympathize with the sporting breeds when they are asked to track mere man. Birds and fur-bearing game are more to their liking. We respect the fact that physical characteristics will aid or handicap the working dog (whichever is the case), and most of all we feel frustrated when attempting to teach a subject about which we know so little. In reality, it is man who should be the pupil!

The tracking test as we know it in relation to obedience training has advantages as well as some disadvantages. We are not required to follow our dogs through heavily wooded areas, swamps, and patches of brambles, such as with Bloodhounds in police work; but, on the other hand, neither are we given the privilege of using a scented article to assure the dog of the correct scent at the start. Picking up an elusive odor from a scuffed-up section of ground (rather than from a scented article) is a more demanding test for which our dogs, just out of the obedience ring, are hardly prepared. To climax the situation, the dog must find, not a human being, but a tiny object dropped enroute, which may be easily overlooked as the tracklayer continues on his way, leaving a trail of scent that goes on indefinitely.

Whether one is training his own dog in tracking or whether he is instructing someone else, he must start with the proper equipment. A tracking harness similar to the one shown in the illustration is practical and will give good results (Figure 34). It may be made of either leather or sturdy webbing. Bloodhounds frequently work on this type of harness where the tracking line fastens into a ring under the tail. The harness acts like a set of traces used to pull a wagon and the dog is free to pivot either to the right or to the left as he tacks back and forth to cover the scented area. The dog is thus permitted almost unlimited freedom of movement and the tracking line will not become tangled around the body when the dog circles.

The tracking line may be made of webbing or clothesline

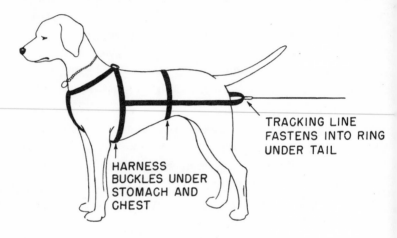

Fig. 34. A tracking harness.

material. One 20 to 40 feet long is specified by the American Kennel Club, but when a dog is learning to track, a longer line has its advantages. It gives the dog greater opportunity to work without interference from the handler. A clothesline, particularly one made of plastic, appears to tangle less frequently and is not so heavy when wet. There should be a snap on one end to fasten to the harness ring and a loop on the opposite end which is held in the hand.

A training collar should be kept on the dog until he learns that the harness is there for a purpose and that while wearing it, he must not be distracted from the task at hand. From the start, the dog is not permitted to stop enroute to lift his leg, to puddle, to sniff interesting smells, or to become curious about surrounding objects. The tracking line is kept fastened to the collar until just before the dog begins to work and it is returned to the collar when the job is completed. Care should be taken to exercise and water the dog prior to training so he will be comfortable and there will be no excuse for misbehavior while he is working. The dog will be quick to distinguish those times when he is at liberty to do what he pleases, and he will soon learn that when he is wearing his harness he must keep his mind on his work.

The next important items are the stakes that will be used to mark the course. These may be made of wood and tied with a piece of colored material, or they can be metal markers painted green to blend into the landscape. The metal is easier to push into the ground and the dark color will discourage the dog from becoming "track-wise," where he will follow the line of stakes with his eyes rather than using his nose. Dogs are quick to spot an obviously marked track and will take advantage.

Training prior to tracking should include teaching the dog to lie down on command, and picking up an article when told, returning with it to the handler. The dog that has had only novice work will be more easily distracted than the utility dog because he lacks experience and the power of concentration acquired over a longer period of training. On the other hand, our U.D. dogs must frequently overcome the problems that arise from their intense training. Tracking will be a new experience and for the first time the dog is encouraged to pull ahead of his handler. Many breeds are by nature reluctant to take the initiative, and obedience training intensifies their attitude. The tightening of the line may cause concern. It will take patience and encouragement to overcome this handicap, but even the highly-trained dog, or the dog that lacks initiative, will eventually learn that he is doing the right thing when, on line, he leads the way instead of staying close at heel.

In the beginning, tracking may be looked upon as an extended seek back. A trainer of Bloodhounds claims the seek back should never be included in a dog's training for police work because the dog must learn not to retrace the person's steps; but there are instances on record where a dog has been known to follow along a road to recover a bundle of clothing and then to return over the same road to locate the criminal. The explanation for the dog's action is that the weight of the body is placed on the heel of the foot when the person steps forward and the dog soon learns that the lighter scent produced from the ball of the foot indicates the direction of travel. This may also explain why the dog does not backtrack, but continues to move forward at all times toward the object he is seeking.

The amateur trainer can start by having his dog do a series of seek backs in long grass or open fields, with the line attached to the harness and dragging on the ground. Since the dog cannot see the article immediately, he will use his nose to find it and, at the same time, will become accustomed to the pull on his harness. Encouraging the dog to use his nose for a specific purpose is the principal factor involved in tracking. Games played around the house where the dog must find a favorite hidden object are also good preliminary training.

Another method that is successful in encouraging the dog to sniff the ground or scent the air is for someone to hold the tracking line while the person the dog is most fond of walks out of sight and hides. The dog is permitted to see the person

leave and when told to "Find!" he should take off immediately, working at the full length of the line. The dog may run
to the spot where the person was last seen and look in all
directions. Small dogs will even stand up on their hind legs to
get a better look. If the person is well hidden and the dog is
unable to find him by sight, he will soon use his nose to gain
his objective—in this case, his favorite person. This type of
game will increase the dog's scenting power and will also
teach him to pull out to the full length of the tracking line.
Praise should be the immediate reward.

The handler should never underestimate the value of praise
or some other compensation as the result of success. Some
recent laboratory research into the learning capacities of dogs
has indicated that they cease to learn under two conditions:
(1) Lack of success, and (2) fear of a new situation (when
timidity is a dominant personality characteristic of the dog).
To this we might add that a dog does not learn when he is in
physical discomfort. Trainers can profit from these accepted
theories and apply them throughout the dog's entire obedience
experience. Where some dogs will work when the owner
shows his approval by giving praise and a loving pat, others
react to the sensation of taste and a titbit is more gratifying.
The dog may be only partially successful in the eyes of the
handler, but the dog must feel that his work was outstanding
and his efforts worth while.

Assuming the dog will seek a lost article in long grass and
return with it to his owner, and providing he has overcome
all fear of the tracking line and of advancing to its full
length, the next step is to lay a single track in a straight line.
The dog, having been given a rest prior to training, is tied
off somewhere by himself. The handler (or a second person)
inserts a stake on ground over which he has not recently
walked and scuffs up the earth close to the stake to leave a

definite mark. (Some trainers prefer to start the dog immediately on the scent of a stranger; others like to work by themselves at first, switching to a stranger's scent later on. Either method will get results.) It is recommended that two people interested in gaining tracking experience work together. They can lay tracks for each other, while the instructor follows the handler to make suggestions or give constructive criticisms.

Taking 4 or 5 stakes and an equal number of articles, the tracklayer proceeds *into* the wind (if there is a wind) for about 20 to 30 feet. He places one of the stakes and drops an article close by. He continues in the same direction for about the same distance, places another stake and drops a second article. This is repeated until all the articles have been dropped. The tracklayer then circles back to the place where the dog was left. The stakes are used to show the exact location of the dropped articles so the handler will not become confused and consequently mislead the dog.

Dogs have been successfully trained by the method where the tracklayer returns to the starting stake by retracing his steps along the same track. There is a possibility that this will cause a conflict in the dog's mind since the tracks lead in *both* directions. If there is plenty of ground, it may prove easier for the beginner dog to have the tracklayer circle back to the original spot, thus leaving a single track line. One or two tests should soon determine how the dog will react to either situation.

The dog, having been kept on his collar during this time, is given the opportunity to relieve himself and take a drink of water. He is taken slowly to the starting mark, made to lie down and the long line is snapped into the ring on the harness. The dog is kept in the down position, close to the scuffed-up area, for 30 to 60 seconds. During this time the handler should see that the line is not tangled or full of knots. The best assurance is to spread it out over the ground. Meanwhile the dog, undisturbed, will be filling his nostrils with scent, which he will retain longer than when he is forced to hold his head down (some dogs resent this), allowed a quick sniff, and sent off in a hurry.

During the first part of the training, the dog works at only a short distance from the handler, who walks along with him toward the second stake (at times, the dog may even have to be led). The handler encourages the dog when he pulls forward and stays close on the line of the track. He makes cautious corrections when the dog strays too far off-course. If the dog is distracted by tempting but obviously irrelevant smells, or if he stops enroute to lift his leg or squat, the line is jerked sharply and the dog is reprimanded. When praise follows immediately, the dog will not be too upset as he will realize he did something wrong and will think twice before repeating his act.

The handler must, at all times, be conscious of wind direction. Even if the track was laid into the wind at the start, he may find it has now shifted and is blowing over his left shoulder. Open fields will frequently have elusive gusts of air that will change direction on a moment's notice. When the wind blows directly into the handler's face or from behind, the dog will weave back and forth across the track; when there is a cross wind from the left, the dog will work to the right of the track; and when the wind comes from the right, he will do the opposite. Handlers frequently make the mistake of insisting that the dog follow the direct line between the two stakes; actually the scent may have been blown either to one side or the other. By checking the wind direction at frequent intervals and using the stakes as a guide, the handler can aid rather than hinder the dog while he is learning.

At first, the dog may pull ahead for some distance, then stop to look back as though to say "Am I doing the right thing?" A word of approval will encourage him to keep on, and when he reaches the first article it should be a momentous occasion in his life. The dog is then sent on to find the second article and the procedure continues. Praise when the dog is on the track, gentle guidance if he strays too far, checking and rechecking the wind directions, and a glorious reward when the dog reaches his goal, are the basic rules of training. When the last article has been retrieved, all stakes are taken up and a new track is laid on fresh ground some distance from the first practice area. If the tracks are short in the beginning, so the dog will immediately be successful, he will gain confidence and thoroughly enjoy the sport of tracking. The dog must never be allowed to give up without finding the article, even if he must be guided to it.

The tone of voice throughout the training should be gentle and reassuring. The demanding tone is used only if the dog becomes interested in other things (cows and woodchucks, for instance) or if he refuses to pick up the article at the end of the track.

The owner who has set out to gain his dog's tracking title might just as well learn to be patient. The process will take a long time and cannot be hurried. The dog may give a good performance one day and the handler will feel that he knows his job well. But the next day the dog may act as if he had never had a tracking lesson in his life! (This may sometimes be due to temporary conditions, health or otherwise, over which the handler has no control.) The owner's reaction will be one of discouragement and frustration. He will become exasperated, lose patience, and even vent his anger on the dog. He must, however, never show his feelings or it will take longer than ever to attain success. A dog can be made to perform some obedience exercises, but he *cannot be forced to track!* Under these circumstances, the handler would do well to start from the beginning and build up the dog's confidence again. Suddenly, for no apparent reason, the time will come when the dog takes a turn for the better. From this point on, his progress will be steady. Owners who are in a hurry for success should remember that trainers of Bloodhounds claim it often takes a year to get satisfactory results. The task of our tracking dogs is not as demanding as that of dogs used for police work; but even so, the owner would do well to figure in terms of months, depending on the amount of time he can give to the training and on the climatic and weather conditions which play such an important role.

As the weeks go by and the dog becomes reliable on a straight track, the turns may be introduced. The stakes are used in the same way as before and either a right-angle or a left-angle turn is made at the spot marked by one of the stakes. The articles are not dropped at the turns, but half way between the two stakes so the dog can concentrate on making the turn and the handler can watch his actions more closely.

This is where observation of the wind direction is of great importance. The track may be laid *with* or *into* the wind during one leg of the course, but have a strong cross wind blowing on another leg. In a stiff breeze, the dog will not follow the direct line walked by the tracklayer. He will be off to one side or the other, will cut corners or perhaps by-pass one entire leg of the trail if another leg runs parallel. As one watches a dog in the act of tracking, it becomes obvious that when the track turns to the right, the dog will often swing to the left, circle back, and then head in the correct direction. When the turn is to the left, the dog will swing to the right, again circling back before he turns left to pick up the trail. This is why it is a good policy for the handler to cast the dog in a circle whenever he feels that the dog has overshot his turn or when the dog indicates by his actions that he is unable to locate the scent. A common failing of the handler is to urge the dog to continue forward (the dog will obey because he is anxious to please his handler). He will overshoot his mark and the tracking line will not be long enough to permit him, even when he circles, to get close enough to the track to pick up the scent again. When in doubt, *stand still!* This is one rule that the handler should learn at the very beginning: When the dog moves along in the right direction, walk cautiously in back of him so he will not be distracted, and when he stops, stop with him. Retrace your steps if necessary to give the dog another chance. Wait and see if he will move on by himself, then give him voice encouragement.

Still another lesson to learn early in tracking is to create as little motion as possible near the dog. Swinging the arms, gathering up the tracking line, or moving around unnecessarily will take the dog's mind off his task. When he is circling around trying to pick up the scent, stand quietly until he starts forward in the right direction. When he is hot on the trail again, noises caused by stepping on sticks or stones will be less disturbing. The line can gradually be fed out so that the dog can travel at some distance from the handler, and in time he will learn to accept distractions and take them in his stride.

The tracklayer plays an important role in the dog's tracking education. Failure may be the result of poor judgment (caused by lack of experience and sufficient knowledge of climatic conditions) when plotting the course. We all suffer in this respect. With practice, one will learn to judge the situation—not through the *eyes* of the human being, but through the *nose* of the dog. If the track is laid close to the boundary of two fields, for instance, the scent may be blown 75 to 150 feet from the original track. The dog may hover close to the fence line or try to cross over into the next field in his attempt to follow the track to the best of his ability. Under these conditions, he is working under a handicap.

One has only to observe how smoke from a cigarette or dust from a passing car will drift great distances to realize that body-scent must do the same thing. When two legs of a track are laid close together and the scent from one conflicts with that from the other, it is little wonder the dog will sometimes fail to make the required turn to the right or left, whatever the case may be.

The various illustrations show how even the inexperienced person can use good judgment when plotting the course so the dog will get off to a good start and not become confused. Needless to say, the tracklayer *should not be within scenting distance of the dog at the start,* and he should be careful to *remain down-wind at all times.*

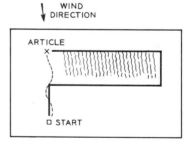

Fig. 35a-1. This track has overlapping scent. The dotted line indicates the course the dog would probably take.

Fig. 35a-2. This is the same field where no two legs of the track interfere.

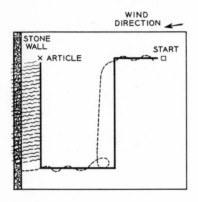

Fig. 35b-1. On this track, the scent has blown into the adjoining field. The stone wall becomes a natural barrier.

Fig. 35b-2. The same field now plotted more carefully. There is still the same number of turns.

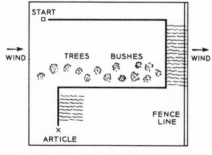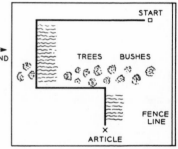

Fig. 35c-1. This track utilizes two adjoining fields, but is badly plotted.

Fig. 35c-2. The same field where the dog is given a reasonable chance to overcome obstacles.

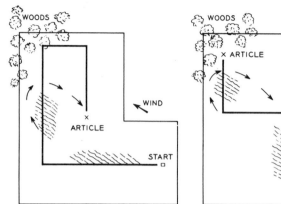

Fig. 35d-1. This track may confuse the dog when a change in wind direction is caused by surrounding topography.

Fig. 35d-2. The same track has now been plotted to allow for tricky wind conditions.

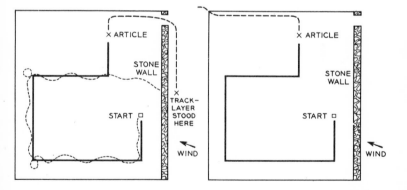

Fig. 35e-1. This tracklayer did not consider the wind direction before leaving the field. Dotted line shows the course taken by the dog.

Fig. 35e-2. This is the same track where the tracklayer should have remained down wind.

The tracks can now be laid by a number of different people. Trainers of Bloodhounds begin by showing the dog an article that has been dropped at the starting stake by the tracklayer. The article is then placed in a bag and carried by the handler so that the dog may be given a sniff at frequent intervals to refresh his memory. This might seem a good way to start our obedience dogs on a stranger's scent. In any case, it is advisable to go back to the beginning and have the strange tracklayer walk a straight course into the wind, dropping several articles at intervals marked by stakes. The handler will know exactly where the trail lies and can encourage the dog at the right moment, check his movements when necessary, and see that the dog doesn't overlook the scented article. Instead of circling back to the starting point, the tracklayer can remain hidden *down-wind* and at some distance from the track. If he is too close, his body scent will overpower that of the dropped article and the dog may try to find the tracklayer.

One will find that during the evening a dog will track with his head low. The air is heavy and the scent lies close to the ground. During the morning the head is carried high because the air is rising, and the strongest scent lies above the ground. This is also true when there is a stiff breeze, for the dog depends upon the air-borne scent rather than on the ground scent. Notice how the dog, when he is working in a strong wind, will lift his head, give a sniff, then immediately start toward the object he is seeking.

During the first few attempts at tracking, the dog may recover the dropped articles simply because he happened to spot them with his eyes, or because he fell over them by accident. When the dog begins to get the idea of using his nose, it is interesting to watch the way in which he approaches the article. The dog's body movements will give every indication that it is near. He will slow down from a fast trot (or almost a run at this point) and assume a stalking attitude as he turns in small circles to get down-wind so it will lead him directly to the article. If the dog failed to pick up the scent where the track began, *the article will have no more meaning for him than a piece of paper lying in the field.* The handler should therefore be careful to give the dog plenty of time at the start so that he will move off slowly and take the scent by himself. The voice should not be too severe when the handler tells the dog to "Find!" In his effort to obey the command, he may dash off without waiting or knowing what he is supposed to look for.

Although the voice must be used in the beginning to correct the dog and to encourage him when he does the right thing, the handler should refrain from doing too much talking as the dog progresses. The command is given at the start, with generous praise when the job is well done, but unless the handler knows exactly where the track is, he may encourage the dog at the wrong time or discourage him by warning him to be careful when actually the dog knows exactly what he is doing. If the dog stops working or becomes interested in other things, he should be given a more definite command. If the line becomes entangled and the dog is jerked accidentally, he will need encouragement; but constant talking or calling the dog by name will only serve to distract him. During the teaching period it is all right to slow the dog down as he approaches a turn and to warn him to be careful, but the track must be well marked. With no stakes to guide him, the handler would do better to say nothing rather than to mislead the dog by saying the wrong thing at the wrong time.

If the handler observes his dog closely, he will gradually learn to recognize when he is working, when he is confused or uncertain, and when he is merely taking his handler for a walk. The dog will usually start off on a businesslike trot and, if working into the wind, will tack back and forth in a rhythmic manner, crossing and re-crossing the trail. Circling to any great extent indicates uncertainty and is often a sign that the track has turned in another direction. An increase of speed shows that the dog is hot on the trail and getting closer to his objective. A stalking motion means he has reached the end of the trail and that somewhere close he will find the article he is seeking. The dog that wanders off in a disinterested sort of way, glancing from side to side with an occasional look over his shoulder to see what his handler is doing, is out for a good time and has nothing more on his mind than to enjoy himself and perhaps spot a chipmunk or two.

There is something about the way a dog holds his body when he is doing a good job of tracking that gives his handler confidence. He will *know*, simply by watching, that the dog is doing the right thing and that, if left alone, he should be successful.

As the dog continues to do good work and the handler learns to read the signs so he will know from the dog's behavior what to expect, the stakes should gradually be eliminated and only one article used. A stake should be left at the starting point and a second one thirty feet further on. It may, even at this point, be advisable to leave a stake close to where the article is dropped to aid the dog in a glorious finish.

The instructor (who is familiar with the course) follows at a distance (or watches through a pair of binoculars) to observe the handler and the way he controls the line. The first two stakes indicate the direction of the track, but from then on the handler must take his clues from the dog. At times the handler will feel certain that the track goes in a different direction from where it actually lies, or he will think he recognizes the track because of crushed grasses, etc. It is probably an old track left by some animal, but the handler feels he knows more than the dog and he may attempt to guide him. The instructor, by using prearranged signals given with a whistle, can prevent the handler from interfering while the dog is working and help him to observe the dog's actions more carefully. For instance, if the dog makes several attempts to go in the right direction and the handler (thinking the dog is wrong) checks him, three blasts on the whistle may mean "Go ahead, what are you waiting for?" If the dog overshoots his mark and the instructor can see from the length of the tracking line that the dog will not be able to retrace his steps sufficiently far enough to pick up the scent again, two blasts may mean "Back up, cast the dog in a circle, and give him another chance!" If the dog circles continuously close to the article (there being no stake to mark the exact spot), one blast may mean "Stand still!—the dog is doing all right and should find the article shortly." This will teach the handler to take his clues from the dog and not to try to do the thinking for both.

The owner who intends to enter his dog in a tracking test would do well to first attend at least one trial as a spectator. From observing the dogs' work and the methods of handling, and listening to the conversation, he will gain insights which will be of value as he continues with his dog's training. It will prepare him for what to expect when his own dog is required to take the test. At that time he can only hope for the breaks, and he should not be disappointed if he fails to make the grade. A few dogs pass their first tracking test, but the majority fail. It takes practice—and then more practice—in all kinds of weather, on all types of terrain, and under all conditions, to be ready for the unexpected. When the day finally arrives and the owner is able to sit down and sigh "Well, we made it!" there will be a glow of satisfaction. Both the owner and the instructor will feel well repaid for the months of hard work and the moments of discouragement they experienced during the training.

THINGS THE INSTRUCTOR SHOULD WATCH FOR WHEN TEACHING A PERSON TO TRAIN HIS DOG IN TRACKING

See that the field is plotted to the best advantage and that the tracks are short and not complicated.

See that the tracklayer is wearing leather-soled shoes.

See that the ground is well scuffed up at the start and request the "tracklayer's shuffle" (dragging the feet) until the dog gains experience.

Ask that all turns be made well in the open and that the track not be laid close to any natural boundary-line.

Observe the tracklayer when he drops the article to see that he continues in a straight line sufficiently far and that he remains down-wind while the dog is in the learning phase.

Be sure that the dog is rested, has had water, and is properly exercised.

Insist that the handler stretch the line to its full length before the dog is permitted to start (nervousness will make the owner keep rolling it up into a ball and it will become tangled and full of knots).

See that the dog is left by himself in the down position, close to the scuffed-up area, for at least 30 seconds.

Listen to the handler's command for the dog to start. It should not be too demanding.

Watch the handler and notice if he is observing the direction of the wind. The dog should be on the down-wind side of the track.

If the dog appears to be scenting, a quiet "Good fellow, that's it" will give the necessary encouragement.

If the dog stops enroute to puddle or lift a leg, or if he sniffs a certain spot indefinitely, advise that the line be snapped sharply and the command "Go find!" be given with more authority.

See that the handler governs the line sufficiently to keep the dog under control and to prevent mistakes. The dog is not given full freedom at first.

Criticize the handler who keeps rolling the line up into a ball. The line is kept taut by sliding it through the hands and playing it out behind.

Suggest that the line be extended smoothly without jerking the dog unnecessarily as he advances.

Request that the handler make as few body motions as possible while the dog is working so that he will not be distracted.

Caution the handler about constant talking to his dog or calling him by name.

If the dog is scenting and begins to circle, see that the handler comes to a halt. Advise him to stand still and wait for the dog's next move before he starts forward.

Insist upon generous praise when the dog finds the article.

As the dog progresses, see that he works at the full length of the line without aid or interference.

The Show Ring

THE REGULATIONS AND STANDARDS for Obedience Trials, published by the American Kennel Club, are final when it comes to the dog competing in Obedience Trials at dog shows. A copy of the rules may be obtained by writing to the American Kennel Club, 51 Madison Avenue, New York, N.Y. Regulations and Standards are occasionally revised and the rules changed to keep abreast of the times. The exhibitor, and of course the judge, should make it his business to familiarize himself with the rules and to know that he has the most recently revised set. In one instance, a judge scored an entire class on the basis of methods that had been outdated the previous year.

The American Kennel Club booklet gives a complete description of each exercise and outlines the show-ring procedure. It explains in detail what can and what cannot be done. By studying the booklet the novice will learn what to expect when he enters an Obedience Trial for the first time and he will not be discouraged with the results. When the home or classroom training has been similar to show conditions and the training area set up to resemble the regulation obedience

READ ALL ABOUT IT
Just What You've Been
Waiting For !
S. O. T. C.'S

SANCTIONED OBEDIENCE TRIAL !

Come and bring your masters ! They need

the practice !!

You might even win one of the swell prizes !!
It's amazing what a lift that would give the boss.

JUDGES

Mrs. Laura A. Dale ——Beginners & Novice A

Mr. Fred Allmann ——Novice B & Grad. Novice

Mr. John Ringwald—— Open A&B, Utility 1&2
(Utility 2 - Exhibition only)

Place - WHITMAN LANES
        Route 110
Just South of Jericho T'pke

Time - 1:00 P.M.

ADMISSION
S.O.T.C. Members--free & $1 per dog.
Non-members-- Adults 50¢, children 25¢
             and $1.50 per dog.

SUNDAY——— MARCH 1ST

Fig. 36. To gain ring experience, the exhibitor should take advantage of
local Sanctioned Obedience Matches.

ring at dog shows, the owner will feel secure in competition. Corrections not permitted at shows may be given in practice and may prevent a dog from becoming ringwise.

If the owner is new in the dog game, there will be a number of things he will have to have explained that the veteran exhibitor takes for granted. For instance, how to get information about the different trials and how to make entries for the show. There are Superintendents who run dog shows to comply with the rules of the American Kennel Club. By writing to the Superintendent that manages the shows in his section of the country, an owner's name may be placed on the list to receive the premium folders that are mailed out in advance. The owner will be aware of the forthcoming trials and he will have ample time to enter his dog. All entries must be in the Superintendent's office almost two weeks before the day of the show. The American Kennel Club, dog publications, kennel owners and professional handlers will furnish the names of the Superintendents. The premium folder will give instructions on how to fill out the entry forms. If the show is what is called a "benched show," it means that the exhibitor must have his dog in the stall that will be assigned to him by a specified time in the morning and that he must leave the dog there until the closing hour of the show. If the show is "unbenched" the dog may be kept in the car, in a crate, tied under a tree, or wherever the owner wishes to keep him. In either case the dog is assigned a number which, together with the dog's name and other data, along with the name of the owner, is published in the show catalogue. The obedience entries will appear at the back of the catalogue unless it is a specialty show and the show-giving club has a catalogue all its own. Castrated dogs and spayed bitches are eligible to compete in Obedience Trials. Every dog must be pure-bred, and over six months of age.

The ruling is not compulsory, but exhibitors are expected to come into the ring in the order in which the names are listed in the catalogue. Frequently the dogs will not have arrived or the owner is showing in the breed ring, in which case the next dog in turn will be called. Upon arrival at the show the exhibitor should immediately look to see how many entries there are in his class and where his name appears. If it is among the first the owner should get ready to be called at the scheduled time. If there are a number of names listed before his, the chances are there will be no immediate rush.

A courtesy due every judge is for the exhibitor whose name is listed first to be ready and willing to enter the ring on time. All too often, the owner of the first dog is not to be found until a number of dogs have been in the ring.

The exhibitor should take care to exercise and water his dog prior to competition. This is especially true of dogs that have been left on the bench for a long period of time or who have traveled great distances to attend the show. If the dog has had no chance to relieve himself it is only natural for him to think the obedience ring is an exercise yard. A mishap even though unavoidable may bring a penalty for misbehavior.

A dog wouldn't be a dog if he were not interested in sniffing places where other dogs have been. The tempting smells that prevail at a show must make our dogs feel they have arrived in doggie heaven. One way to avoid these outside distractions is to let the obedience-trained dog know from the moment he enters the show ground he will not be permitted to sniff or perform an act of tracking. The owner should carry the leash short in the left hand and every time the dog lowers his head, he should be snapped up sharply. The point to keep in mind is that when entering or leaving the show grounds, while traveling to and from the bench or the obedience ring, or while standing or sitting at the ringside, the dog must never be permitted to lower his head out of curiosity. This extra precaution will help to overcome one of the greatest problems that faces the obedience exhibitor—the dog that sniffs the ground while working.

The owner will learn by experience to what extent his dog must be left alone before he competes. A dog may do his best work when he hasn't seen his owner for a long time. The dog will be excited when he is taken off the bench and he will show his willingness to please in the way he performs. Another dog will work himself into a frenzy when he is left by himself for even a few moments. Such a dog will be on the verge of a nervous collapse and when required to do the obedience routine will be completely out of control. By watching how the dog behaves at one or two shows the owner can judge what precautions to take.

The exhibitor (providing, of course, he is not the first) should stand at the ringside and observe the other exhibitors as they work. A lot can be learned from watching. There is a certain etiquette maintained in every obedience ring, and the exhibitor should be aware of it and follow it to the best of his ability. Each judge has his own judging procedure, and it will be to the exhibitor's advantage to know what the requirements will be that day.

The moment the exhibitor and his dog enter the obedience ring they become the center of attention and the subject of conversation. There are eccentrics who wait for opportunities to display themselves, but the obedience ring is not the place for exhibitionists. Unwarranted actions should be avoided. Manners and personal appearance should bring only admiration.

It is normal to feel nervous and keyed up but one should act as natural as possible under the circumstances. The owner's attitude will reflect on the dog and influence his work. Almost every judge remembers the first time he walked into the obedience ring as an exhibitor and he will be sympathetic in spite of the scowl he is wearing. It is not advisable to have long discussions with a judge prior to working in the ring, but the owner should not hesitate to ask a question if something is not clear and if it has a bearing on the trial that day. Usually the judge will give the exhibitor all special instructions so a great deal of talking will not be necessary. A pleasant "Good morning" or "How do you do" is always welcome and will give no cause for complaint.

The numbered arm band the exhibitor must wear is obtained from the ring steward prior to the judging. When fastened securely with a safety pin (be sure to take one with you to the show), the dog will not be distracted by the arm band falling off. In the novice and open classes the exhibitor should enter the ring with his dog on leash. He should assume the position where the preceding dogs began their heeling exercises. This is usually off center and close to one side and facing the length of the ring. This position will permit the judge to call the right and left turns with a minimum of confusion. The dog should be made to sit immediately at heel and, if entered in the open class, the leash should be removed and placed on the judge's table or given to the ring steward. In the utility class the dog enters the ring off lead. It is not necessary to watch the dog constantly, but the owner should *know where the dog is and what he is doing* every minute of the time.

Each exercise will come naturally if the owner has trained his dog correctly from the beginning. The heeling calls for walking in a brisk manner. The turns should be sharp and done with the correct footwork. The judge is not an army drill master, so he will not always call for the turns on the proper foot. The exhibitor must use his own judgment and make the turns so it will be to the dog's advantage. When the judge calls for a right turn, the weight of the body is placed on the left foot and right foot swings to the right. When the judge calls for a left turn, the weight is put on the right foot and the left foot swings to the left. This will avoid hesitation on the dog's part because the action will be continuous. When the feet are brought together before making the turn, the dog may try to sit because he will think the owner is going to halt. When the judge asks for a Fast, the owner should glide into a fast forward run, so the dog must change pace. A Slow means a slow walk that will not immobilize the dog to the extent that he will start to sit down at every step because he thinks the trainer is going to halt. When doing an about-turn, although the handler was told to step backward with one foot while training to give the leash a better snap, this extra motion should now be eliminated. The about-turn should be done smoothly by pivoting quickly and in such a manner the owner will not walk away from his dog.

At all times the owner should walk in a straight line parallel to the sides of the ring, avoid diagonal wandering and wait for the judge to call the turns. If the owner is nervous and unconsciously moves his left hand, he should clinch his fingers tight or hold his hand in back of his body so the dog is not penalized for the handler's body motions. When the time comes for the Figure-8, the owner should walk to where the two ring stewards are standing and halt with his dog sitting at heel position. When possible, he should face the judge. The Figure-8 will be done in both directions. It is not necessary to ask which direction to take first. If the judge has a preference he will inform the exhibitor at the time. The owner should remember to lengthen his steps when the dog is on the outside of the circle and to shorten his steps when the dog is on the inside. The Figure-8 will in this way be done smoothly and the exhibitor and dog will work as one.

All commands should be spoken clearly and distinctly and all signals made definite. The manner in which the commands and signals are used will be determined by the dog's attitude. When exhibiting a Novice dog, the owner should take advantage of using his name along with the command. A dog distracted by unusual surroundings of a show will be kept under control and more obedient when the commands are given in a demanding tone, with authority, and when the signals are made with a forceful gesture. It is not necessary to yell at the dog. Handle him in such a way that there will be no doubt in his mind but that he is expected to do his best work. A display of affection by giving the dog a pat and a kind word between exercises is a natural reaction and should be evident even in the obedience ring. The owner should not be ashamed to let the spectators know he approves of the way his dog has behaved. The offering of food in the ring is prohibited. Another thing that is on the black list is correcting the dog severely or exhibiting uncontrolled temper. It is agreed that when a dog gets away with making a mistake it is a disadvantage. The same mistake will be repeated at some future show. But most persons are not careful when they correct their dog and moreover, the spectators do not understand the corrections. If the obedience ring were permitted to be used as a training yard, obedience on the whole would suffer.

The owner should guard against talking unnecessarily about the dog while he is in the ring. He should not attempt to inform the judge of what dog he has in the ring that day nor of the dog's previous high scores—if any. Calling the dog by name is allowed but it shouldn't be overdone.

Before he is entered in an Obedience Trial, the dog should

be trained to the point where the owner will have confidence in the way he works. A tendency among amateurs is to work in close to their dogs and to cover a limited area of ground, because they are not sure of their dog. The result is they make a poor showing among some of the other more experienced dogs and handlers. When the judge asks to have the dumbbell thrown, the exhibitor should toss it out a reasonable distance—not just a few feet. When required to do the recall or the drop on recall, the dog should be left sitting at one end of the ring while the exhibitor goes to the opposite end. On the other hand, there is the exhibitor who just doesn't use his head. In the retrieve on the flat he will throw the dumbbell so far it goes out of the ring completely or he will throw it in the most difficult of places. We have all watched while an exhibitor carelessly tossed the dumbbell so it landed underneath the four hurdles that make up the broad jump. Such action is not good handling.

There are exhibitors who like to impress the judge with their knowledge and those who are sticklers when it comes to rules. If the hurdle deviates half an inch, one hears, "I shall report it." A scrap of paper, until removed by the steward, looms up as a mountainous object. An exhibitor is entitled to fair play but he shouldn't be overly demanding. A trained dog must be obedient even though ring conditions are not always perfect.

In the novice class, the stand for examination follows heeling on leash. The owner, with his dog sitting at heel position, removes the leash and hands it to the ring steward. He waits for the judge to say "Pose or stand your dog for examination." Instead of lifting a heavy dog to the standing position, why not take one step forward to bring the dog to all four feet? The dog is not judged until he is in the standing position and has been told to stay! When the dog is standing, the owner gives the command and signal to stay, and faces him approximately six feet away. Care must be taken, without consuming a great deal of time, to see that the dog is standing in a comfortable position with all feet securely planted. Prolonged posing of every part of the dog's anatomy is not necessary. The stand for examination is a test for temperament, not conformation. When the examination is completed and the judge says "Return to your dog," the handler returns to heel position by going to the right and in back of the dog. At this point many dogs receive a penalty because they sit before the judge says "Exercise finished."

Heeling off leash is performed in the same way as heeling on leash. The handler again assumes the starting position without waiting to be told. A dog will invariably make the same mistakes off leash he made when the leash was on. The owner should make every attempt to have his dog work accurately in training with the leash in hand and to give sufficient training so frequent corrections will not be necessary. The voice command is important in the off-leash exercise and should be authoritative. Using the dog's name will make him more attentive. A brisk pace will encourage close heeling and give a better impression.

The final exercise performed individually in the novice class is the recall. The judge may have a preference as to which end of the ring he wants the dog left and will tell the exhibitor at the time. If not, the exhibitor should walk immediately to one end of the ring and make his dog sit at heel position. When the judge gives the command "Leave your dog," the command and signal to stay are given together and the owner walks to the opposite end of the ring and turns to face his dog. When the judge tells him "Call your dog," he gives the signal or the command to come and the dog must sit in front of his handler. Here again, the owner would do well to use the dog's name and to exaggerate his command. There is a great deal of noise at dog shows and many sounds are similar. Dogs are inattentive and easily distracted. If the dog's name and the command to come is given in a loud clear voice there will be less chance of the dog not hearing and failing the exercise.

Fig. 37. The next step (dog show) where the dog gains his obedience titles.
Courtesy: Louise Branch.

The dogs in the novice and open classes perform the sit and down exercises as a group. The exhibitor who is considerate of the judge and of the other exhibitors will stay close to the ring, reporting in at intervals to find out how soon these exercises will take place. Nothing is more annoying to the judge and his ring stewards than having to hunt for a number of owners who have vanished into thin air.

In the sit and down exercises the dogs are lined up in catalogue order. The exhibitor should take his position with an equal distance between his dog and the dogs on either side. In the long sit, the dog should be left sitting squarely on both hips. In the long down, a crouched position will often tempt the dog to get up.

A demanding tone of voice should be used in both exercises to warn the dog that disobedience may bring drastic results. (As a matter of fact, every time the inexperienced dog is left by himself, as in the stand for examination, the recall, and the long sit and down, the owner should put real authority in the "Stay" command. The dog must feel that he has more to fear from disobeying his owner than from outside distractions that might tempt him to move from position.) In the novice classes, where the handler remains in sight, it is extremely important that he refrain from making idle gestures or body motions. The dog may misinterpret such motions and come in to the handler.

By the time the exhibitor enters the open class he will have had enough ring experience to feel more at ease. Nonetheless, the owner must be on the alert to take advantage of every opportunity to assist rather than hinder the dog. Before attending a trial, the dog should be posed with head erect and the distance measured from the high point of the dog's shoulder to the floor. A ruler laid flat across the shoulder blades and another used for measuring, will determine his height. Upon entering the ring, the exhibitor should glance at the hurdle and the broad jump to see if they are the correct height and width. If the measurements appear to be inaccurate, he can speak to the judge or ring steward so the jumps can be adjusted before the dog starts to work. The dog is now measured in the ring by the judge, but it still helps when the owner knows the dog's height.

After the heeling exercises and the Figure-8 have been performed off leash, the exhibitor should prepare for the drop on recall. The dog that is trained to drop on either signal or command has the advantage over the dog trained to obey in only one manner. At the time the dog is made to lie down he may be looking in the opposite direction. A loud "Down" given in a demanding tone should cause the dog to drop at once. The demanding voice will often prevent anticipating the second command to come after the dog has dropped. If the signal is used, the owner should be certain the dog is looking at him.

The next exercise is the retrieve on the flat. The exhibitor should get his dumbbell without waiting and take his position to be ready for the exercise. If the judge wants the dumbbell thrown in any special way, he will tell the exhibitor. Occasionally the dumbbell will roll off to the side or bounce after hitting a stone, but the owner should attempt to throw it so it does not stop under the feet of the spectators or against the wall; and, most important of all, he should make certain the dog sees the dumbbell when he throws it. The owner should get his dog's attention, then throw the dumbbell in an underhand motion so the dog will see the action of the hand when it moves forward. During the retrieve on the flat and over the hurdle, the exhibitor should encourage the dog to follow the path of the dumbbell with his eyes. When the retrieve is done on the flat, the dog can see where the dumbbell stopped moving and he will respond more quickly when given the command "Take it." Although he will not see the dumbbell land when it is thrown over the hurdle, he will know it is there. If the dumbbell is painted white, the dog will see it more easily. The command for both retrieves should be a cheerful one to keep the dog gay in spirit.

Immediately following the retrieve on the flat, the owner should take his position in front of the hurdle. A judge is not usually particular about the direction the dog must jump, so unless the exhibitor is told to do it in a special way, he should use his judgment and select the direction most suited to the occasion. When the hurdle is placed close to the side of the ring, if the dog starts the retrieve by sitting between the handler and the wall or group of spectators, he will be more inclined to take the hurdle than if he sits on the open side toward the center of the ring when he may be tempted to go around the jump. Another suggestion is for the owner to stand with his back to a setting sun so the dog will not have to jump toward the sun. If the dog is blinded by the glare he may go around the first time and be tempted to do the same on the return. The dumbbell should not be thrown such a distance the dog will not see it immediately when he jumps the hurdle. If the dog is not familiar with difficult retrieves, it may cause him to come back without it. Neither should the dumbbell be tossed so that it will fall so close to the hurdle that the dog will be limited in his natural take-off on the return. In practice, the dumbbell should be thrown off-center to prepare the dog for the unexpected at shows, but during competition, the exhibitor should try to keep the dumbbell as close to the center line as possible.

The owner with a fast-working dog would do well to stand back from the hurdle so the dog will have ample room to correct himself and sit straight on the return. The owner whose dog is tempted to run around the hurdle should do the opposite. By standing close, the dog is more likely to take the jump. To complete the exercise, the dumbbell, when taken from the dog, is held in the right hand close to the body and hidden behind the wrist. This will encourage the dog to do a more accurate finish. Some dogs like to play with their dumbbell and they think retrieving is a game. By removing the tempting object and using a demanding tone of voice, the dog will be more obedient in the less exciting part of the exercise.

When the retrieve over the hurdle has been completed, the exhibitor should go immediately to the broad jump and take his position within the ten feet stipulated by the rules. The broad jump requires a thrust forward rather than the upward thrust necessary in the high jump, and a greater distance is needed for the take-off. The exhibitor should select the position (within the designated ten feet) which is most suited to his own dog. A thought to keep in mind is to center the dog before leaving him so he will be less tempted to run around the jump. When taking his position at the side of the broad jump, the exhibitor should face it at a distance of about two feet. The owner whose dog is inclined to anticipate the command to jump, or to come without jumping, would do well to keep his head turned away from the dog instead of looking directly at him as he waits for the judge's order. The voice command, if used, should be given with authority. If the signal is preferred, it should be forceful and the gesture made with the left arm.

A dog that has become ringwise will very often refuse the broad jump (or the hurdle, for that matter) at a show, even though he performs perfectly at home or in class. To overcome this tendency, the owner should move the jumps to a different location in practice, and permit only one attempt at the exercise before moving the jumps again. It is the *first correction* in unfamiliar surroundings that makes the impression and convinces the dog that he cannot take advantage.

The utility class exercises require the exhibitor to use more common sense and forethought than ever. In scent discrimination the exhibitor who makes his dog sit at heel where he can watch the unscented articles being put down gives him an advantage. Many dogs, particularly at outdoor shows where the grass is long, fail in this exercise because they do not see the articles and run around the ring seeking for something that belongs to the owner.

The exhibitor should rub the scent article firmly in the palm of his hand. There is more moisture there than anywhere else, especially when one is nervous and excited. A well-scented article will make it easy for the dog, and when the owner is careful to give the proper scent by cupping his hand under the dog's nose, there should be little cause for error.

In the signal exercise, each signal must be clear and distinct. Dogs do not see well at a distance and signals are sometimes confusing. When the dog has been left in a standing position the owner should remain motionless so the dog will not misinterpret the slightest movement. When giving all signals, the hand should be held so the arm does not blend into the body when seen from far away. The signals should be similar to those used throughout the basic training. The signal to heel is a motion forward with the left hand. The signal to stand should be given while the dog is still moving. This is really the signal to stay and the dog must be on all four feet at the time he receives it. When the signal is repeated to make the dog remain where he is, the owner must give the signal before he steps away from the dog. Either the right or the left hand may be used. When giving the signal to lie down the arm should be brought up with a forceful gesture and lowered slowly. If dropped quickly, the dog may interpret it as the signal to come. The signal to sit at a distance is given with the right hand, palm up, which is brought forward with force and stopped so the dog can see the palm of the hand. This will remind the dog of his previous training when he was taught to sit from the down position. When the sit signal continues to shoulder height, the hand, as it is lowered to the side, becomes still another motion and the dog will be more confused than ever. The signal to come may be given with either hand in a downward gesture or one across the body depending on the dog's early leash training. The signal to finish is given with the left hand and the exhibitor should remember to snap the arm around to the left side with force. If the arm is held in back of the body until the judge says "Exercise finished," it will insure a more complete turn. Throughout the signal exercise the exhibitor should refrain from giving a signal if the dog is not looking.

The success of the directed go in the obedience ring will depend upon the results in the training yard. Practice with the hurdles set close together as well as far apart will season the dog for work under all conditions. The dog must learn to "Go" when told and to continue going until he is stopped. In the obedience ring, the exhibitor should assume his position as close to the hurdles as the rules permit so the dog will be encouraged to proceed sufficiently far before he is called upon to stop. The dog will then have room to take the designated hurdle. When the owner starts his dog too far back, the distance he must travel may be greater than that to which he is accustomed and he may anticipate the command to sit. This will place the dog at a disadvantage for jumping.

A dog that will not sit when told should be given the command in a demanding tone. If the dog's name is used before the command, there should be no pause between the two words and the emphasis should be placed on the word "Sit!" Calling the dog by name will encourage him to return without jumping unless he is given immediate instructions that will make him sit at once. When the exhibitor signals the jump, the arm should be brought out from the body with force. Care should be taken to hold the palm of whichever hand is used so the dog can see it clearly at a distance. The command to jump is given after the dog starts moving to encourage him to take the hurdle in case he is thinking otherwise. Keep in mind the arm is the signal to start the dog in the right direction. The command follows to encourage the dog to jump before he returns to the owner. Correct timing in this exercise will bring success where the dog might otherwise fail.

In the group examination, the suggestions made previously

Fig. 38. This obedience-trained Dalmatian shows his ability at the broad jump.

for the stand for examination and the long sit and down apply. The dog must be standing comfortably on all feet at an equal distance from the other dogs. A demanding tone of voice when the dog is told to stay and lack of movement on the part of the handler during the exercise so the dog will not misinterpret the action, will help in an effort to pass the test.

The obedience dog is, or at least should be, scored on his willingness to obey and his enjoyment of his work. The owner should make an effort to have his dog exhibit a happy attitude throughout every performance in the obedience ring. If, for any reason, the dog should stop working, the owner would do well to give a second command and take a penalty. Where the rules definitely state a second command warrants a failing score, the owner is tempted to wait and see if the dog will do the exercise in time, but when the dog gets into the habit of working slowly he will do the same thing at every show. It gets monotonous when a dog is permitted to stand idle. The judge stares at the exhibitor! The exhibitor glares at the dog! The dog continues his ringwise attitude! It is better to sacrifice one entry fee and stop such nonsense then and there.

Good sportsmanship and good fellowship in the obedience ring are qualities upon which no value can be placed. Judges do not always interpret the rules the same way. There will be times—and rightfully so—when the exhibitor will feel he has not had a square deal, but, win or lose, a smile should be in evidence. The exhibitor who complains and makes excuses for his dog soon gains the reputation of being a poor sport and a bad loser.

The exhibitor will find that judges vary as much in their scoring of the dogs as the dogs do in the way they work. Some judges prefer to be considered tough, and they will boast of how few qualifying scores they give. A slight error deserving a minor deduction becomes a major fault and results in failure or a substantial drop in points. Other judges will add flourishes to their methods of judging and ring procedure to confuse the owner and disarm the dog completely. On the other hand, many judges are far too lenient. When this is the case the exhibitor is fortunate and reaps the reward. There will be days when an exhibitor receives all the lucky breaks and times when the cards appear stacked against him. Obedience training is a sporting venture. It was not meant to be taken dead seriously. We should enjoy it and profit from our experiences. If the dog doesn't make the grade that day—there are other shows! In spite of the result, the owner will still have his trained dog. The disappointed exhibitor whose dog fails to make the grade may console himself with these few lines:

> Tomorrow is another day. With tomorrow comes
>   another show,
> There are always more tomorrows— And so it goes.
> Time cannot wither—nor custom stale,
> The dog show—or the wagging tail.

Exercises for Team Competition

FIRST DOG TRAINING CLUB OF NORTHERN NEW JERSEY, INC. *

I & III HEELING (On Leash and Free)	II FIGURE EIGHT (8) (On Leash)

This exercise will be done on leash and repeated off, each after the figure eight exercise.

In addition to calling the turns the judge will give the commands, "FAST, SLOW, NORMAL, and HALT."

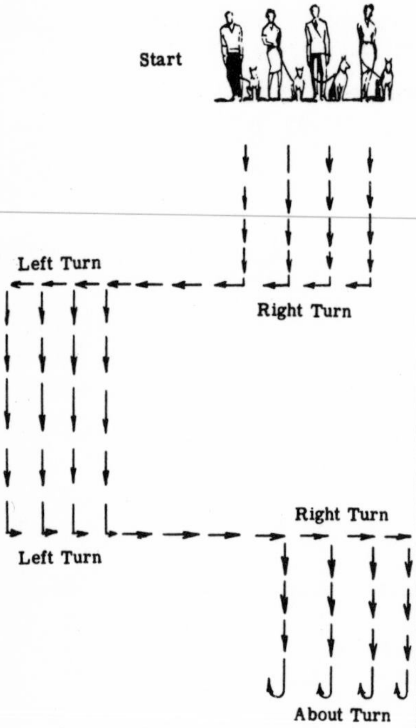

On command, "Prepare for Figure 8," handlers and dogs will take position as shown in diagram.   At command, "FORWARD," do the figure 8, making first turn to left and proceding as indicated below, working around the stewards who were at your right and left at the start of the exercise.

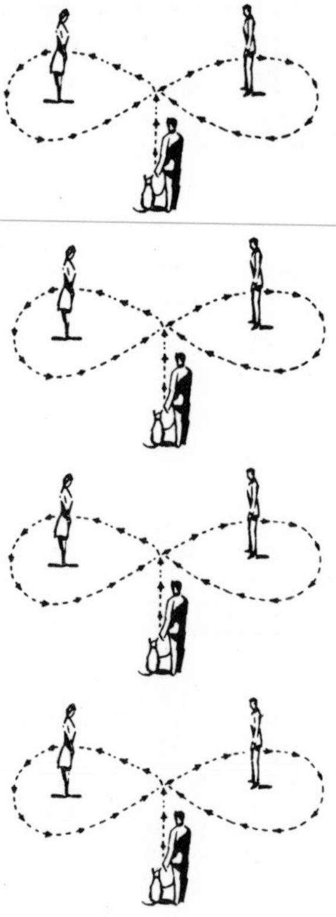

Start

Left Turn

Right Turn

Right Turn

Left Turn

Right Turn

About Turn

Fig. 39a

THE SHOW RING

TEANECK, N. J.

JUNE 22, 1947

IV RECALL

On command, "Prepare for Recall," handlers will prepare to leave dogs in sitting position and on command,"Leave your dogs," will do so, and proceed forward until the judge gives the commands, "Halt" and "About Turn." The judge will then command,"Call the first dog," the first dog on the handlers' right will be called, and when it is sitting in front of its handler, the next dog will be called. This wil be repeated until all four dogs are sitting in front of their handlers. On command, "Exercise Finished," all four dogs will go smartly to heel.

Handlers forward - leave your dogs.

Halt - About Turn

V DROP ON RECALL

The Drop on Recall will be done the same as the Recall except that the dogs will be left in the Down position, and when the command,"Call the First Dog," is given, the first dog on the handlers' right will be called, and the handler will drop his dog (without command from the judge) midway between the dogs and the handlers. The dog will remain in the Down position until all four dogs have been called and dropped.

On command,"Call All Dogs," all dogs will be called in together and sit in front of handlers until the judge gives the command,"Exercise Finished," then all four dogs will go smartly to heel.

Courtsey: Jerry Behrend

VI STAND-STAY

The "Stand-Stay" exercise will be done as above, except dogs will be left in a standing position.

After the judge has circled the dogs, the command "Return to Your Dogs" will be given.

Return as in Utility Exercise.

On command "Exercise Finished," all four dogs will sit.

VII LONG SIT AND DOWN

The long sit (1 minute), and the long down (3 minutes), will be done with no more than 4 teams (16 dogs) in the ring at one time.

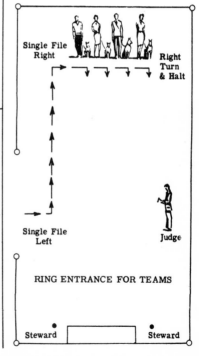

Fig. 39b

Appendix

SUGGESTIONS FOR EXHIBITIONS AND DEMONSTRATIONS

Study the size and shape of the demonstration area so it will be used to the best advantage.

Plan the exhibition from the spectator's point of view. (Whether observed from one side, such as off stage, or from all sides similar to a boxing ring.)

Outline the plan on paper. Make sketches and diagrams if necessary.

Keep the program simple if the dogs have not had much experience.

Take into consideration the type of audience that will be watching, and dress up the exhibition to meet the occasion.

Divide the group according to the size of the dogs. This will avoid adjusting the hurdles which can be left sufficiently low to accommodate all the dogs in that group.

Eliminate dogs that are generally disobedient and not under control. Select happy workers (even though they perform with less accuracy). Those that lack spirit have little ringside appeal.

Insist upon two or three rehearsals, even though it may not be convenient.

Select a good master of ceremonies, who will turn an embarrassing situation into a humorous one.

Call out all commands in a loud clear voice so the audience will know what the dogs are expected to do.

A short explanation of each exercise is educational and will make the gallery familiar with obedience training. Avoid long lectures and periods of idleness.

Minimize the heeling and the less important parts of the exercise.

Include such things as the sit- and down-stays, retrieving and jumping. These exercises are favored by the crowd.

Uniforms add gaiety and color.

Music (at least during the entrance and exit) makes for a more festive occasion.

Vary the obedience exercises for greater amusement. During the sit-stay, test the dogs' steadiness by rolling balls along the floor in front of them.

Use baseballs, the dog's favorite toy, unusually large objects (such as an oversize dumbbell or a large ball wrapped in netting, which will make it easy to pick up), for the retrieve on the flat and over the hurdle.

Train the dogs to carry pennants that can be lettered with the dog's name or the occasion for which the demonstration is being given.

Teach two dogs to hold the ends of a single bar in their mouth, over which the others can retrieve.

When the audience is some distance away, use colored baskets or large-size objects for scent discrimination. In a small group, the regular scent articles can be used.

Work the program up to a spectacular climax and permit as much jumping as time will allow.

Include such things as the "Hup-Heel" and the recall over three or four hurdles. Let the dogs carry dumbbells or pennants while jumping. Use hoops occasionally instead of the regulation hurdles and train some of the dogs to jump through a hoop covered with paper.

Have one or two persons responsible for setting up the jumps and to be on hand to supply the extra equipment.

Use the bar jump whenever possible. It will avoid long delays and is more convenient than setting up the solid and broad. The bar jump is spectacular and the dog is visible at all times.

Avoid long drawn out demonstrations. Twenty to thirty minutes is sufficient and the spectators will not become bored.

Don't attempt to create a humorous situation. The dogs' natural mistakes will provide adequate laughter and amusement.

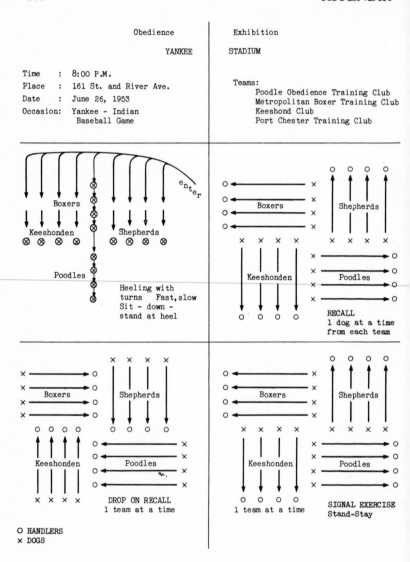

Fig. 40a. The nine diagrams represent a planned exhibition by the author in an unlimited working area.

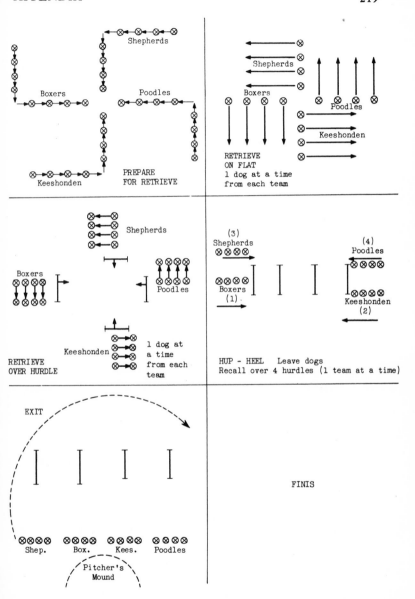

Fig. 40b

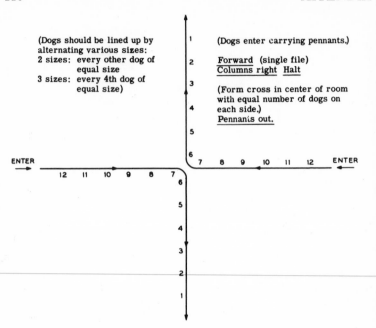

(Dogs should be lined up by
alternating various sizes:
2 sizes: every other dog of
equal size
3 sizes: every 4th dog of
equal size)

(Dogs enter carrying pennants.)

Forward (single file)
Columns right Halt

(Form cross in center of room
with equal number of dogs on
each side.)
Pennants out.

ENTER

ENTER

Fig. 41a. The thirteen diagrams represent an exhibition staged and directed
by the author at Madison Square Garden during the 1949 Westminster
Kennel Club Dog Show.

Forward (Odd numbers circle left...even numbers circle right.)

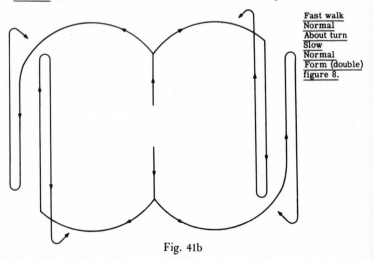

Fast walk
Normal
About turn
Slow
Normal
Form (double)
figure 8.

Fig. 41b

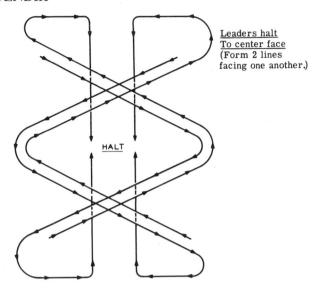

Leaders halt
To center face
(Form 2 lines
facing one another.)

HALT

Fig. 41c

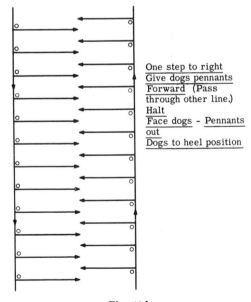

One step to right
Give dogs pennants
Forward (Pass
through other line.)
Halt
Face dogs - Pennants
out
Dogs to heel position

Fig. 41d

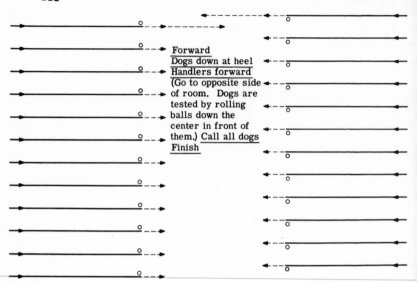

Fig. 41e

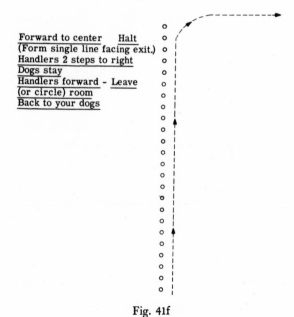

Fig. 41f

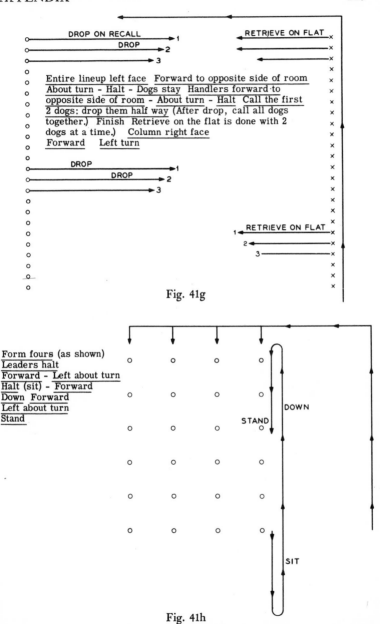

DROP ON RECALL
DROP
RETRIEVE ON FLAT

Entire lineup left face   Forward to opposite side of room
About turn - Halt - Dogs stay   Handlers forward to
opposite side of room - About turn - Halt   Call the first
2 dogs: drop them half way (After drop, call all dogs
together.)   Finish   Retrieve on the flat is done with 2
dogs at a time.)   Column right face
Forward   Left turn

DROP
DROP

RETRIEVE ON FLAT

Fig. 41g

Form fours (as shown)
Leaders halt
Forward - Left about turn
Halt (sit) - Forward
Down   Forward
Left about turn
Stand

DOWN

STAND

SIT

Fig. 41h

(Dogs go to stand-stay.)
Handlers forward
About turn - Halt
Back to your dogs

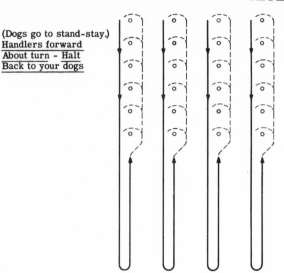

Fig. 41i

Forward
Columns 1 and 3 about turn
Prepare for retrieve over
hurdle (4 dogs at one time)
Throw it - Send them
(Finish to be done without
command.) Line up for
next exercise.)

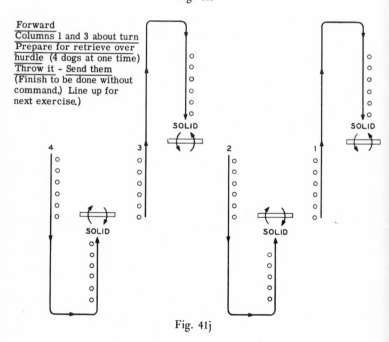

Fig. 41j

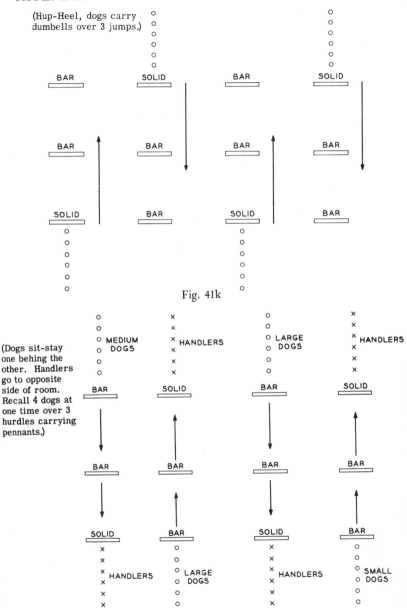

Fig. 41k

Fig. 41l

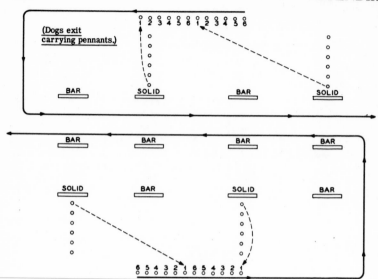

Fig. 41m

Regulations for

American Kennel Club

Licensed Obedience Trials

(As in effect July 1, 1969)

Purpose

Obedience trials are a sport and all participants should be guided by the principles of good sportsmanship both in and outside of the ring. The purpose of
obedience trials is to demonstrate the usefulness of the pure-bred dog as a companion of man, not merely the dog's ability to follow specified routines in the
obedience ring. While all contestants in a class are required to perform the same
exercises in substantially the same way so that the relative quality of the various
performances may be compared and scored, the basic objective of obedience trials
is to produce dogs that have been trained and conditioned always to behave in
the home, in public places, and in the presence of other dogs, in a manner that will
reflect credit on the sport of obedience. The performances of dog and handler in
the ring must be accurate and correct and must conform to the requirements of
these regulations. However, it is also essential that the dog demonstrate willingness and enjoyment of its work, and smoothness and naturalness on the part of
the handler are to be preferred to a performance based on military precision and
peremptory commands.

CHAPTER 1

General Regulations

Section 1. **Obedience Clubs.** An obedience club that meets all the requirements of The American Kennel Club and wishes to hold an Obedience Trial at which qualifying scores toward an obedience title may be awarded, must make application to The American Kennel Club on the form provided for permission to hold such trial. Such a trial, if approved, may be held either in conjunction with a dog show or as a separate event. If the club is not a member of The American Kennel Club it shall pay a license fee for the privilege of holding such trial, the amount of which shall be determined by the Board of Directors of The American Kennel Club. If the club fails to hold its trial at the time and place which have been approved, the amount of the license fee paid will be returned.

Section 2. **Dog Show and Specialty Clubs.** A dog show club may be granted permission to hold a licensed or member obedience trial at its dog show, and a specialty club may also be granted permission to hold a licensed or member obedience trial if, in the opinion of the Board of Directors of The American Kennel Club, such clubs are qualified to do so.

Section 3. **Obedience Classes.** A licensed or member obedience trial need not include all of the regular obedience classes defined in this chapter, but a club will be approved to hold Open classes only if it also holds Novice classes, and a club will be approved to hold a Utility class only if it also holds Novice and Open classes. A specialty club which has been approved to hold a licensed or member obedience trial, if qualified in the opinion of the Board of Directors of The American Kennel Club, or an obedience club which has been approved to hold a licensed or member obedience trial may, subject to the approval of The American Kennel Club, offer additional non-regular classes for dogs not less than six months of age, provided a clear and complete description of the eligibility requirements and performance requirements for each such class appears in the premium list. Pre-Novice classes will not be approved at licensed or member obedience trials.

Section 4. **Tracking Tests.** A club that has been approved to hold licensed or member obedience trials and that meets the requirements of The American Kennel Club, may also make application to hold a Tracking Test. A club may not hold a tracking test on the same day as its show or obedience trial, but the tracking test may be announced in the premium list for the show or trial, and the tracking test entries may be included in the show or obedience trial catalog. If the entries are not listed in the catalog for the show or obedience trial, the club must provide, at the tracking test, several copies of a sheet, which may be typewritten, giving all the information that would be contained in the catalog for each entered dog. If the tracking test is to be held within 7 days of the obedience trial the entries must be sent to the same person designated to receive the obedience trial entries, and the same closing date should apply. If the tracking test is not to be held within 7 days of the obedience trial the club may name someone else in the premium list to receive the tracking test entries, and may specify a different closing date for entries at least 7 days before the tracking test.

The presence of a veterinarian shall not be required at a tracking test.

Section 5. **Obedience Trial Committee.** If an obedience trial is held by an obedience club, an Obedience Trial Committee must be appointed by the club, and this committee shall exercise all the authority vested in a dog show's Bench Show Committee. If an obedience club holds its obedience trial in conjunction with a dog show, then the Obedience Trial Committee shall have sole jurisdiction only over those dogs entered in the obedience trial and their handlers and owners; provided, however, that if any dog is entered in both obedience and breed classes, then the Obedience Trial Committee shall have jurisdiction over such dog, its owner, and its handler, only in matters pertaining to the Obedience Regulations, and the Bench Show Committee shall have jurisdiction over such dog, its owner and handler, in all other matters.

When an obedience trial is to be held in conjunction with a dog show by the club which has been granted permission to hold the show, the club's Bench Show Committee shall include one person designated as "Obedience Chairman". At such event the Bench Show Committee of the show-giving club shall have sole jurisdiction over all matters which may properly come before it, regardless of whether the matter has to do with the dog show or with the obedience trial.

Section 6. **Sanctioned Matches.** A club may hold an Obedience Match by obtaining the sanction of The American Kennel Club. Sanctioned obedience matches shall be governed by such regulations as may be adopted by the Board of Directors of The American Kennel Club. Scores awarded at such matches will not be entered in the records of The American Kennel Club nor count towards an obedience title.

All of these Obedience Regulations shall also apply to sanctioned matches except for those sections in which it is specified that the provisions apply to licensed or member trials, and except where specifically stated otherwise in the Regulations for Sanctioned Matches.

Section 7. **American Kennel Club Sanction.** American Kennel Club sanction must be obtained by any club that holds American Kennel Club obedience trials, for any type of match for which it solicits or accepts entries from non-members.

Section 8. **Dog Show Rules.** All the Dog Show Rules, where applicable, shall govern the conducting of obedience trials and tracking tests, and shall apply to all persons and dogs participating in them except as these Obedience Regulations may provide otherwise.

Section 9. **Immediate Family.** As used in this chapter, "immediate family" means husband, wife, father, mother, son, daughter, brother, or sister.

Section 10. **Pure-Bred Dogs Only.** As used in these Regulations the word "dog" refers to either sex but only to dogs that are pure-bred of a breed eligible or registration in the American Kennel Club stud book or for entry in the Miscellaneous Class at American Kennel Club dog shows, as only such dogs may compete in obedience trials, tracking tests, or sanctioned matches. A judge must report to The American Kennel Club after the trial or tracking test any dog shown under him which in his opinion appears not to be pure-bred.

Section 11. **Unregistered Dogs.** Chapter 16, Section 1 of the Dog Show Rules shall apply to entries in licensed or member obedience trials and tracking tests, except that an eligible unregistered dog for which an ILP number has been issued by The American Kennel Club may be entered indefinitely in such events provided the ILP number is shown on each entry form.

Section 12. **Dogs That May Not Compete.** No dog belonging wholly or in part to a judge or to a Show or Obedience Trial Secretary, Superintendent, or veterinarian, or to any member of such person's immediate family or household, shall be entered in any dog show, obedience trial, or tracking test at which such person officiates or is scheduled to officiate. This applies to both obedience and dog show judges when an obedience trial is held in conjunction with a dog show. However, a tracking test shall be considered a separate event for the purpose of this section.

No dog shall be entered or shown under a judge at an obedience trial or tracking test if the dog has been owned, sold, held under lease, handled in the ring, boarded, or has been regularly trained or instructed, within one year prior to the date of the obedience trial or tracking test, by the judge or by any member of his immediate family or household, and no such dog shall be eligible to compete. "Trained or instructed" applies equally to judges who train professionally or as amateurs, and to judges who train individual dogs or who train or instruct dogs in classes with or through their handlers.

Section 13. **When Titles Are Won.** Where any of the following sections of the regulations excludes from a particular obedience class dogs that have won a particular obedience title, eligibility to enter that class shall be determined as follows: a dog may continue to be shown in such a class after its handler has been notified by three different judges that it has received three qualifying scores for such title, but may not be entered or shown in such a class in any obedience trial of which the closing date for entries occurs after the owner has received official notification from the American Kennel Club that the dog has won the particular obedience title.

Where any of the following sections of the regulations requires that a dog shall have won a particular obedience title before competing in a particular obedience class, a dog may not be shown in such class at any obedience trial before the owner has received official notification from The American Kennel Club that the dog has won the required title.

Section 14. **Disqualification and Ineligibility.** A dog that is blind or deaf or that has been changed in appearance by artificial means (except for such changes as are customarily approved for its breed) may not compete in any obedience trial or tracking test and must be disqualified. Blind means having useful vision in neither eye. Deaf means without useful hearing.

If a judge has evidence of any of these conditions in any dog he is judging at an obedience trial he must, before proceeding with the judging, notify the Superintendent or Show or Trial Secretary and must call an official veterinarian to examine the dog in the ring and give to the judge an advisory opinion in writing on the condition of the dog. Only after he has seen the opinion of the veterinarian in writing shall the judge render his own decision and record it in the judge's book, marking the dog disqualified and stating the reason if he determines that disqualification is required under this section. The judge's decision is final and need not necessarily agree with the veterinarian's opinion. The written opinion of the veterinarian shall in all cases be forwarded to The American Kennel Club by the Superintendent or Show or Trial Secretary.

The judge must disqualify any dog that attempts to attack any person in the ring. He may excuse a dog that attacks another dog or that appears dangerous to other dogs in the ring. He shall mark the dog disqualified or excused and state the reason in his judge's book, and shall give the Superintendent or Show or Trial Secretary a brief report of the dog's actions which shall be submitted to AKC with the report of the show or trial.

When a dog has been disqualified under this section as being blind or deaf or having been changed in appearance by artificial means or for having attempted to attack a person in the ring, all awards made to the dog at the trial shall be cancelled by The American Kennel Club and the dog may not again compete unless and until, following application by the owner to The American Kennel Club, the owner has received official notification from The American Kennel Club that the dog's eligibility has been reinstated.

Spayed bitches, castrated dogs, monorchid or cryptorchid males, and dogs that have faults which would disqualify them under the standards for their breeds, may compete in obedience trials if otherwise eligible under these regulations.

A dog that is lame in the ring at any obedience trial may not compete and shall not receive any score at the trial. It shall be the judge's responsibility to determine whether a dog is lame. He shall not obtain the opinion of the show veterinarian. If in the judge's opinion a dog in the ring is lame, he shall not score such dog, and shall promptly excuse it from the ring and mark his book "Excused—lame".

No dog shall be eligible to compete if it appears to have been dyed or colored in any way or if the coat shows evidence of chalk or powder, or if the dog has anything attached to it whether for medical or corrective purposes, for protection, for adornment or for any other reason, except for certain breeds to the extent only that they are normally shown in the breed ring with the hair over the eyes tied back. The judge, at his sole discretion, may agree to judge such a dog at a later time if the offending condition has been corrected.

An obedience judge is not required to be familiar with the breed standards nor to scrutinize each dog as in dog show judging, but shall be alert for conditions which may require disqualification or exclusion under this section.

Section 15. **Disturbances.** Bitches in season are not permitted to compete. The judge of an obedience trial or tracking test must remove from competition any bitch in season, any dog which its handler cannot control, any handler who interferes willfully with another competitor or his dog, and any handler who abuses his dog in the ring, and may excuse from competition any dog which he considers unfit to compete, or any bitch which appears so attractive to males as to be a disturbing element. In case of doubt an official veterinarian shall be called to give his opinion. If a dog or handler is expelled or excused by a judge, the reason shall be stated in the judge's book or in a separate report.

Section 16. **Novice A Class.** The Novice A class shall be for dogs not less than six months of age that have not won the title C.D. No person who has previously handled a dog that has won a C.D. title in the obedience ring at a licensed or member trial, and no person who has regularly trained such a dog, may enter or handle a dog in this class. Each dog in the class must have a separate handler, who must be its owner or a member of the owner's immediate family. The same person must handle each dog in all exercises.

Section 17. **Novice B Class.** The Novice B class shall be for dogs not less than six months of age that have not won the title C.D. Dogs in this class may be handled by the owner or any other person. A person may handle more than one dog in this class, but each dog must have a separate handler for the Long Sit and Long Down exercises when judged in the same group. No dog may be entered in both Novice A and Novice B classes at any one trial.

Section 18. **Novice Exercises and Scores.** The exercises and maximum scores in the Novice classes are:

1. Heel on Leash	35 points
2. Stand for Examination	30 points
3. Heel Free	45 points
4. Recall	30 points
5. Long Sit	30 points
6. Long Down	30 points
Maximum Total Score	200 points

Section 19. **C.D. Title.** The American Kennel Club will issue a Companion Dog

certificate for each registered dog, and will permit the use of the letters "C.D." after the name of each dog that had been certified by three different judges to have received scores of more than 50% of the available points in each of the six exercises and final scores of 170 or more points in Novice classes at three licensed or member obedience trials, provided the sum total of dogs that actually competed in the regular Novice classes at each trial is not less than six.

Section 20. **Open A Class.** The Open A class shall be for dogs that have won the C.D. title but have not won the title C.D.X. Obedience judges and licensed handlers may not enter or handle dogs in this class. Each dog must be handled by its owner or by a member of his immediate family. Owners may enter more than one dog in this class but the same person who handled each dog in the first five exercises must handle the same dog in the Long Sit and Long Down exercises, except that if a person has handled more than one dog in the first five exercises he must have an additional handler, who must be the owner or a member of his immediate family, for each additional dog, when more than one dog he has handled in the first five exercises is judged in the same group for the Long Sit and Long Down.

Section 21. **Open B Class.** The Open B class will be for dogs that have won the title C.D. or C.D.X. A dog may continue to compete in this class after it has won the title U.D. Dogs in this class may be handled by the owner or any other person. Owners may enter more than one dog in this class but the same person who handled each dog in the first five exercises must handle each dog in the Long Sit and Long Down exercises, except that if a person has handled more than one dog in the first five exercises he must have an additional handler for each additional dog, when more than one dog that he has handled in the first five exercises is judged in the same group for the Long Sit and Long Down. No dog may be entered in both Open A and Open B classes at any one trial.

Section 22. **Open Exercises and Scores.** The exercises and maximum scores in the Open classes are:

1. Heel Free	40 points
2. Drop on Recall	30 points
3. Retrieve on Flat	25 points
4. Retrieve over High Jump	35 points
5. Broad Jump	20 points
6. Long Sit	25 points
7. Long Down	25 points
Maximum Total Score	200 points

Section 23. **C.D.X. Title.** The American Kennel Club will issue a Companion Dog Excellent certificate for each registered dog, and will permit the use of the letters "C.D.X." after the name of each dog that has been certified by three different judges of obedience trials to have received scores of more than 50% of the available points in each of the seven exercises and final scores of 170 or more points in Open classes at three licensed or member obedience trials, provided the sum total of dogs that actually competed in the regular Open classes at each trial is not less than six.

Section 24. **Utility Class.** The Utility class shall be for dogs that have won the title C.D.X. Dogs that have won the title U.D. may continue to compete in this class. Dogs in this class may be handled by the owner or any other person. Owners may enter more than one dog in this class, but each dog must have a separate handler for the Group Examination when judged in the same group.

Section 25. **Division of Utility Class.** A club may choose to divide the Utility class into Utility A and Utility B classes, provided such division is approved by The American Kennel Club and is announced in the premium list. When this is done the Utility A class shall be for dogs which have won the title C.D.X. and have not won the title U.D. Obedience judges and licensed handlers may not enter or handle dogs in this class. A dog may be handled in the Group Examination by a person other than the person who handled it in the individual exercises, but each dog must be handled in all exercises by the owner or by a member of his immediate family. All other dogs that are eligible for the Utility class but not eligible for the Utility A class may be entered only in the Utility B class to which the conditions listed in Section 24 shall apply. No dog may be entered in both Utility A and Utility B classes at any one trial.

Section 26. **Utility Exercises and Scores.** The exercises and maximum scores in the Utility classes are:

1. Scent Discrimination—Article No. 1	....	30 points
2. Scent Discrimination—Article No. 2	....	30 points
3. Directed Retrieve	....	30 points
4. Signal Exercise	....	35 points
5. Directed Jumping	....	40 points
6. Group Examination	....	35 points
Maximum Total Score	....	200 points

Section 27. **U.D. Title.** The American Kennel Club will issue a Utility Dog certificate for each registered dog, and will permit the use of the letters "U.D." after the name of each dog that has been certified by three different judges of obedience trials to have received scores of more than 50% of the available points in each of the six exercises and final scores of 170 or more points in Utility classes at three licensed or member obedience trials in each of which three or more dogs actually competed in the Utility class or classes.

Section 28. **Tracking Test.** This test shall be for dogs not less than six months of age, and must be judged by two judges. With each entry form for a licensed or member tracking test for a dog that has not passed a tracking test there must be filed a written statement, dated within six months of the date the entry is received, signed by a person who has been approved by The American Kennel Club to judge tracking tests, certifying that the dog is considered by him to be ready for such a test. These original statements cannot be used again and must be submitted to The American Kennel Club with the entry forms. Written permission to waive or modify this requirement may be granted by The American Kennel Club in unusual circumstances. Tracking tests are open to all dogs that are otherwise eligible under these Regulations.

This test cannot be given at a dog show or obedience trial. The duration of this test may be one day or more within a 15 day period after the original date in the event of an unusually large entry or other unforeseen emergency, provided that the change of date is satisfactory to the exhibitors affected.

Section 29. **T.D. Title.** The American Kennel Club will issue a Tracking Dog certificate to a registered dog, and will permit the use of the letters "T.D." after the name of each dog which has been certified by the two judges to have passed a licensed or member tracking test in which at least three dogs actually competed.

The owner of a dog holding both the U.D. and T.D. titles may use the letters "U.D.T." after the name of the dog, signifying "Utility Dog Tracker".

Section 30. **Obedience Ribbons.** At licensed or member obedience trials the following colors shall be used for prize ribbons or rosettes in all regular classes:

First Prize......................................Blue
Second Prize....................................Red
Third Prize.....................................Yellow
Fourth Prize....................................White
Special Prize...................................Dark Green

and the following colors shall be used for non-regular classes:

First Prize......................................Rose
Second Prize....................................Brown
Third Prize.....................................Light Green
Fourth Prize....................................Gray

Each ribbon or rosette shall be at least two inches wide and approximately eight inches long, and shall bear on its face a facsimile of the seal of The American Kennel Club, the words "Obedience Trial", the name of the prize, the name of the trial-giving club, the date of the trial, and the name of the city or town where the trial is given.

Section 31. **Match Ribbons.** If ribbons are given at sanctioned obedience matches they shall be of the following colors and shall have the words "Obedience Match" printed on them, but may be of any design or size:

First Prize...............................Rose
Second Prize..............................Brown
Third Prize...............................Light Green
Fourth Prize..............................Gray
Special Prize.............................Green with pink edges

Section 32. **Prizes.** Ribbons for the four official placings and all other prizes offered for competition within a single regular class at a licensed or member trial, shall be awarded only to dogs that earn scores of more than 50% of the available points in each exercise and final scores of 170 or more points.

Prizes for which dogs in one class compete against dogs in one or more other classes at a licensed or member trial may, at the option of the club holding the trial, specify that scores of more than 50% of the available points in each exercise and final scores of 170 or more points, are required.

Ribbons and all prizes offered at sanctioned obedience matches, and in non-regular classes at licensed and member trials, shall be awarded on the basis of final scores without regard to more than 50% of the points in each exercise.

Prizes at a licensed or member obedience trial must be offered to be won outright, with the exception that a prize which requires three wins by the same owner, not necessarily with the same dog, for permanent possession, may be offered for the dog with the highest qualifying score in one of the regular classes, for the highest scoring dog in the regular classes, or for the highest combined score in the Open B and Utility classes.

Subject to the provisions of paragraphs 1 and 2 of this section, prizes may be offered for the highest scoring dogs of the Groups as defined in Chapter 2 of the Dog Show Rules, or for the highest scoring dogs of any breeds, but not for a breed variety. Show varieties are not recognized for obedience. In accordance with Chapter 2, all Poodles are in the Non-Sporting Group and all Manchester Terriers in the Terrier Group.

Prizes offered only to members of certain clubs or organizations will not be approved for publication in premium lists.

Section 33. **Risk.** The owner or agent entering a dog in an obedience trial does so at his own risk and agrees to abide by the rules of The American Kennel Club, and the Obedience Regulations.

Section 34. **Decisions.** At the trial the decisions of the judge shall be final in all matters affecting the scoring and the working of the dogs and their handlers. The Obedience Trial Committee, or the Bench Show Committee if the trial is held by a show-giving club, shall decide all other matters arising at the trial, including protests against dogs made under Chapter 20 of the Dog Show Rules, subject, however, to the rules and regulations of The American Kennel Club.

Section 35. **Dogs Must Compete.** Any dog entered and received at a licensed or member obedience trial must compete in all exercises of all classes in which it is entered unless disqualified, expelled, or excused by the judge or by the Bench Show or Obedience Trial Committee, or unless excused by the official veterinarian to protect the health of the dog or of other dogs at the trial. The excuse of the official veterinarian must be in writing and must be approved by the Superintendent or Show or Trial Secretary, and must be submitted to The American Kennel Club with the report of the trial. The judge must report to The American Kennel Club any dog that is not brought back for the group exercises.

Section 36. **Judging Program.** Any club holding a licensed or member obedience trial must prepare, after the entries have closed, a program showing the time scheduled for the judging of each of the classes. A copy of this program shall be mailed to the owner of each entered dog and to each judge, and the program shall be printed in the catalog. This program shall be based on the judging of no more than 8 Novice entries, 7 Open entries, or 5 Utility entries, per hour during the time the show or trial will be open as published in the premium list, taking into consideration the starting hour for judging if published in the premium list, and the availability of rings. No judge shall be scheduled to exceed this rate of judging. In addition, one hour for rest or meals must be allowed if, under this formula, it will take more than five hours of actual judging to judge the dogs entered under him. No judge shall be assigned to judge for more than eight hours in one day under this formula, including any breed judging assignment if the obedience trial is held in conjunction with a dog show.

If any non-regular class is to be judged in the same ring as any regular class, or by the judge of any regular class, the non-regular class must be judged after the regular class.

Section 37. **Limitation of Entries.** If a club holding a licensed or member trial anticipates an entry in excess of the club's facilities, it may limit entries in any or all classes by prominent announcement on the title or cover page of its premium list, or immediately under the obedience heading in the premium list for a dog show, stating that entries in one or more specified classes or in the obedience trial will automatically close when a certain limit or limits have been reached, even though the official closing date for entries has not arrived. If entries in the regular classes are limited, non-regular classes will not be approved.

Section 38. **Additional Judges, Reassignment, Split Classes.** If when the entries have closed, it is found that the entry under one or more judges exceeds the limit established in Section 36, the club shall immediately secure the approval of The American Kennel Club for the appointment of one or more additional judges, or for reassignment of its advertised judges, so that no judge will be required to exceed the limit.

If a judge with an excessive entry was advertised to judge more than one class, one or more of his classes shall be assigned to another judge. The class or classes selected for reassignment shall first be any non-regular classes for which he was advertised, and shall then be those with the minimum number of entries which will bring the advertised judge's schedule within the maximum limit. If a judge with an excessive entry was advertised to judge only one class, the Superintendent, Show Secretary, or Obedience Trial Secretary, shall divide the entry as evenly as possible between the advertised judge and the other judge by drawing lots.

The club shall promptly mail to the owner of each entry affected, a notification of any change of judge. The owner shall be permitted to withdraw such entry at any time prior to the day of the show, and the entry fee shall then be refunded. If the entry in any one class is split in this manner, the advertised judge shall judge the run-off of any tie scores that may develop between the two groups of dogs, after each judge has first run-off any ties resulting from his own judging.

Section 39. **Split Classes in Premium List.** A club may choose to announce two or more judges for any class in its premium list. In such case the entries shall be divided by lots as proviced above, but no announcement of the drawing need be made to the owners in advance of the trial, and no owner shall be entitled to a refund of entry fee. In such case the premium list shall also specify the judge for the run-off of any tie scores which may develop between the dogs in the different groups, after each judge has first run-off any ties resulting from his own judging.

Section 40. **Split Classes, Official Ribbons.** A club which gives a split class, whether the split is announced in the premium list or made after entries have closed, shall not award American Kennel Club official ribbons in either section, but may offer prizes on the basis of qualifying scores made within each section if the split class is announded in the premium list. The four dogs with the highest qualifying scores in the class regardless of the section in which they were made, shall be called back into the ring and awarded the four American Kennel Club official ribbons by one of the judges of the class who shall be responsible for recording the entry numbers of the four placed dogs in one of the judges' books.

Section 41. **Training of Dogs.** There shall be no drilling nor intensive or corrective training of dogs on the grounds or premises at a licensed or member obedience trial. No practice rings or areas shall be permitted at such events. All dogs shall be kept on leash except when in the obedience ring or exercise ring. Spiked or other special training collars shall not be used on the grounds or premises at an obedience trial or match. These requirements shall not be interpreted as preventing a handler from moving normally about the grounds or premises with his dog at heel on leash, nor from giving such signals or such commands in a normal tone, as are necessary and usual in everday life in heeling a dog or making it stay, but physical or verbal disciplining of dogs shall not be permitted except to a reasonable extent in the case of an attack on a person or another dog. The Superintendent, or Show or Trial Secretary, and the members of the Bench Show or Obedience Trial Committee, shall be responsible for compliance with this section, and shall investigate any reports of infractions.

Section 42. **Abuse of Dogs.** The Bench Show or Obedience Trial Committee shall also investigate any reports of abuse of dogs or severe disciplining of dogs on the grounds or premises of a show, trial, or match. Any person who, at a licensed or member obedience trial, conducts himself in such manner or in any other manner prejudicial to the best interests of the sport, or who fails to comply with the requirements of Section 41 above after receiving a warning, shall be dealt with promptly, during the trial if possible, after the offender has been notified of the specific charges against him, and has been given an opportunity to be heard in his own defense, in accordance with Section 43 below.

Article XII Section 2 of the Constitution and By-Laws of The American Kennel Club provides:

Section 43. **Discipline.** The Bench Show, Obedience Trial or Field Trial Committee of a club or association shall have the right to suspend any person from the privileges of The American Kennel Club for conduct prejudicial to the best interests of pure-bred dogs, dog shows, obedience trials, field trials or The American Kennel Club, alleged to have occurred in connection with or during the progress of its show, obedience trial or field trial, after the alleged offender has been given an opportunity to be heard.

Notice in writing must be sent promptly by registered mail by the Bench Show, Obedience Trial or Field Trial Committee to the person suspended and a duplicate notice giving the name and address of the person suspended and full details as to the reasons for the suspension must be forwarded to The American Kennel Club within seven days.

An appeal may be taken from a decision of a Bench Show, Obedience Trial or Field Trial Committee. Notice in writing claiming such appeal together with a deposit of five ($5.00) dollars must be sent to The American Kennel Club within thirty days after the date of suspension. The Board of Directors may itself hear said appeal or may refer it to a committee of the Board, or to a Trial Board to be heard. The deposit shall become the property of The American Kennel Club if the decision is confirmed, or shall be returned to the appellant if the decision is not confirmed.

(*See Guide for Bench Show and Obedience Trial Committees in Dealing with Misconduct at Dog Shows and Obedience Trials for proper procedure at licensed or member obedience trials.*)

(*The Committee at a Sanctioned event does not have this power of suspension, but must investigate any allegation of such conduct and forward a complete and detailed report of any such incident to The American Kennel Club.*)

CHAPTER 2

Regulations for Performance

Section 1. **Ring Conditions.** If the judging takes place indoors the ring should be rectangular and should be at least 35' wide and 50' long for all obedience classes. In no case shall the ring for a Utility class be less than 35' by 50', and in no case shall the ring for a Novice or Open class be less than 30' by 40'. The floor shall have a surface or covering that provides firm footing for the largest dogs, and rubber or similar non-slip material must be laid for the take off and landing at all jumps unless the surface, in the judge's opinion, is such as not to require it. At an outdoor show or trial the rings shall be about 40' wide and 50' long. The ground shall be clean and level, and the grass, if any, shall be cut short. The Club and Superintendent are responsible for providing, for the Open classes, an appropriate place approved by the judge, for the handlers to go completely out of sight of their dogs. If inclement weather at an outdoor trial necessitates the judging of obedience under shelter, the requirements as to ring size may be waived.

Section 2. **Obedience Rings at Dog Shows.** At an outdoor dog show a separate ring or rings shall be provided for obedience, and a sign forbidding anyone to permit any dog to use the ring, except when being judged, shall be set up in each such ring by the Superintendent or Show Secretary. It shall be his duty as well as that of the Show Committee to enforce this regulation. At an indoor show where limited space does not permit the exclusive use of any ring for obedience, the same regulation will apply after the obedience rings have been set up. At a dog show the material used for enclosing the obedience rings shall be at least equal to the material used for enclosing the breed rings. The ring must be thoroughly cleaned before the obedience judging starts if it has previously been used for breed judging.

Section 3. **Compliance with Regulations and Standards.** In accordance with the certification on the entry form, the handler of each dog and the person signing each entry form must be familiar with the Obedience Regulations applicable to the class in which the dog is entered. A handler with a physical handicap may compete, provided he can move himself about the ring as required, without physical assistance or guidance from another person, except for guidance to the proper location in the ring which may be given by the judge or, in the group exercises, by a person who is handling a competing dog in the ring.

Section 4. **Praise and Handling between Exercises.** Praise and patting are allowed between exercises, but points must be deducted from the total score for a dog that is not under reasonable control while being praised. A handler must not carry or offer food in the ring.

Imperfections in heeling between exercises will not be judged. In the Novice classes the dog may be guided gently by the collar between exercises and to get it into proper position for the next exercise. There shall be a substantial penalty for any dog that is picked up or carried at any time in the obedience ring, and for a dog in the Open or Utility classes that is not readily controllable or that is physically controlled at any time, except for permitted patting between exercises. Minor penalties shall be imposed for a dog that does not respond promptly to its handler's commands or signals between exercises in the Open and Utility classes.

Section 5. **Use of Leash.** All dogs shall be kept on leash except when in the obedience ring or exercise ring. Dogs should be brought into the ring and taken out of the ring on leash. Dogs may be kept on leash in the ring when brought in to receive awards, and when waiting in the ring before and after the group exercises. The leash shall be left on the judge's table between the individual exercises, and during all exercises except the Heel on Leash and group exercises. The leash may be of fabric or leather and, in the Novice classes, shall be of sufficient length to provde adequate slack in the Heel on Leash exercise.

Section 6. **Collars.** Dogs in the obedience ring must wear well-fitting plain buckle or slip collars of leather, fabric, or chain. Fancy collars, spiked collars or other special training collars, or collars that are either too tight or so large that they hang down unreasonably in front of the dogs, are not permitted, nor may there be anything hanging from the collars.

Section 7. **Misbehavior.** Any disciplining by the handler in the ring, any display of fear or nervousness by the dog, or any uncontrolled behavior of the dog such as snapping, barking, relieving itself in the ring, or running away from its handler, whether it occurs during an exercise, between exercises, or before or after judging, must be penalized according to the seriousness of the misbehavior, and the judge may expel or excuse the dog from further competition in the class. If such behavior occurs during an exercise, the penalty must first be applied to the score for that exercise. Should the penalty be greater than the value of the exercise during which it is incurred, the additional points shall be deducted from the total score under Misbehavior. If such behavior occurs before or after the judging or between exercises, the entire penalty shall be deducted from the total score.

Section 8. **Commands and Signals.** Whenever a command or signal is mentioned in these regulations, a single command or signal only may be given by the handler, and any extra commands or signals must be penalized; except that whenever the regulations specify "command and/or signal" the handler may give either one or the other or both command and signal simultaneously. When a signal is permitted and given, it must be a single gesture with one arm and hand only, and the arm must immediately be returned to its normal position. Delay in following a judge's order to give a command or signal must be penalized, unless the delay is directed by the judge because of some distraction or interference.

The signal for downing a dog may be given either with the arm raised or with a down swing of the arm, but any pause in holding the arm upright followed by a down swing of the arm will be considered an additional signal.

Signaling correction to a dog is forbidden and must be penalized. Signals must be inaudible and the handler must not touch the dog. Any unusual noise or motion may be considered to be a signal. Movements of the body shall be considered additional signals except that a handler may bend as far as necessary to bring his hand on a level with the dog's eyes in giving a signal to a dog in the heel position, and that in the Directed Retrieve exercise the body and knees may be bent to the extent necessary to give the direction to the dog. Whistling or the use of a whistle is prohibited.

The dog's name may be used once immediately before any verbal command or before a verbal command and signal when these regulations permit command and/or signal. The name shall not be used with any signal not given simultaneously with a verbal command. The dog's name, when given immediately before a verbal command, shall not be considered as an additional command, but a dog that responds to its name without waiting for the verbal command shall be scored as having anticipated the command. The dog should never anticipate the handler's directions, but must wait for the appropriate commands and/or signals.

Loud commands by handlers to their dogs create a poor impression of obedience and should be avoided. Shouting is not necessary even in a noisy place if the dog is properly trained to respond to a normal tone of voice. Commands which in the judge's opinion are excessively loud will be penalized.

Section 9. **Heel Position.** The heel position as used in these regulations whether the dog is sitting, standing, or moving at heel, means that the dog shall be straight in line with the direction in which the handler is facing, at the handler's left side, and as close as practicable to the handler's left leg without crowding, permitting the handler freedom of motion at all times. The area from the dog's head to shoulder shall be in line with the handler's left hip.

Section 10. **Heel on Leash.** The handler shall enter the ring with his dog on a loose leash and shall stand still with the dog sitting in the heel position until the judge asks if the handler is ready and then gives the order "Forward". The handler may give the command or signal to Heel, and shall start walking briskly and in a natural manner with the dog on loose leash. The dog shall walk close to the left side of the handler without crowding, permitting the handler freedom of motion at all times. At each order to "Halt", the handler will stop and his dog shall sit straight and smartly in the Heel position without command or signal and shall not move until ordered to do so. It is permissible after each Halt before moving again, for the handler to give the command or signal to Heel.

The leash may be held in either hand or in both hands, at the handler's option,

provided the hands are in a natural position. However, the handler and dog will
be penalized if, in the judge's opinion, the leash is used to signal or give assistance
to the dog.

Any tightening or jerking of the leash or any act, signal or command which in
the opinion of the judge gives the dog assistance shall be penalized. The judge
will give the orders "Forward", "Halt", "Right turn", "Left turn", "About turn",
"Slow", "Normal", and "Fast", which order signifies that both the handler and
dog must run, changing pace and moving forward at noticeably accelerated speed.
These orders may be given in any sequence and may be repeated if necessary. In
executing the About Turn, the handler will do a Right About Turn in all cases.
The judge will say "Exercise finished" after the heeling and then "Are you ready?"
before starting the Figure Eight.

The judge will order the handler to execute the "Figure Eight" which signifies
that the handler shall walk around and between the two stewards who shall stand
about 8 feet apart, or if there is only one steward, shall walk around and between
the judge and the steward. The Figure Eight in the Novice classes shall be done
on leash only. The handler may choose to go in either direction. There shall be
no About Turn in the Figure Eight, but the handler and dog shall go twice completely around the Figure Eight with at least one Halt during and another Halt
at the end of the exercise.

Section 11. **Stand for Examination.** The judge will give the order for examination and the handler will stand or pose his dog off leash, give the command
and/or signal to Stay, walk forward at least six feet in front of his dog, turn
around, and stand facing his dog. The method by which the dog is made to stand
or pose is optional with the handler who may take any reasonable time in posing
the dog, as in the show ring, before deciding to give the command and/or signal
to Stay. The judge will approach the dog from the front and will touch its head,
body and hindquarters only, and will then give the order "Back to your dog",
whereupon the handler will walk around behind his dog to the heel position.
The dog must remain in a standing position until the judge says "Exercise finished". The dog must show no shyness nor resentment at any time during the
exercise.

Section 12. **Heel Free.** This shall be executed in the same manner as Heel on
Leash except that the dog is off the leash. Heeling in both Novice and Open
classes is done in the same manner except that in the Open classes all work is
done off leash, including the Figure Eight.

Section 13. **Recall and Drop on Recall.** To execute the Recall to handler,
upon order or signal from the judge "Leave your dog", the dog is given the command and/or signal to stay in the sitting position while the handler walks towards
the other end of the ring, the distance to be about 40 feet. Upon order or signal
from the judge "Call your dog", the handler calls or signals the dog, which in
the Novice class must come straight in at a brisk pace and sit straight, centered
immediately in front of the handler's feet and close enough so that the handler
could readily touch its head without moving either foot or having to stretch forward. The dog shall not touch the handler nor sit between his feet. Upon order
or signal from the judge to "Finish", the dog on command or signal must go
smartly to the heel position and sit.

In the Open class, at a point designated by the judge, the dog must drop completely to a down position immediately on command or signal from the handler,
and must remain in the down position until, on order or signal from the judge,
the handler calls or signals the dog which must rise and complete the exercise

as in the Novice class. The method by which the dog goes to the heel position shall be optional with the handler provided it is done smartly and the dog sits straight at heel.

Section 14. **Long Sit.** In the Long Sit in the Novice classes all the competing dogs in the class take the exercise together, except that if there are 12 or more dogs they shall, at the judge's option, be judged in groups of not less than 6 nor more than 15 dogs. Where the same judge does both classes the separate classes may be combined provided there are not more than 15 dogs competing in the two classes combined. The dogs that are in the ring shall be lined up in catalog order along one of the four sides of the ring. Handlers' armbands, weighted with leashes or other articles if necessary, shall be placed behind the dogs. On order from the judge the handlers shall sit their dogs, if they are not already sitting, and on further order from the judge to "Leave your dogs" the handlers shall give the command and/or signal to Stay and immediately leave their dogs, go to the opposite side of the ring, and line up facing their respective dogs. After one minute from the time he has ordered the handlers to leave their dogs, the judge will order the handlers "Back to your dogs" whereupon the handlers must return promptly to their dogs, each walking around and in back of his own dog to the heel position. The dogs must not move from the sitting position until after the judge says "Exercise finished".

Section 15. **Long Down.** The Long Down in the Novice classes is done in the same manner as the Long Sit except that instead of sitting the dogs the handlers, on order from the judge, will down their dogs without touching the dogs or their collars, and except further that the judge will order the handlers back after three minutes. The dogs must stay in the down position until after the judge says "Exercise finished".

Section 16. **Open Classes, Long Sit and Long Down.** These exercises in the Open classes are performed in the same manner as in the Novice classes except that after leaving their dogs the handlers must cross to the opposite side of the ring, and then leave the ring in single file as directed by the judge and go to a place designated by the judge, completely out of sight of their dogs, where they must remain until called by the judge after the expiration of the time limit of three minutes in the Long Sit and five minutes in the Long Down, from the time the judge gave the order to "Leave your dogs". On order from the judge the handlers shall return to the ring in single file in reverse order, lining up facing their dogs at the opposite side of the ring, and returning to their dogs on order from the judge.

Section 17. **Retrieve on the Flat.** In retrieving the dumbbell on the flat, the handler stands with his dog sitting at the heel position in a place designated by the judge, and the judge gives the orders "Throw it", whereupon the handler may give the command and/or signal to Stay, which may not be given with the hand that is holding the dumbbell, and throws the dumbbell; "Send your dog", whereupon the handler gives the command or signal to his dog to retrieve; "Take it", whereupon the handler may give a command or signal and takes the dumbbell from the dog; "Finish", whereupon the handler gives the command or signal to heel as in the Recall. The dog shall not move forward to retrieve nor deliver to hand on return until given the command or signal by the handler following order by the judge. The retrieve shall be executed at a fast trot or gallop, without unnecessary mouthing or playing with the dumbbell. The dog shall sit straight, centered immediately in front of its handler's feet and close enough so that the handler can readily take the dumbbell without moving either foot or having to stretch forward. The dog shall not touch the handler nor sit between his feet.

The dumbbell, which must be approved by the judge, shall be made of one or more solid pieces of one of the heavy hardwoods, which shall not be hollowed out. It may be unfinished, or coated with a clear finish, or painted white. It shall have no decorations or attachments but may bear an inconspicuous mark for identification. The size of the dumbbell shall be proportionate to the size of the dog. The judge shall require the dumbbell to be thrown again before the dog is sent if, in his opinion, it is thrown too short a distance, or too far to one side, or against the ringside.

Section 18. **Retrieve over High Jump.** In retrieving the dumbbell over the High Jump, the exercise is executed in the same manner as the Retrieve on the Flat, except that the dog must jump the High Jump both going and coming. The High Jump shall be jumped clear and the jump shall be as nearly as possible one and one-half times the height of the dog at the withers, as determined by the judge, with a minimum height of 8 inches and a maximum height of 36 inches. This applies to all breeds with the following exceptions:

The jump shall be once the height of the dog at the withers or 36 inches, whichever is less, for the following breeds—

Bloodhounds, Bullmastiffs, Great Danes, Great Pyrenees, Mastiffs, Newfoundlands, St. Bernards.

The jump shall be once the height of the dog at the withers or 8 inches, whichever is greater, for the following breeds—

Spaniels (Clumber), Spaniels (Sussex), Basset Hounds, Dachshunds, Welsh Corgis (Cardigan), Welsh Corgis (Pembroke), Australian Terriers, Cairn Terriers, Dandie Dinmont Terriers, Norwich Terriers, Scottish Terriers, Sealyham Terriers, Skye Terriers, West Highland White Terriers, Maltese, Pekingese, Bulldogs, French Bulldogs.

The handler has the option of standing any reasonable distance from the High Jump, but must stay in the same spot throughout the exercise.

The side posts of the High Jump shall be 4 feet high and the jump shall be 5 feet wide and shall be so constructed as to provide adjustment for each 2 inches from 8 inches to 36 inches. It is suggested that the jump have a bottom board 8 inches wide including the space from the bottom of the board to the ground or floor, together with three other 8 inch boards, one 4 inch board, and one 2 inch board. The jump shall be painted a flat white. The width in inches, and nothing else, shall be painted on each side of each board in black 2 inch figures, the figure on the bottom board representing the distance from the ground or floor to the top of the board.

Section 19. **Broad Jump.** In the Broad Jump the handler will stand with his dog sitting at the heel position in front of and anywhere within 10 feet of the jump. On order from the judge to "Leave your dog", the handler will give his dog the command and/or signal to stay, and go to a position facing the right side of the jump, with his toes about 2 feet from the jump, and within the range of the first and last hurdles. On order from the judge the handler shall give the command or signal to jump and the dog shall clear the entire distance of the Broad Jump without touching and, without further command or signal, return to a sitting position immediately in front of the handler as in the Recall. The handler shall change his position by executing a right angle turn while the dog is in mid-air, but shall remain in the same spot. On order from the judge, the handler will give the command or signal to Heel and the dog shall finish as in the Recall.

The Broad Jump shall consist of four hurdles, built to telescope for convenience, made of boards about 8 inches wide, the largest measuring about 5 feet in length and 6 inches high at the highest point, all painted a flat white. When set up they shall be arranged in order of size and shall be evenly spaced so as to cover a distance equal to twice the height of the High Jump as set for the particular dog, with the low side of each hurdle and the lowest hurdle nearest the dog. The four hurdles shall be used for a jump of 52" to 72", three for a jump of 32" to 48", and two for a jump of 16" to 28". The highest hurdles shall be removed first.

Section 20. **Scent Discrimination.** In each of these two exercises the dog must select by scent alone and retrieve an article which has been handled by its handler. The articles shall be provided by the handler and these shall consist of two sets, each comprised of five identical articles not more than six inches in length, which may be items of everyday use. One set shall be made entirely of rigid metal, and one of leather of such design that nothing but leather is visible except for the minimum amount of thread or metal necessary to hold the article together. The articles in each set must be legibly numbered each with a different number, and must be approved by the judge.

The handler shall present all ten articles to the judge and the judge shall designate one article from each of the two sets, and shall make a written note of the numbers of the two articles he selects. These two handler's articles shall be placed on a table or chair in the ring until picked up by the handler who shall hold in his hand only one article at a time. The handler's scent may be imparted to the article only from his hands which must remain in plain sight. The handler has the option as to which article he picks up first. Before the start of the Scent Discrimination exercises the judge or the steward will handle each of the remaining 8 articles before placing them at random in the ring about 6 inches apart. The handler will stand about 15 feet from the articles with the dog sitting at heel position with their backs to the articles. On order from the judge, the handler immediately will place his article on the judge's book or work sheet and the judge, without touching the article with his hands, will place it among the other articles.

On order from the judge to "Send your dog", the handler and dog will execute a Right About Turn to face the articles and the handler will simultaneously give the command or signal to retrieve. The dog shall not again sit after turning, but shall go directly to the articles. The handler may give his scent to the dog by gently touching the dog's nose with the palm of one open hand, but this may only be done while the dog is sitting at heel and the hand must be returned to the handler's side before handler and dog turn to face the articles. The dog shall go at a brisk pace to the articles. It may take any reasonable time to select the right article, but only provided it works continuously and does not pick up any article other than the one with its handler's scent. After picking up the right article the dog shall return at a brisk pace and complete the exercise as in the Retrieve on the Flat.

The same procedure is followed in each of the two Scent Discrimination exercises. Should a dog retrieve a wrong article in the first exercise, it shall be placed on the table or chair, and the handler's article must also be taken up from the remaining articles. The second exercise shall then be completed with one less article in the ring.

Section 21. **Directed Retrieve.** In this exercise the handler will stand with his dog sitting in the heel position, midway between the two jumps. The handler will provide three short, predominantly white, work gloves, which must be open and must be approved by the judge. The judge or steward shall place the three gloves across the end of the ring in front of the handler and dog, one in each corner and one in the center, about three feet from the end and/or side of the ring. There shall be no table or chair at this end of the ring.

The judge will give the order "Left" or "Right" or "Center". The handler must give the command to Heel and turn with his dog to face the designated glove, if necessary, but may not turn completely around nor touch the dog to get it in position. The handler will then give his dog the direction to the designated glove with his left hand and arm, and the command to retrieve. The dog shall go directly to the glove at a brisk pace and retrieve it without unnecessary mouthing or playing with it, completing the exercise as in Retrieve on the Flat.

The handler may bend his knees and body in giving the direction to the dog and in giving the command to retrieve, after which the handler will stand erect with his arms at his sides. The exercise shall consist of a single retrieve, but the judge shall designate different glove positions for successive dogs.

Section 22. **Signal Exercise.** In the Signal Exercise the heeling is done in the same manner as in the Heel Free exercise except that throughout the entire exercise the handler uses signals only and must not speak to his dog at any time. On order from the judge "Forward", the handler signals his dog to walk at heel and then, on specific order from the judge in each case, the handler and the dog execute a "Left turn", "Right turn", "About turn", "Halt", "Slow", "Normal", "Fast." These orders may be given in any sequence and may be repeated if necessary. Then on order from the judge, and while the dog is walking at heel, the handler signals his dog to Stand in the heel position near the end of the ring, and on further order from the judge "Leave your dog", the handler signals his dog to Stay, goes to the far end of the ring, and turns to face his dog. Then on separate and specific signals from the judge in each case, the handler will give the signals to Drop, to Sit, to Come and to Finish as in the Recall. During the heeling part of this exercise the handler may not give any signal except where a command or signal is permitted in the Heeling exercises.

Section 23. **Directed Jumping.** In the Directed Jumping exercise the jumps shall be placed midway in the ring at right angles to the sides of the ring and 18 to 20 feet apart, the Bar Jump on one side, the High Jump on the other. The handler from a position on the center line of the ring and about 20 feet from the line of the jumps, stands with his dog sitting in the heel position. On order from the judge "Send your dog", he commands and/or signals his dog to go forward at a brisk pace toward the other end of the ring to an equal distance beyond the jumps and in the approximate center where the handler gives the command to Sit, whereupon the dog must stop and sit with its attention on the handler, but need not sit squarely. The judge will then designate which jump is to be taken first by the dog, whereupon the handler commands and/or signals his dog to return to him over the designated jump, the dog sitting in front of the handler and finishing as in the Recall. While the dog is in mid-air the handler may turn so as to be facing the dog as it returns. The judge will say "Exercise finished" after the dog has returned to the heel position. When the dog is again sitting in the heel position for the second part of the exercise, the judge will ask "Are you ready?" before giving the order "Send your dog" for the second jump. The same procedure is to be followed for the dog taking the opposite jump. It is optional with the judge which jump is taken first but both jumps must be taken to complete the exercise and the judge must not designate the jump until the dog is at the far end of the ring.

The height of the jumps shall be the same as required in the Open classes. The High Jump shall be the same as that used in the Open classes, and the Bar Jump shall consist of a bar between 2 and 2½ inches square with the four edges rounded sufficiently to remove any sharpness. The bar shall be painted a flat black and white in alternate sections of about 3 inches each. The bar shall be supported by two unconnected 4 foot upright posts about 5 feet apart. The bar shall be adjustable for each 2 inches of height from 8 inches to 36 inches, and the jump shall be so constructed and positioned that the bar can be knocked off without disturbing the uprights. The dog shall clear the jumps without touching them.

Section 24. **Group Examination.** All the competing dogs take this exercise together, except that if there are 12 or more dogs, they shall be judged in groups of not less than 6 nor more than 15 dogs, at the judge's option. The handlers and dogs that are in the ring shall line up in catalog order, side by side down the center of the ring with the dogs at heel position. Each handler shall place his armband, weighted with leash or other article, if necessary, behind his dog. On order from the judge to "Stand your dogs", all the handlers will stand or pose their dogs, and on order from the judge "Leave your dogs", all the handlers will give the command and/or signal to Stay, walk forward to the side of the ring, then about turn and face their dogs. The judge will approach each dog in turn from the front and examine it, going over the dog with his hands as in dog show judging. When all dogs have been examined, and after the handlers have been away from their dogs for at least three minutes, the judge will promptly order the handlers "Back to your dogs", and the handlers will walk around behind their dogs to the heel position, after which the judge will say "Exercise finished". Each dog must remain standing at its position in the line from the time its handler leaves it until the end of the exercise, and must show no shyness nor resentment.

Section 25. **Tracking.** The tracking test must be performed with the dog on leash, the length of the track to be not less than 440 yards nor more than 500 yards, the scent to be not less than one half hour nor more than two hours old and that of a stranger who will leave an inconspicuous glove or wallet, dark in color, at the end of the track where it must be found by the dog and picked up by the dog or handler. The article must be approved in advance by the judges. The tracklayer will follow the track which has been staked out with flags a day or more earlier, collecting all the flags on the way with the exception of one flag at the start of the track and one flag about 30 yards from the start of the track to indicate the direction of the track; then deposit the article at the end of the track and leave the course, proceeding straight ahead at least 50 feet. The tracklayer must wear his own shoes which, if not having leather soles, must have uppers of fabric or leather. The dog shall wear a harness to which is attached a leash between 20 and 40 feet in length. The handler shall follow the dog at a distance of not less than 20 feet, and the dog shall not be guided by the handler. The dog may be restrained by the handler, but any leading or guiding of the dog constitutes grounds for calling the handler off and marking the dog "Failed". A dog may, at the handler's option, be given one, and only one, second chance to take the scent between the two flags, provided it has not passed the second flag.

The Club or Tracking Test Secretary, after a licensed or member tracking test, shall forward the two copies of the judges' marked charts, the entry forms with certifications attached, and a marked and certified copy of the catalog pages or sheets listing the dogs entered in the tracking test, to The American Kennel Club so as to reach its office within seven days after the close of the test.

CHAPTER 3

Regulations for Judging

Section 1. **Standardized Judging.** Standardized judging is of paramount importance. Judges are not permitted to inject their own variations into the exercises, but must see that each handler and dog executes the various exercises exactly as described in these regulations. A handler who is familiar with these regulations.

should be able to enter the ring under any judge without having to inquire how the particular judge wishes to have any exercise performed, and without being confronted with some unexpected requirement.

Section 1-A. **Handicapped Handlers.** Judges may modify the specific requirements of these regulations for handlers to the extent necessary to permit physically handicapped handlers to compete, provided such handlers can move about the ring without physical assistance or guidance from another person, except for guidance from the judge or from the handler of a competing dog in the ring for the group exercises. Dogs handled by such handlers shall be required to perform all parts of all exercises as described in these regulations, and shall be penalized for failure to perform any part of an exercise.

Section 2. **Judge's Report on Ring and Equipment.** The Superintendent and the officials of the club holding the obedience trial are responsible for providing rings and equipment which meet the requirements of these regulations. However, the judge must check the ring and equipment provided for his use before starting to judge, and must report to The American Kennel Club after the trial any undesirable ring conditions or deficiencies that have not been promptly corrected at his request.

Section 3. **Stewards.** The judge is in sole charge of his ring until his assignment is completed. Stewards are provided to assist him, but they may act only on the judge's instructions. Stewards shall not give information or instructions to owners and handlers except as specifically instructed by the judge, and then only in such a manner that it is clear that the instructions are those of the judge.

Section 4. **Training and Disciplining in the Ring.** The judge shall not permit any handler to train his dog nor to practice any exercise in the ring either before or after he is judged, and shall deduct points from the total score of any dog whose handler does this. A handler who disciplines his dog in the ring must be severely penalized. The penalty shall be deducted from the points available for the exercise during which the disciplining may occur, and additional points may be deducted from the total score if necessary. If the disciplining does not occur during an exercise the penalty shall be deducted from the total score. Any abuse of a dog in the ring must be immediately reported by the judge to the Bench Show or Obedience Trial Committee for action under Chapter 1, Section 43.

Section 5. **Catalog Order.** Dogs should be judged in catalog order to the extent that it is practicable to do so without holding up the judging in any ring for a dog that is entered in more than one class at the show or trial.

Judges are not required to wait for dogs for either the individual exercises or the group exercises. It is the responsibility of each contestant to be ready with his dog at ringside when required, without waiting to be called. The judge's first consideration should be the convenience of those exhibitors who are at ringside with their dogs when scheduled, and who ask no favors.

A judge may agree, on request in advance, to judge a dog earlier or later than the time scheduled by catalog order if the same dog is entered in another class which may conflict. However, a judge should not hesitate to mark absent and to refuse to judge any dog and handler that are not at ringside ready to be judged in catalog order if no such arrangement has been made in advance, nor if the dog is available while its handler is occupied with some other dog or dogs at the show or trial.

Section 6. **Judge's Book and Score Sheets.** The judge must enter the scores and sub-total score of each dog in the official judge's book immediately after each dog has been judged on the individual exercises and before judging the next dog. Scores for the group exercises and total scores must be entered in the official judge's book immediately after each group of dogs has been judged. No score may be changed except to correct an arithmetical error or if a score has been entered in the wrong column. All final scores must be entered in the judge's book before prizes are awarded. No person other than the judge may make any entry in the judge's book. Judges may use separate score sheets for their own purposes, but shall not give out nor allow exhibitors to see such sheets, nor give out any other written scores, nor permit anyone else to distribute score sheets or cards prepared by the judge. Carbon copies of the sheets in the official judge's book shall be made available through the Superintendent or Show or Trial Secretary for examination by owners and handlers immediately after the prizes have been awarded in each class. If score cards are distributed by a club after the prizes are awarded they must contain no more information than is shown in the judge's book and must be marked "unofficial score".

Section 7. **Announcement of Scores.** The judge shall not disclose any score or partial score to contestants or spectators until he has completed the judging of the entire class or, in case of a split class, until he has completed the judging of his division; nor shall he permit anyone else to do so. After all the scores are recorded for the class, or for the division in case of a split class, the judge shall call for all available dogs that have won qualifying scores to be brought into the ring. Before awarding the prizes, the judge shall inform the spectators as to the maximum number of points for a perfect score, and shall then announce the score of each prize winner, and announce to the handler the score of each dog that has won a qualifying score.

Section 8. **Explanations and Errors.** The judge is not required to explain his scoring, and should not enter into any discussion with any contestant who appears to be dissatisfied. Any interested person who thinks that there may have been an arithmetical error or an error in identifying a dog may report the facts to one of the stewards or to the Superintendent or Show or Trial Secretary so that the matter may be checked.

Section 9. **Rejudging.** If a dog has failed in a particular part of an exercise, it shall not ordinarily be rejudged nor given a second chance; but if in the judge's opinion the dog's performance was prejudiced by peculiar and unusual conditions, the judge may at his own discretion rejudge the dog on the entire exercise.

Section 10. **Ties.** In case of a tie for any prize in a class, the dogs shall be tested again by having them perform at the same time all or some part of one or more of the regular exercises in that class. In the Utility class the dogs shall perform at the same time all or some part of the Signal exercise. The original scores shall not be changed.

Section 11. **Judge's Directions.** The judge's orders and signals should be given to the handlers in a clear and understandable manner, but in such a way that the work of the dog is not disturbed. Before starting each exercise, the judge shall ask "Are you ready?" At the end of each exercise the judge shall say "Exercise finished". Each contestant must be worked and judged separately except for the Long Sit, Long Down, and Group Examination exercises, and in running off a tie.

Section 12. **A and B Classes and Different Breeds.** The same methods and standards must be used for judging and scoring the A and B Classes, and in judging and scoring the work of dogs of different breeds.

Section 13. **No Added Requirements.** No judge shall require any dog or handler to do anything, not penalize a dog or handler for failing to do anything, that is not required by these regulations.

Section 14. **Additional Commands or Signal and Interference.** If a handler gives an additional command or signal not permitted by these regulations, either when no command or signal is permitted, or simultaneously with or following a permitted command or signal, or if he uses the dog's name with a permitted signal but without a permitted command, the dog shall be scored as though it had failed completely to perform that particular part of the exercise. A judge who is aware of any assistance, interference, or attempts to control a dog from outside the ring, must act promptly to stop any such double handling or interference, and should penalize the dog or give it less than a qualifying score if in his opinion it received such aid.

Section 15. **Standard of Perfection.** The judge must carry a mental picture of the theoretically perfect performance in each exercise and score each dog and handler against this visualized standard which shall combine the utmost in willingness, enjoyment and precision on the part of the dog, and naturalness, gentleness, and smoothness in handling. Lack of willingness or enjoyment on the part of the dog must be penalized, as must lack of precision in the dog's performance, and roughness in handling. There shall be no penalty of less than ½ point or multiple of ½ point.

Section 16. **Qualifying Performance.** A judge's certification in his judge's book of a qualifying score for any particular dog constitutes his certification to The American Kennel Club that the dog on this particular occasion has performed all of the required exercises at least in accordance with the minimum standards and that its performance on this occasion would justify the awarding of the obedience title associated with the particular class. A qualifying score must never be awarded to a dog whose performance has not met the minimum requirements, nor to a dog that shows fear or resentment, or that relieves itself at any time in an indoor ring, or that relieves itself while performing any exercise indoors or outdoors, nor to a dog whose handler disciplines or abuses it in the ring, or carries or offers food in the ring.

In deciding whether the faulty performance of a particular exercise by a particular dog warrants a qualifying score or a score that is something less than 50% of the available points, the judge shall consider whether the awarding of an obedience title would be justified if all dogs competing in the class performed the exercise in a similar manner; and must give a score of less than 50% of the available points if he decides that it would be contrary to the best interests of the sport if all dogs competing in the class performed in a similar manner on all occasions.

Section 17. **Orders and Minimum Penalties.** The orders for the exercises and the standards for judging are set forth in the following sections. The lists of faults are not intended to be complete but minimum penalties are specified for most of the more common and serious faults. There is no maximum limit on penalties. A dog which makes none of the errors listed may still fail to qualify or may be scored zero for other reasons.

Section 18. **Heel on Leash.** The orders for this exercise are "Forward", "Halt", "Right turn", "Left turn", "About turn", "Slow", "Normal", "Fast", "Figure eight". These orders may be given in any order and may be repeated, if necessary, but the judge shall attempt to standardize the heeling pattern for all dogs in any class. The principal feature of this exercise is the ability of the dog to work as a team with its handler. A dog that is unmanageable must be scored zero. Where a handler continually tugs on the leash or adapts his pace to that of the dog, the judge must score such a dog less than 50% of the available points. Substantial deductions shall be made for additional commands or signals to Heel and for failure of dog or handler to change pace noticeably for Slow and Fast. Minor deductions shall be made for such things as poor sits, occasionally guiding the dog with the leash, heeling wide, and other imperfections in heeling. In judging this exercise the judge shall follow the handler at a discreet distance so that he may observe any signals or commands given by the handler to the dog, but without interfering with either dog or handler.

Section 19. **Stand for Examination.** The orders for this exercise are "Stand your dog for examination", "Back to your dog". The principal features of this exercise are to stand in position before and during examination and to show no shyness nor resentment. A dog that sits before or during the examination or growls or snaps must be marked zero. A dog that moves away from the place where it was left before or during the examination, or a dog that shows any shyness or resentment, must receive less than 50% of the available points. Depending on the circumstances in each case, minor or substantial deductions must be made for any dog that moves its feet at any time, or that sits, or moves away after the examination is completed. The examination shall consist of touching only the dog's head, body and hindquarters with the fingers and palm of one hand. The scoring of this exercise will not start until the handler has given the command and/or signal to Stay, except for such things as rough treatment of the dog by its handler or active resistance by the dog to its handler's attempts to make it stand, which shall be penalized substantially.

Section 20. **Heel Free.** The orders and scoring for this exercise shall be the same as for Heel on Leash except that the Figure Eight is omitted in the Heel Free exercise in the Novice classes.

Section 21. **Recall.** The orders for this exercise are "Leave your dog", "Call your dog", "Finish". The principal features of this exercise are the prompt response to the handler's command or signal to Come, and the Stay from the time the handler leaves the dog until he calls it. A dog that does not come on the first command or signal must be scored zero. A dog that does not stay without extra command or signal, or that moves from the place where it was left, from the time the handler leaves until it is called, or that does not come close enough so that the handler could readily touch its head without moving either foot or having to stretch forward, must receive less than 50% of the points. Substantial deductions shall be made for a slow response to the Come, depending on the specific circumstances in each case; for extra commands or signals to Stay if given before the handler leaves the dog; for a dog that stands or lies down; for extra commands or signals to Finish; and for failure to Sit or Finish. Minor deductions shall be made for poor or slow Sits or Finishes, and for a dog that touches the handler on coming in or sits between his feet.

Section 22. **Long Sit and Long Down.** The orders for these exercises are "Sit your dogs" or "Down your dogs", "Leave your dogs", "Back to your dogs". The principal features of these exercises are to stay, and to remain in the sitting or down position, whichever is required by the particular exercise. A dog that at any time during the exercise moves a substantial distance away from the place where it was left, or that goes over to any other dog, must be marked zero. A dog that stays on the spot where it was left but that fails to remain in the sitting or down position, whichever is required by the particular exercise, until the handler has returned to the heel position, and a dog that repeatedly barks or whines, must receive less than 50% of the available points. A substantial deduction shall be made for any dog that moves even a minor distance away from the place where it was left or that barks or whines only once or twice. Depending on the circumstances in each case, a substantial or minor deduction shall be made for touching the dog or for forcing it into the Down position. There shall be a minor deduction for sitting after the handler is in the heel position but before the judge has said "Exercise finished" in the Down exercises. The dogs shall not be required to sit at the end of the Down exercises.

If a dog gets up and starts to roam or follows its handler, the judge shall promptly instruct the handler or one of the stewards to take the dog out of the ring or to keep it away from the other dogs. The judge should not attempt to judge the dogs or handlers on the manner in which they are made to Sit. The scoring of the Long Sit exercise will generally start after the judge has given the order "Leave your dogs", except for such general things as rough treatment of a dog by its handler or active resistance by a dog to its handler's attempts to make it Sit.

During these exercises the judge shall stand in such a position that all of the dogs are in his line of vision, and where he can see all the handlers in the ring, or leaving and returning to the ring, without having to turn around.

Section 23. **Drop on Recall.** The orders for this exercise are the same as for the Recall, except that the dog is required to drop when coming in on command or signal from its handler when ordered by the judge, and except that an additional order or signal to "Call your dog" is given by the judge after the Drop. The dog's prompt response to the handler's command or signal to Drop is a principal feature of this exercise, in addition to the prompt responses and the Stays as described under Recall above. A dog that does not stop and drop completely on a single command or signal must be scored zero. Minor or substantial deductions shall be made for a slow drop, depending on whether the dog is just short of perfection in this respect, or very slow in dropping or somewhere between the two extremes. All other deductions as listed under Recall above shall also apply.

The judge may designate the point at which the handler is to give the command or signal to drop by some marker placed in advance which will be clear to the handler but not obvious to the dog, or he may give the handler a signal for the Drop, but such signal must be given in such a way as not to attract the dog's attention.

If a point is designated, the dog is still to be judged on its prompt response to the handler's command or signal rather than on its proximity to the designated point.

Section 24. **Retrieve on the Flat.** The orders for this exercise are "Throw it", "Send your dog", "Take it", "Finish". The principal feature of this exercise is to retrieve promptly. Any dog that fails to go out on the first command or a dog that fails to retrieve, shall be marked zero. A dog that goes to retrieve before the command or signal is given, or that does not return with the dumbbell sufficiently close so that the handler can readily take it without moving either foot or stretching forward, must receive less than 50% of the points. Depending on the specific circumstances in each case, minor or substantial deductions shall be made for slowness in going out or returning or in picking up the dumbbell, mouthing or playing with the dumbbell, dropping the dumbbell, slowness in releasing the dumbbell to the handler, touching the handler on coming in, sitting between his feet, failure to sit in front or to Finish. Minor deductions shall be made for poor or slow Sits or Finishes.

Section 25. **Retrieve over High Jump.** The orders for this exercise are "Throw it", "Send your dog", "Take it", and "Finish". The principal features of this exercise are that the dog must go out over the jump, pick up the dumbbell and promptly return with it over the jump. The minimum penalties shall be the same as for the Retrieve on the Flat, and in addition a dog that fails both going and returning to go over the High Jump, must be marked zero. A dog that retrieves properly but goes over the High Jump in only one direction, must receive less than 50% of the available points. Substantial deductions must be made for a dog that climbs the jump or uses the top of the jump for aid in going over, in contrast to a dog that merely touches the jump. Minor deductions shall be made for touching the jump in going over.

The jumps may be preset by the stewards based on the handler's advice as to the dog's height. The judge must make certain that the jump is set at the required height for each dog. He shall verify with an ordinary folding rule or steel tape to the nearest one-half inch, the height at the withers of each dog that jumps less than 36 inches. He shall not base his decision as to the height of the jump on the handler's advice.

Section 26. **Broad Jump.** The orders for this exercise are "Leave your dog", "Send your dog", and "Finish". Any dog that refuses the jump on the first command or signal or walks over any part of the jump must be marked zero. A dog that fails to stay until the handler gives the command or signal to jump, or that fails to clear the full distance with its forelegs, shall receive less than 50% of the available points. There shall be minor penalties for failure to return smartly to the handler and to sit straight in front of the handler or finish correctly, as in the Recall. It is the judge's responsibility to see that the distance jumped is that required by these Regulations for the particular dog.

Section 27. **Scent Discrimination.** The orders for each of these two exercises are "Send your dog", "Take it", and "Finish". The principal features of these exercises are the selection of the handler's article from among the other articles by scent alone, and the prompt carrying of the right article to the handler after its selection. The minimum penalties shall be the same as for the Retrieve on the Flat and in addition a dog that fails to go out to the group of articles, or that retrieves a wrong article, or that fails to bring the right article to the handler, must be marked zero for the particular exercise. Substantial deductions shall be made for a dog that picks up a wrong article, even though it puts it down again immediately, and for any roughness by the handler in imparting his scent to the dog. Minor or substantial deductions, depending on the circumstances in each case, shall be made for a dog that is slow or inattentive, or that does not work continuously. There shall be no penalty for a dog that takes a reasonably long time examining the articles, provided it is working smartly and continuously.

The judge shall select one article from each of the two sets and shall make written notes of the numbers of the two articles selected. The handler has the option as to which article he picks up first, but must give up each article immediately when ordered by the judge. The judge must see to it that the handler imparts his scent to the article only with his hands and that, between the time the handler picks up each article and the time he gives it to the judge, the article is held continuously in the handler's hands which must remain in plain sight. The judge or his steward must handle each of the eight other articles as he places them in the ring. The judge must make sure that they are properly separated before the dog is sent so that there may be no confusion of scent between articles.

Section 28. **Directed Retrieve.** The orders for this exercise are "Right", or "Center", or "Left", "Take it" and "Finish". The principal features of this exercise are that the dog stay until directed to retrieve, that it go directly to the designated glove, and that it retrieve promptly. A dog that fails to go out on command or that fails to go directly in a straight line to the glove designated, or that fails to retrieve the glove shall be marked zero. A dog that goes to retrieve before the command is given or that does not return promptly with the glove sufficiently close so that the handler can readily take it without moving either foot or stretching forward, must receive less than 50% of the available points. Depending on the specific circumstances in each case, minor or substantial deductions shall be made for touching the dog or for excessive movements in getting it to heel facing the designated glove, for slowness or hesitation in going out or returning or in picking up the glove, for mouthing or playing with the glove, for dropping the glove, for slowness in releasing it to the handler, and for failure to sit in front or to Finish. Minor deductions shall be made for poor or slow Sits or Finishes.

Section 29. **Signal Exercise.** The orders for this exercise are "Forward", "Left turn", "Right turn", "About turn", "Halt", "Slow", "Normal", "Fast", "Stand", and "Leave your dog", and in addition the judge must give the handler signals to signal his dog to Drop, to Sit, to Come, to Finish. The orders for those parts of the exercise which are done with the dog at heel may be given in any order and may be repeated if necessary, except that the order to "Stand" shall be given when the dog and handler are walking at a normal pace. The signals given the handler after he has left his dog in the Stand position shall be given in the order specified above. The principal features of this exercise are the heeling of the dog and the Come on signal as described for the Heel and Recall exercises, and the prompt response to the other signals given to the dog at a distance. A dog that fails, on a single signal from the handler, to stand or remain standing where left, or to drop, or to sit and stay, or to come, or that receives a command or audible signal from the handler to do any of these parts of the exercise, shall receive less than 50% of the available points. All of the deductions listed under the Heel and Recall exercises shall also apply to this exercise.

Section 30. **Directed Jumping.** The judge's first order is "Send your dog". Then, after the dog has stopped at the far end of the ring, the judge shall designate which jump is to be taken by the dog, whereupon the handler commands and/or signals his dog to return to him over the designated jump, the dog sitting in front of the handler and finishing as in the Recall. After the dog returns to the handler the order "Finish" is given followed by "Exercise Finished". The same sequence is then followed for the other jump. The principal features of this exercise are that the dog goes away from the handler in the direction indicated, stops when comanded, jumps as directed, and returns as in the Recall.

A dog that, in either half of the exercise, anticipates the handler's command and/or signal to go out, that does not leave its handler, that does not go out between the jumps and a substantial distance beyond, that does not stop on command, that anticipates the handler's command and/or signal to jump, that does not jump as directed, or a dog that knocks the bar off the uprights or climbs over the High Jump or uses the top of the High Jump for aid in going over, must receive less than 50% of the available points. Substantial deductions shall be made for anticipating the Turn, Stop or Sit, and for failure to Sit. Substantial or minor deductions shall be made for faults such as slowness in going out or returning, slow response to direction, and poor sits or finishes, depending on the specific circumstances in each case.

The judge must make certain that the jumps are set at the required height for each dog by following the same procedure described for the Retrieve over High Jump.

Section 31. **Group Examination.** The orders for this exercise are "Stand your dogs", "Leave your dogs", and "Back to your dogs". The principal features of this exercise are that the dog must stand and stay, and must show no shyness nor resentment. A dog that moves a substantial distance away from the place where it was left, or that goes over to any other dog, or that sits or lies down before the handler returns to the heel position, or that growls or snaps at any time, must be marked zero. A dog that remains standing but that moves a minor distance away from the place where it was left, or a dog that shows any shyness or resentment or that repeatedly barks or whines, must receive less than 50% of the available points. Depending on the specific circumstances in each case, minor or substantial deductions must be made for any dog that moves its feet at any time during the exercise, or sits or lies down after the handler has returned to the heel position. The judge should not attempt to judge the dogs or handlers on the manner in which the dogs are made to stand. The scoring will normally start after the judge has given the order "Leave your dogs", except for such general things as rough treatment of a dog by its handler, or active resistance by a dog to its handler's attempts to make it stand. The dogs are not required to sit at the end of this exercise. The examination shall be conducted as in dog show judging, the judge going over each dog carefully with his hands. The judge must make a written record of any deductions immediately after examining each dog, subject to further deduction of points for subsequent faults. The judge must instruct one or more stewards to watch the other dogs while he conducts the individual examinations, and to call any faults to his attention.

Section 32. **Tracking Tests.** For obvious reasons these tests cannot be held at a dog show, and a person, though he may be qualified to judge Obedience Trials, is not necessarily capable of judging a tracking test. He must be familiar with the various conditions that may exist when a dog is required to do nose work. Scent conditions, weather, lay of the land, etc., must be taken into consideration, and a thorough knowledge of this work is necessary.

One or both of the judges must personally lay out or walk over each track after it has been laid out, a day or so before the test, so as to be completely familiar with the location of the track, landmarks and ground conditions. At least two of the major turns shall be well out in the open country where there are no fences or other boundaries to guide the dog. No major part of any track shall follow along any fence or boundary within 15 yards of such boundary. The track shall include at least two right angle turns and should include more than two such turns so that the dog may be observed working in different wind directions. Acute angle turns should be avoided whenever possible. No conflicting tracks shall be laid. No track shall cross any body of water. No part of any track shall be laid within 75 yards of any other track. In the case of two tracks going in opposite directions, however, the first flags of these tracks may be as close as 50 yards from each other. The judges shall make sure that the track is no less than 440 yards and that the tracklayer is a stranger to the dog in each case. It is the judges' responsibility to instruct the tracklayer to insure that each track is properly laid and that each tracklayer carries a copy of the chart with him in laying the track. The judges must approve the article to be left at the end of each track and must see that it is thoroughly impregnated with the tracklayer's scent and that the tracklayer's shoes meet the requirements of these regulations.

There is no time limit provided the dog is working, but a dog that is off the track and is clearly not working should not be given any minimum time, but should be marked Failed. The handler may not be given any assistance by the judges or anyone else. If a dog is not trailing it shall not be marked Passed even though it may have found the article. In case of unforseen circumstances, the judges may in rare cases, at their own discretion, give a handler and his dog a second chance on a new track. A track for each dog entered shall be plotted on the ground not less than one day before the test, the track being marked by flags which the tracklayer can follow readily on the day of the test. A chart of each track shall be made up in duplicate, showing the approximate length in yards of each leg, and major landmarks and boundaries, if any. Two of these charts shall be marked, one by each of the judges, at the time the dog is tracking, so as to show the approximate course followed by the dog. The judges shall sign their charts and show on each whether the dog "Passed" or "Failed", the time the tracklayer started, the time the dog started and finished tracking, a brief description of ground, wind and weather conditions, the wind direction, and a note of any steep hills or valleys.

NEW

OBEDIENCE JUDGE'S WORKSHEET
For Judge's Use ONLY — Not to be distributed or shown to exhibitors

DATE . . . .

SHOW . . . .

NOVICE......CLASS
(A or B)

BREED. . . . .

DOG No. . . . . . .

EXERCISE	NON QUALIFYING ZERO	NON QUALIFYING LESS THAN 50%	QUALIFYING SUBSTANTIAL	QUALIFYING MINOR	Maximum Points	Points Lost	NET SCORE
HEEL ON LEASH AND FIGURE 8	Unmanageable ......☐ Unqualified heeling..☐	Handler continually adapts pace to dog..☐ Constant tugging on leash or guiding....☐	Heeling Fig.8 ☐... Improper heel position ....☐ ☐ ☐... Occasional tight leash........☐ ☐ ☐... Forging .. ☐ Crowding handler..☐ ☐ ☐... Lagging .. ☐ Sniffing..........☐ ☐ ☐... Extra command to heel ....☐ ☐... Heeling wide ☐ Turns ☐ Abouts☐ ☐... No change of pace ☐ Fast ☐Slow☐ ☐... No sits.............Poor sits☐ ☐ ☐... Lack of naturalness smoothness ☐ ☐		**35**		
STAND FOR EXAMINATION	Sits before or during examination ....☐ Growls or snaps ....☐	Moves away before or during examination ....☐ Shows shyness or resentment ....☐	☐... Resistance to handler posing ....☐ ☐... Extra command to stay ....☐ ☐... Moving slightly during exam........☐ ☐... Moving after examination ....☐ ☐... Sits as handler returns ....☐ ☐... Lack of naturalness smoothness .....☐		**30**		
HEEL OFF LEASH	Unmanageable ......☐ Unqualified heeling..☐	Handler continually adapts pace to dog ....☐ Leaving handler.....☐	☐... Improper heel position ....☐ ☐... Forging ....☐ Crowding handler ☐ ☐... Lagging ....☐ Sniffing ....☐ ☐... Extra command to heel ☐... No change of pace ☐Fast ☐ Slow ☐... No sits ....Poor sits☐ ☐... Lack of naturalness smoothness ....☐		**45**		
RECALL	Didn't come on first command or signal ....☐	Extra command or signal to stay .....☐ Moved from position .☐ Anticipated recall command ....☐ Sat out of reach.....☐ Leaving handler.....☐	☐ Stood or lay down Touched handler ☐ ☐ Slow response Sat between feet ☐ ☐ No sit Poor sit ☐ ☐ No finish Poor finish ☐ ☐ Extra command to Lack of naturalness finish or smoothness ☐		**30**		
			MAX SUB-TOTAL		**140**		
LONG SIT (1 Minute)	Did not remain in place ....☐ Goes to another dog...............☐	Stood or lay down before handler returns .☐ Repeated whines or barks ....☐	☐ Forcing into position ☐ Minor move before handler returns ☐ Minor whine or bark	Stood or lay down after handler returns to heel position ....☐	**30**		
LONG DOWN (3 Minutes)	Did not remain in place ....☐ Goes to another dog...............☐	Sat or stood before handler returns.....☐ Repeated whines or barks ....☐	☐ Forcing into position ☐ Minor move before handler returns ☐ Minor whine or bark	Sat or stood after handler returns to heel position ....☐	**30**		
			MAX. POINTS ➡		**200**		

☐ H. Disciplining ☐ Shows fear ☐ Fouling ring ☐ Disqualified ☐ Expelled ☐ Excused   Less Penalty for Unusual Behavior ➡

EXPLANATION OF PENALTY   **TOTAL NET SCORE** ➡

Fig. 42a. This chart, and the four that follow are reproduced by courtesy of the Ralston Purina Company. Training clubs may obtain free copies of the charts from the Purina Pet Care Center, St. Louis, Mo. 63199.

OBEDIENCE TRIAL SCORE BREAKDOWN

GRADUATE NOVICE CLASS   Dog No. ....

SHOW...

DATE...

JUDGE...   BREED...

EXERCISE	MAXIMUM POINTS	NON-QUALIFYING		QUALIFYING (OVER 50%)		SCORE
		ZERO	LESS THAN 50%	SUBSTANTIAL	MINOR	
HEEL ON LEASH	**35**	Unmanageable......☐ Unqualified Heeling..☐	Handler continually adapts pace to dog..☐ Constant tight leash, or guiding..........☐	☐........Dog interferes with handler........☐ ☐........Extra commands or signals........☐ ☐.................Sluggish.................☐ ☐..................Sniffing..................☐ ☐...................Lagging...................☐ ☐...................Forging...................☐ ☐........Heeling wide—turns—abouts......☐ ☐................Poor sits................☐ ☐ Handler error................................☐	
STAND FOR EXAMINATION OFF LEAD	**30**	Sits before or during examination.........☐ Growls or snaps......☐	Moves away before or during examination..........☐ Shows shyness or resentment.........☐	☐.........Extra command or signal.........☐ ☐.................Moving feet.................☐ ☐....Moves after examination completed....☐ ☐.........Sits as handler returns...........☐ ☐ Handler error................................☐	
HEEL FREE AND FIGURE 8	**45**	Unmanageable......☐ Unqualified heeling..☐	Handler continually adapts self to dog...☐	Heeling Fig.8 ☐.....Extra commands or signals......☐....☐ ☐.....Forging ....☐....☐ ☐.....Crowding handler..............☐....☐ ☐.....Sniffing.....................☐....☐ ☐.....Lagging......................☐....☐ ☐.Heeling wide - on turns - abouts.....☐....☐ ☐....Poor sits.....................☐....☐ ☐ Handler error....................☐....☐	
DROP ON RECALL	**30**	Does not come on first command or signal...............☐ Does not drop on first command or signal...............☐	Extra command or signal to stay after handler leaves......☐ Does not wait for recall...............☐ Anticipated come after drop..........☐ ☐.............Anticipated drop.............☐	Extra command or signal to stay ☐...........before handler leaves...........☐ ☐................Holds Signal................☐ ☐ Extra command or signal to finish ☐ No sit in front Poor sit............☐ ☐ No finish Poor finish........☐	
SUB-TOTAL	**140**					
LONG SIT (3 MINUTES) Handler out of sight	**30**	Did not remain in place..............☐ Disturbed other dog..☐	Stood or lay down before handler returns to heel position.............☐	☐ Minor move before handler returns to heel position	Minor move after handler returns to heel positio... ☐	
LONG DOWN (5 MINUTES) Handler out of sight	**30**	Did not remain in place..............☐ Disturbed other dog..☐	Sat or stood before handler returns to heel position.............☐	☐ Minor move before handler returns to heel position	Minor move after handler returns to heel position....☐	
Total Score	**200**					
Less Penalty for Un-controlled Behavior		Disciplining ☐ Snapping ☐ Barking ☐ Leaving Ring ☐ Handler error ☐ Other*				
		COMMENTS*			TOTAL SCORE	

Fig. 42b

OBEDIENCE JUDGE'S WORKSHEET

For Judge's Use ONLY — Not to be distributed or shown to exhibitors

DATE ....   OPEN ...... CLASS   DOG No. ....
(A or B)

SHOW ....   BREED .... HEIGHT .... JUMPS ....
At Withers

EXERCISE	NON QUALIFYING		QUALIFYING		Maximum Points	Points Off	NET SCORE
	ZERO	LESS THAN 50%	SUBSTANTIAL	MINOR			
HEEL FREE AND FIGURE 8	Unmanageable ... ☐ Unqualified heeling ☐	Handler continually adapts pace to dog ☐ Leaving handler ...☐	Heeling Fig. 8 ☐ ... Improper heel position .... ☐ ☐ Forging.. ☐ Crowding handler . ☐ Lagging.......... ☐ Sniffing ☐ .... Extra command to heel ..... ☐ Heeling wide ☐ on turns ☐ abouts No change of pace ☐ fast ☐ slow ...... No sit ... Poor sits ... ☐ , Lacks naturalness snoothness . ☐		40		
DROP ON RECALL	Does not come on first command or signal .... ☐ Does not drop on first command or signal .... ☐	Extra com. or sig. to stay after handler leaves ...☐ Moved from place left .... ☐ Anticipated: Recall .... ☐ Drop .... ☐ Come in ..... ☐ Sat out of reach ..☐	☐ Stood or lay down Touching handler ☐ ☐ Extra com. or sig. Sat between feet ☐ ☐ Before leaving ☐ Finish Poor sit ☐ ☐ Slow response Poor finish ..... ☐ ☐ Slow return Lack of naturalness ☐ Slow drop smoothness ...☐ ☐ No sit in front ☐ No finish		30		
RETRIEVE ON FLAT	Fails to go out on first command or signal ..... ☐ Fails to retrieve . ☐	Goes before command or signal ... ☐ Extra command or signal .... ☐ Sat out of reach ☐	☐ . Slow ... ☐ Going ... ☐ Returning. ☐ ☐ ....Mouthing or Playing .... ☐ ☐ Dropping dumbbell Touching handler ☐ ☐ Poor delivery Sat between feet ☐ ☐ No sit in front Poor sit .... ☐ ☐ No finish Poor finish ..... ☐ ☐ Handler error		25		
RETRIEVE OVER HIGH JUMP	Fails to go out on first command or signal .... ☐ Fails to jump going and returning .... ☐ Fails to retrieve . ☐	Goes before command or signal ...☐ Jumps only one direction........ ☐ Sat out of reach .. ☐ Extra command or signal ....☐	☐ . Slow ....☐ Going... ☐ Returning ...☐ ☐ .... Mouthing or Playing .... ☐ ☐ Dropping dumbbell Touching handler ..☐ ☐ Poor delivery Sat between feet ..☐ ☐ Climbing jump Poor sit ☐ ☐ No sit in front Poor finish ....☐ ☐ No finish ☐ Handler error		35		
BROAD JUMP	Refuses to jump on first command or signal .... ☐ Walks over any part ☐	Goes before command or signal .....☐ Does not clear jump ☐ Sat out of reach ...☐	☐ Minor jump touch Touching handler ..☐ ☐ Poor return Sat between feet ..☐ ☐ No sit in front Poor sit ....☐ ☐ No finish Poor finish ....☐		20		
				MAX. SUB-TOTAL ➡	150		
LONG SIT (3 Minutes)	Did not remain in place .... ☐ Goes to another dog .... ☐	Stood or lay down before handler returns .... ☐ Repeated whines or barks .... ☐	☐ Forced into position Minor move after ☐ Minor move before handler returns handler returns to heel position . ☐ ☐ Minor whine or bark Handler error ....☐		25		
LONG DOWN (5 Minutes)	Did not remain in place .... ☐ Goes to another dog .... ☐	Stood or sat before handler returns .. ☐ Repeated whines or barks .... ☐	☐ Forced into position Minor move after ☐ Minor move before handler returns handler returns to heel position.. ☐ ☐ Minor whine or bark Handler error ....☐		25		
				MAXIMUM POINTS ➡	200		

☐ H. Disciplining ☐ Shows fear ☐ Fouling ring ☐ Disqualified ☐ Expelled ☐ Excused   Less Penalty for ➡ Unusual Behavior

EXPLANATION OF PENALTY   TOTAL NET SCORE ➡

Fig. 42c

NEW

OBEDIENCE JUDGE'S WORKSHEET
For Judge's Use ONLY — Not to be distributed or shown to exhibitors

DOG No. . . . .

DATE. . . . .

UTILITY . . . . . . CLASS
(A or B)

SHOW. . . . .

ARTICLES NO. . . . .   BREED . . . .   HEIGHT. . . . . . . .JUMPS. . . . .
at withers

EXERCISE	NON QUALIFYING					QUALIFYING		Maximum Points	Points Lost	NET SCORE
	ZERO			LESS THAN 50%		SUBSTANTIAL	MINOR			
SCENT DISCRIMI-NATION	No go out 1st comm. ☐L ☐M	No retrieve ☐L ☐M	Wrong article ☐L ☐M	Anticipated . . . . . ☐ Double command . ☐ Sat out or reach: LEATHER. . . . .☐ METAL . . . . .☐		L M ☐ ☐ . . Handler roughness . . . ☐ ☐ ☐ ☐ . . . .Sat after turn . . . . ☐ ☐ ☐ ☐ Doesn't work continuously ☐ ☐ ☐ ☐ Dropping article on return ☐ ☐ Picks up wrong Mouthing . ☐ ☐ article then dropped: Touched ☐ ☐ handler . ☐ ☐ ☐ Slow response Sat between ☐ No sit in front feet . . .☐ ☐ ☐ No finish Poor sit . . .☐ ☐ ☐ Handler error Poor finish .☐		LEATHER **30** METAL **30**		
DIRECTED RETRIEVE	Does Not: Go out on command ☐ Go directly to glove . . . . ☐ Retrieve right article . . . . ☐ Fails to retrieve . . ☐			Anticipated . . . . .☐ Sat out of reach . . ☐		☐ . . . . . Touching dog sending . . . . . ☐ ☐ . . . . . .Excessive signals . . . . . . ☐ ☐ . . . . . . Slow response to command . . ☐ ☐ . . . Mouthing. ☐ Playing. ☐ . . ☐ ☐ Dropping article Touching handler . ☐ ☐ Poor delivery . . . Sat between feet . ☐ ☐ No sit in front Poor sit . . . . . . ☐ ☐ No finish Poor finish . . . . ☐ ☐ Lack of naturalness smoothness. . . . ☐		**30**		
SIGNAL EXERCISE	Unmanageable . . . . ☐ Unqualified heeling .☐			Any audible comm. ☐ Handler adapting self to dog pace . ☐ Failure on first signal to: Stand . . .☐ Stay . . . .☐ Drop . . . .☐ Sit . . . .☐ Come . . .☐ Anticipated . . . . .☐ Sat out of reach . .☐		☐ . . . Forging . . . Crowding handler . ☐ ☐ . . .Lagging . . . Sniffing . . . .☐ ☐ No change of pace ☐ Fast ☐ Slow ☐ ☐ . Heeling wide — on turns — abouts . ☐ ☐ . Extra signal to heel ☐ . . ☐ Sit . . ☐ ☐ . . . . . Holding signals . . . . Slow response to signal to ☐ . . Stand . . Down . . Sit . . Come . . .☐ ☐ No sit front-finish Touching handler ☐ ☐ Lack of Sat between feet . ☐ naturalness Poor sits . . . . ☐ smoothness Poor finish. . . . . ☐		**35**		
DIRECTED JUMPING	HIGH JUMP Does Not: Leave on order . . ☐ Go substantially in right direction .☐ Stop on command . ☐ Jump as directed . ☐ Climbing jump . . . ☐ ☐ . . . . . . Anticipated		BAR JUMP Does Not: Leave on order . . . ☐ Go substantially in right direction . ☐ Stop on command . ☐ Jump as directed . ☐ Knocking bar off . . ☐ command . . . . . . ☐		☐ . . . . . . Holding signals . . . . ☐ ☐ . . . Slow response to directions . . . ☐ ☐ . . . . . Slightly off direction . . . . . ☐ ☐ . . . . . Not back for enough. . . . . .☐ ☐ . . Anticipated ☐Turn ☐ Stop ☐ Sit ☐ . . . . . Does not sit on command ☐ No sit in front Touched handler ☐ ☐ No finish Sat between feet ☐ ☐ Lack of naturalness Poor sits . . . . ☐ —smoothness Poor finishes . . ☐		**40**		
						MAX. SUB-TOTAL ➡		**165**		
GROUP EXAMI-NATION	Substantial move . ☐ Growls or snaps . . ☐ Goes to another dog . . . . . . ☐ Sits or lies down be-fore handler returns☐		Minor move away. . .☐ Shows shyness. . . .☐ Resentment. . . . ☐ Repeated barks or whines . . ☐		☐ . .Resistance to handler posing . . . ☐ ☐ . . . . Moved feet slightly . . . . ☐ ☐ . . . . . Minor whine or bark . . . . . ☐ ☐ Sits or lies down after handler returns to heel position . . . . .☐		**35**		
						MAXIMUM POINTS ➡		**200**		

☐ H. Disciplining ☐ Shows Fear ☐ Fouling Ring ☐ Disqualified ☐ Example ☐ Excused Less Penalty for ➡ Unusual Behavior

EXPLANATION OF PENALTY

TOTAL NET SCORE ➡

Fig. 42d

NEW

OBEDIENCE JUDGE'S WORKSHEET — not to be distributed

LONG SIT • LONG DOWN • GROUP EXAMINATION CHART

SHOW _____

DATE _____ CLASS _____ GROUP NO. _____

BREED

DOG NUMBER														

LONG SIT														
SCORE														

LONG DOWN														
SCORE														

GROUP EXAM.														
SCORE														

COMMENTS

NOVICE CLASSES — 30 POINTS each

| 1 Min. LONG SIT | 3 MIN. LONG DOWN |

ZERO
A—Moved substantial distance out of position
B—Goes to or disturbed another dog

LESS THAN 50%
C—Stood or lay down before handler returns | D—Sat or stood before handler returns to heel
E—Repeated barks or whines

SUBSTANTIAL (QUALIFYING) MINOR
F—Break of position after handler returns
G—Forcing into position ☐ Sit ☐ Down
H—Minor wine or barks

OPEN CLASSES — 25 POINTS each

| 3 min. LONG SIT | 5 min. LONG DOWN |

ZERO
A—Moves substantial distance out of position
B—Goes to or disturbed another dog

LESS THAN 50%
C—Stood or lay down before handler returns | D—Sat or stood before handler returns
E—Repeated whines or barks

SUBSTANTIAL (QUALIFYING) MINOR
F—Minor move before handler returns | FF—Minor move after handler returns
G—Forcing into position . ☐ Sit .. ☐ Down
H—Minor whine or bark

UTILITY CLASS — 35 POINTS

GROUP EXAMINATION minimum 3 minutes

ZERO
A—Moves a substantial distance out of position
B—Goes to another dog
C—Growls or snaps during exercise
D—Sits or lies down before handler returns

LESS THAN 50%
E—Moves minor distance out of position
F—Shows shyness or resentment
G—Repeated whines or barks

SUBSTANTIAL (QUALIFYING) MINOR
H—Moves feet slightly during exercise
I —Minor whine or bark
J—Sits or lies down after handler returns to heel position

Fig. 42e

Index

Other Books by Blanche Saunders

THE COMPLETE NOVICE OBEDIENCE COURSE
THE COMPLETE OPEN OBEDIENCE COURSE
THE COMPLETE UTILITY OBEDIENCE COURSE (with TRACKING)
DOG TRAINING FOR BOYS AND GIRLS

Published by Howell Book House Inc.
845 Third Avenue, New York, N.Y. 10022